PREACHING

ON THE BOOKS

OF THE

OLD TESTAMENT

PREACHING

ON THE BOOKS

OF THE

OLD TESTAMENT

BY

DWIGHT E. STEVENSON

HARPER & BROTHERS PUBLISHERS

NEW YORK

To My Wife

CONTENTS

PREFACE

The simplest and clearest thing to say about the present book is that it is a sequel and companion to my earlier work, *Preaching on the Books of the New Testament*.[1] The same purpose undergirds both books; that is to provide one way among many for a return from the fragmented world of textual preaching to the wholeness of the biblical view upon life and destiny. One obvious road back is that of biblical theology; those seeking this trail do not speak with a single voice but they do work from the same aim—that of rediscovering the Bible as a book of faith and redemption. Another road back is the one offered here—that of rediscovering the unity of the biblical books.

The division of the Bible into chapters and verses is a marvelous device for quick reference, but it is highly unfortunate when used as a key to biblical life and thought. The numbers, bold upon the page, invite us to chop the living book asunder and deal with the scattered fragments as living wholes. Think what this would mean, by way of illustration, if applied to the plays of Shakespeare. We should then be confronted with theater audiences who had heard Shakespeare all their lives: lectures upon selected lines from the plays, fragments of scenes and episodes—but never a whole play! A given theater audience could have heard the whole of Shakespeare in this manner without having gained the faintest glimmer of the dramatic world that Shakespeare sought to create. Similarly, a congregation reared and nurtured on textual preaching can even be strangers to the life and thought of the Bible—because they have never seen the drama through from beginning to end.

There is a single biblical drama. This is the drama of redemption. The books are scenes and episodes—some minor, some major. But they are natural wholes through which we may enter into the drama and move with its action.

We have become so accustomed to shredding the Bible into

[1] New York: Harper & Brothers (1956).

separated texts that we suppose that this is the only proper way to preach upon it. We even suppose that any other way is both un-natural and impossible. A little reflection should teach us that a text out of context is a very dangerous guide to thought and conduct. It is so easy to empty such a tiny vessel of its biblical content and fill it with our hobbies and the world's prejudices. Thus the conviction gradually overtakes us that the only textual preaching that we should allow ourselves is contextual preaching. Any part of Scripture should be seen, not in isolation, but in relation to the living whole. By *context* we should mean not only the immediate setting of a verse of Scripture, but the whole book from which it is taken, and the whole biblical drama of which it is a part.

Therefore, it matters little whether we intend to preach many sermons upon whole books of Scripture. We need to *prepare* all our sermons within that larger perspective and with that wider point of view. Any sermon, textual or otherwise, will be more truly repre-sentative of the biblical revelation if the preacher has first put him-self through the discipline of studying biblical books as wholes.

When we turn to the Old Testament with such a purpose, there are some "books" that require special treatment. For example, Isaiah appears to be not one book but two. And Samuel and Kings on closer study turn out to be not four books but one. The same is true of the history of the Chronicler—Ezra, Nehemiah, and Chron-icles. In the arrangement of the chapters that follow, we have made these concessions to logic. But we have followed the biblical order.

This does not mean that the chapters should be read in their present order, any more than that we would advise a reader of the Bible to begin with Genesis and read straight through, book after book. The present volume is not so much a reading book as a study guide. Those who get the most from it will read a chapter at a time, meanwhile looking up and reading each scriptural reference as it is called for, and afterward lingering to read and reread the biblical book again and again.

This book, because it is concerned with biblical wholes, does not dwell upon many of the assured results of the analytical approach. Therefore, it has little to say about literary sources, authorship, edit-ing, and the refinements of dating. The writer does not dispute or discredit these. Rather, he takes each Old Testament book in its present form to be a unit, created not so much by individual authors and editors as by the congregation of Israel, the covenant community, of whom the actual authors and editors were servants.

Preaching on whole books of Scripture is demanding, but it is also rewarding both to preacher and to congregation. Its greatest danger is heaviness. Such a sermon, as Halford E. Luccock observed, may be "heavy enough to sink a battleship." But it need not be. If the preacher has grasped his message at center and if he has learned the arts of selectivity and of modern relevance, he may well find his people listening to him with glad surprise because he has enabled them to see a fresh vision.

The author is indebted to his colleague, William L. Reed, Professor of Old Testament at The College of the Bible in Lexington, Kentucky, and Executive Assistant to the President of the American Schools of Oriental Research, for reading the entire book in manuscript and for his many helpful suggestions. Dr. Reed is not to be blamed for the shortcomings of this book, but he has undoubtedly prevented it from being more inadequate than it is.

Several of the faculty secretaries at The College of the Bible have had a hand in the typing of the manuscript: Janice Bell, Eleanor Ivy Drash, and Kathryn Jones. Another colleague, Roscoe M. Pierson, Librarian of the Bosworth Memorial Library at the College of the Bible, generously read galley and page proof after the author had begun a sabbatical leave in the Near East.

DWIGHT E. STEVENSON

American School of Oriental Research
Jerusalem, Jordan
January, 1961

PREACHING

ON THE BOOKS

OF THE

OLD TESTAMENT

1

THE OLD TESTAMENT
AND THE WORD OF GOD

THE Old Testament is much misunderstood. For many Christians, some ministers included, it is a lost book. And for nearly all the rest it is a neglected book.

I

There is, for example, the misconception implicit in a widely current sermon outline on the topic "How to Spell God." It goes something like this: (1) the patriarchs spelled God "F-E-A-R"; (2) Moses spelled God "L-A-W"; (3) the prophets spelled God "J-U-S-T-I-C-E"; but (4) Christ spelled God "L-O-V-E." This is an appealing outline; many have used it. But it is almost completely false. It makes the mistake of dividing law and gospel between the Testaments, assigning law to the Old Testament and grace to the New Testament. But is there no grace in the Old Testament? To say there is none is to assert that there was no calling of Israel to be God's people, no deliverance from bondage, no covenant, no steadfast love shown toward men, no call to repentance, no mercy, and no pardon.

The love of God is so germane to Old Testament thought that we could fill the book with supporting quotations. Let a single example suffice. The covenant—a ruling idea of both Testaments—is rooted in the love of God, as we see when we read Deuteronomy 7:6–8: "For you are a people holy to the Lord your God; the Lord your God has chosen you to be a people for his own possession, out of all the peoples that are on the face of the earth. It was not because you were more in number than any other people that the Lord set his love upon you and chose you, for you were the fewest of all peoples; but it is because the Lord loves you, and is keeping the oath which he swore to your fathers, that the Lord has brought you out with a mighty hand, and redeemed you from the house of bondage . . ." A quotation like this is simply shattering to any neat scheme for the confining of grace to the New Testament. The God of the Old Testament appears as Creator and Redeemer, not merely as Lawgiver and Judge. Even when he appears in these latter roles he does so upon the basis of his prior acts of deliverance and instruction, and for the ultimate purpose of quickening repentance so that there can be forgiveness and renewal. The God revealed in the Old Testament does not call upon man to act before he himself has acted; rather, he takes the initiative. Therefore, the pattern of the Old Testament in this respect is like that of the New: God's gift; man's response.

Preachers using the Old Testament need to keep this in mind in order to avoid the trap of moralism. This trap has two jaws. One is religion as burdensome duty. The other is salvation by human merit. Religion always tends to fall into these twin jaws, but biblical religion does not do so. Not even the Old Testament tells us what man ought to do before it tells us what God has done and is doing for us. And even the justice that God requires of us is only the human reflection of the steadfast love of God. When preaching on the Prophets or upon the Torah we do well to remember this.

II

Another misconception would turn the Old Testament into the museum of the Christian Church. The idea is that the Old Testament is not only old and superannuated; it is actually dead. A trip through some of the legal books—Leviticus in particular—is not unlike a visit to the Early American Room in a museum. There we view the open fireplace with its crane and huge copper kettle, the spinning wheel, the bootjack and the flintlock musket. These all belong to a bygone era. The suggestion that we might move in and make ourselves at home may appear less absurd than that we should try to find a contemporary voice of God in the ancient oracles of the Old Testament. This is to say that there is a strong tendency to regard the Old Testament as a rich treasure trove for historians, but nothing more.

It is a repository for an ancient event, but it is not regarded as a source of new life.

To this we should reply that there are many things in the Old Testament that do belong exclusively to the past. They perished with their times and have in themselves no power of resurrection. Thus, outmoded institutions and customs, such as sacrificing sheep upon altars and taking off one's shoe to seal a contract, are curios in the museum of history. On the other hand, there are two ways in which the Old Testament lives for us and by means of which its personages may become our contemporaries. One is universal; the other is particular.

III

The universal appeal of the Old Testament lies close to the realm of art. It has little to do with dates and places but much to do with the ageless yearnings, struggles, guilts, expiations, and aspirations of the human spirit. It has to do with man's dealing with man—not at the level of commerce or politics, but at the level of personal life and ultimate meaning. It has to do with that yearned-for-and-dreaded meeting of self with self and with God. When a Jacob or a Jonah comes marching out of the pages of the Old Testament and begins to live before our eyes in the living element of his own throbbing times, the years that separate us begin to melt away, and, as in any work of art, we identify ourselves with our hero or discover ourselves in our villain—waking at Bethel in shuddering awe at the uncomfortable nearness of God, or fleeing to Joppa with bag packed for faraway places to escape divine mandates that call us out of our narrowness to the wideness of God's mercy.

There are analogies by which we may understand this. This morning's newspaper lies crumpled in my wastebasket, but Shakespeare's *Macbeth* sits waiting on the shelf, ready to speak its urgent, searing lines to anyone who will reach up his hand and take down the book. And though Shakespeare is dead, and was buried at Stratford-on-Avon more than three hundred years ago, Macbeth may leap to life tonight at the little theater on the village green, or upon the stage of your imagination by your reading lamp. What is more, you will be closer to reality in that meeting than you were this afternoon when you chatted amiably about trivialities with five flesh-and-blood companions at the coffee break. If Shakespeare—and Aeschylus and Sophocles—can speak to us in this way across the gulf of centuries, why should it surprise us that the personalities of the Old Testament should rise and seek us out? Thus do the universal powers of the human spirit bridge the centuries to make of the Bible a living book and of our reading the revelation of a light that never shone on sea or land, but in our hearts. It is the "light that enlightens every man." It comes to us upon the plane of the universal.

IV

The second way in which the Old Testament lives is through particular, unique events. Meaning does not brood above the world in timeless invitation to the human spirit. It enters the world. It has a time, a place, a people, and a story. In other words, the Old Testament is the story of the Chosen People. If we dismiss this idea as the idolization of the corporate pride which we may find among any people, we will be unable to read the Old Testament on the plane of revelation. We will see it instead as one more example of human pretension and pride, and read it as one more chapter in secular history. As long as we are thinking of the history of Israel in this light, the story of this people may be as significant as the story of any other people, but no more so.

But the biblical idea of the Chosen People is not an idolization of human pride. It is, in fact, quite the reverse. This is not to say that Israel never fell into the trap of human pretension, that the Israelites never thought of themselves (as all human groups tend to do) as somehow superior and entitled to special privileges. The Israelites often did this, but when they did so their prophets were quick to remind them that they were breaking their covenant with God and setting up their own will in place of God's (Jer. 31:32; Amos 11:25; Deut. 31:16, 17, 20). For the call of God to his people was not a call to special privilege but to service; and it was a call not to pride in human merit but to obedience (and to repentance for disobedience). To be God's Chosen People is to belong to God and not to self; it is a relationship that shatters pride and produces a broken and a contrite heart. This fact is seen in Israel's national festivals. Two of the most significant are the Passover and Yom Kippur. In the Passover the Jews celebrate God's grace toward Israel in the deed of deliverance from the bondage of Egypt. And on Yom Kippur the whole people gather before God in repentance for their sins. This constant renewal of divine grace and human repentance makes all the difference. Without them we have nothing but the unregenerate self-deification of a nation; but with them we have a people whom God can use for his purposes among all nations. This, in fact, is the central idea in the notion of a Chosen People: "By you all the families of the earth will bless themselves" (Gen. 12:3).

The Old Testament, therefore, makes the stupendous claim that the story of Israel is the key to the whole human story for the whole of mankind. It is the clue to history. The life line of Israel is not laid down beside the life lines of other nations in monotonous parallel. It is the hub of a wheel in which all others, as spokes, find their coherence and their meaning. This is a staggering claim, but the Old Testament makes it. We may call it revelation or we may call it rubbish, but we cannot be indifferent to it. (Here is at least one of the roots of history's long story of anti-Semitism. A claim so stupendous must be accepted with gladness or it will be repudiated with violence. Never, if we take it seriously, can we regard it with indifference or amused tolerance.)

The covenant was the obverse side of being the Chosen People. For only to the extent that they kept the covenant could Israel be and act as God's people. This is why the idea of the remnant (the faithful few) emerged. And it is also why the Christian sees Jesus Christ as the Chosen People concentrated in one man.

How are Christians connected to all of this? To use the language of Paul, "if you are Christ's, then you are Abraham's offspring, heirs according to promise" (Gal. 3:29). This tradition is our tradition; this is our heritage. For we are the New Israel, the new covenant community standing in direct line of succession. This is the thought of 1 Peter 2:9 which echoes for the Christian Church the covenant call of Israel in Exodus 19:5–6. And it is the idea informing Paul's analogy of a wild olive tree in Romans 11:17–24. A Christian sees ancient Israel as his spiritual homeland and the Israelites as his spiritual forefathers. This, incidentally, is the thought of Hebrews 11:39–40 where, after the roll call of heroes, the writer makes our connection with them quite explicit: "And all these, though well attested by their faith, did not receive what was promised, since God had foreseen something better for us, that apart from us they should not be made perfect."

This is to say that the biblical drama of redemption is a single drama. Speaking figuratively, we may say that the events of the Old Testament are like the first two acts of a play, incomplete in themselves without the final act. We should also say that though the events of the New Testament contain the crisis and denouement of the final act, they cannot be fully understood without the first two acts. The early church understood the Old Testament in this light. We should never forget that the Old Testament was the Holy Scripture of the early church—the only Scripture it had at first. It was the Bible of Jesus and of Paul.

This does not mean that the Bible is a level book, that the insights of the Old Testament are as penetrating or as ennobling as the central insights of the New Testament. We must not make the Old Testament say what it does not say. We must not read New Testament meanings into it. Job does not rise to the heights of the Apostle Paul. Second Isaiah does not climb Calvary with Jesus, not quite. We must be on guard against the old use of symbols, archetypes, and predictions by which the Old Testament was reduced to a shadow of the New Testament, casting its events before. Such a method of Old Testament interpretation leads only to obscurantism. The historical discipline cannot be slighted. We can never know what the Bible says to us now until we first know what it said then in the uniqueness of past events. Nevertheless the Old Testament still stands, the indispensable foundation of the New.

V

One more introductory word must be given. This touches the nature of the Word of God through Scripture. There is always the temptation to downgrade the Word into words—that is to say, into bits of secret information, or into orthodox doctrines, or into isolated commands, or even into magic formulas. The Bible contains not the words of God but the words of men; but God uses these words to transmit his Word.

The Word is fundamentally personal. It intends communication, meeting. But when God meets man through his Word it is not merely to greet him, to impart information, or to give externalized commands. It is to come to him as Lord, as Holy Spirit, as Creator, Judge, and Redeemer. When God meets us it is with his sovereign personal claim upon us as persons, at the core of our being. This is to say that the content of God's revelation through his Word is God himself. Through his Word he gives himself.

Biblically considered, there are three phases to the Word of God as it comes to us. First, there is the Deed of God. Second, there is the covenant community called into being by the Deed of God, his mighty acts of deliverance, and transmitting his Word to the individual believer. Finally, there is the ever-new life of the Spirit as it comes from these sources and through these corporate channels in profound immediacy to the individual person.

In its first phase the Word of God is an act in history, a unique and unrepeatable complex of events. For the Old Testament this is the deliverance of Israel from Egyptian bondage, the making of the covenant and the giving of the law. For the New Testament this Deed was the life, teachings, death, and resurrection of Jesus Christ, and the coming of the Holy Spirit to the church.

In its second phase the Word of God is the life of God in the midst of his people. It is the saving life of the covenant community. This community creates the Scriptures as one expression of its life with God. And since the Scriptures rose as the record of that life, and welled up from the source of inspiration, it has always the capacity of quickening the life of the Spirit for those who come to it in faith. Here we need to stress the fact that the covenant community to which the Bible is related is not merely the church of the ancient past; it is the living community, a mighty cable of life, stretching out of the long past, gathering us into its vital strands in this present hour, and stretching on into God's future. The Bible rose in the church; when it is read in faith it claims us for the church, which is to say that it quickens us to the rebirth by which we may enter the community of God's people or it calls us back through repentance to a renewal of the bonds that we have broken. To open the Bible as a book of faith is to open and pass through the door into the covenant community.

The third phase of the life of God's Word as it comes to us we have already discussed as an integral part of the second phase. But, while it may not be separated in experience, we can discuss it separately. Neither the Deed of God nor his life in the covenant community can be the Word of God for us until it comes home to us and takes us captive, heart and soul. To put it as Acts does of Pentecost, we must be "pricked in our hearts" by it. The Word must become a personal word calling us by name. God does not tyrannize the human heart; he does not break and enter. He does not coerce. He persuades, which means that he always asks for human consent. Without the human response, the Word of God comes to naught. This means that the Bible needs more than inspired writers. It needs inspired *readers*. In fact, without human response we cannot even hear the word as the Word. A man who receives the Word is not like a person who has picked up a bundle; he has not added *something* he did not have before. Rather he has entered into a new relationship with God, and hence with his fellows and with himself. Henceforth he is not his own, but God's. And he has not something but Someone; or, to put it more accurately, Someone has him, and he is born anew. This individuality and intimacy of the Word of God as it comes home to us is nowhere more aptly expressed than in Hebrews 4:12. "For the word of God is living and active, sharper than any two-edged sword, piercing to the division of soul and spirit, of joints and marrow, and discerning the thoughts and intentions of the heart."

Such is revelation. Rooted in an ancient event, and transmitted by the covenant community, it comes to us, one person at a time, in this present day; it is living and active, quickening the new life of the Spirit.

Not everything that is said or done within the covenant community, even when it is said and done in faith, is the Word of God. But all is done before God's face, subject to the testing of his Spirit. The content of a specific revelation is always to be seen in the light of the nature of God. "Beloved, do not believe every spirit, but test the spirits to see whether they are of God" (1 John 4:1). Applied to the practical problem of Old Testament exegesis, this means that we must read Scripture contextually, in the light of the whole. Thus, for example, Obadiah and Nahum, with their bitter nationalism, are in some senses obstructive of the light of revelation, while in other respects they are transmissive of that light. Although the books of the Old Testament are for the most part literary wholes, no one of them should stand alone as a complete packet of divine truth. The covenant community not only transmits God's Word, it also stands under his judgment. The ultimate light of that judgment is the light that shone in the face of Jesus Christ.

2

IN HIS IMAGE

Genesis

"So God created man in his own image, in the image of God he created him; male and female he created them. And God blessed them, and God said to them, 'Be fruitful and multiply, and fill the earth and subdue it; . . .'" (Gen. 1:27–28). These words suggest both the lordly power and the intimate involvement of God in making man. If he had not made man so lofty, man could not have fallen so low. If he had not made man for love, man could not have lusted. If he had not made man for companionship, man could not have hated so cruelly. If he had not made man to subdue the earth, man could not have learned how to exploit and despoil it. When God created man in his image, he undertook a task which he could accomplish only by further expending himself in the work of redemption.

These are the themes of Genesis: creation, fall, and redemption. Let us be careful not to export these themes out of our lives into the dim ancestral past, for they lie at the foundation of every life and pervade every act and concern of civilization.

I. WORKING YOUR WAY INTO THE BOOK

Genesis abounds in critical problems which have agitated the Jewish and Christian world for at least a century. How are we to reconcile its two accounts of creation with each other and with the findings of science? To what extent are the patriarchs historical individuals; are they perhaps personifications of clans and tribes? How much does the book reveal of the history of religions and of comparative religions; what indications of religious primitivism are re-

corded here, and what interpolations from the much later times of
the editors? What of the tangled problem of the many literary
strands which were finally woven into one fabric to form the book
as we have it? The answering of these and other questions has produced the fascinating story of "higher criticism" recorded in books
numerous enough to fill a library; it is an important story and should
not be neglected by anyone who wants to grasp the Bible as a living
book which emerged out of the living past. The main results of that
critical study can be read in a competent commentary.

Space does not permit us to deal with these critical questions. We
do not wish to ignore them here; we shall simply assume them and
pass on through them, as it were, to see if we can grasp Genesis from
the standpoint of its own original thesis—as a unity and as a book of
faith. It is really not difficult to see the book's point of view nor to
follow its unfolding plan. Whoever put it together has, in fact, produced a very simple story out of exceedingly complex materials.
Once the focus of our attention is withdrawn from the study of his
sources and is given to the book as it is, we begin to see it as a book
of faith in its original, simple grandeur and quiet power.

God's Prologue

Early we get the idea that we are witnessing the prologue to a
vast, cosmic drama. It is the story of God's dealings with man, and
of man's response. The events of the main drama will be acted out
upon a tiny stage by a little nation in an obscure land; but the purpose of these events will be for all mankind, and their meaning will
reach to the highest heaven.

The stage at first is as wide as the universe itself. We are present
as God creates the heavens and the earth, peopling the far immensities with stars, and the earth itself with plants and animals—and with
man. Man comes into the good earth and he is given dominion in it.
He gropes for companionship and knowledge. In rebellion and in
fear he becomes separated from his Creator. And this mingled creature, compounded of the stuff of divinity and the dross of his own
willful pride and rebellion, multiplies and populates the earth. He
discovers the arts of civilization, and practices them for his own
glory. The shining image of God in man is marred by selfish ambition, by hatred, by murder, and by self-worship. And God ponders

what he will do with his perverse creation. At first he decides to destroy it, to blot it out from his sight forever; and he begins to do this, but he finds that he cannot. And so he saves a remnant, and from these he makes a new beginning, only to find the same perverse tendency repeated. Instead of becoming a family, they break community with each other and with God; they divide into warring camps, and go their separate ways—lost from each other, confused within themselves, and strayed from God.

Now it becomes clear that creation and providence, and even judgment, are not enough. God must learn to speak a deeper word. As the prologue continues to unfold we see him preparing to speak this word. At first we are permitted to look upon the whole divided family of man. And then our view is limited to one great segment of mankind, to the Semites. Finally among the swarming Semitic peoples the narrowing spotlight singles out a tiny clan, the Hebrews. At first we see only Abraham, the father of the Hebrews; he has separated himself from his kinsmen and from their corrupt civilization to answer the call of God. He does not know whither God is beckoning him. But, prototype of all questing souls who are trying to find their way back to God, he answers the call and begins the uncertain, heroic adventure of faith. Now it is that God speaks the first syllables of his new word. That word is "redemption." Abraham and his descendants are singled out for a mission of redemption to all mankind:

Read Genesis 12:1–3; 18:17–19; 22:17–18; 26:3–5; 28:13–15.

Aside from this initial response of faith and from God's secret purpose for them, Abraham and his descendants seem to be not greatly different from other peoples. They are human, all too human. They are filled with the jealousies and ambitions that plague all mankind. They feud among themselves; they deceive and despoil each other; and they even sell their choicest spirit into slavery. Thus the story that began in the blazing light of creation and that found its human response in the daring adventure of Abraham seems to fade into dimness and night. It is like a stream that rose out of Mesopotamia, that swelled into a small but confident river, only to lose itself in the sands of Egypt. But God is able to use this perverse people and to turn their evil intentions to good account. Even the selling of Joseph into Egypt is a part of the grand design:

Read Genesis 45:4–8; 50:15–21.

The whole atmosphere of Genesis is one of suspenseful preparation. The need of rebellious man is desperate and universal, extending even to the people whom God purposes to use in meeting the need. But the promise of redemption is luminous, and as the curtain closes on the prologue, we keenly await the beginning of the first act.

OUTLINE OF GENESIS

The final editor of Genesis has his own outlining device; it is a long genealogy, which is broken into fragments; each fragment is then inserted to serve as a bridge from one part of the story to its sequel. A study of these genealogies will reveal the main outlines of the book:

Read Genesis 2:4; 5:1; 6:9; 10:1; 11:10; 11:27; 25:12; 36:1.

The units which thus emerge are: (1) the creation, climaxing in the making of mankind, and the fall of mankind into sin; (2) from Adam to the Flood; (3) Noah and the Flood; (4) the separation of the peoples of the earth; (5) focus upon the Semitic peoples; (6) narrowing of focus to Abraham and his descendants; (7) Isaac and his sons Esau and Jacob; (8) Joseph and his father and brothers in Egypt.

A somewhat simpler outline might unfold on these lines:

I. Creation and civilization, chapters 1–11
   A. Creation, 1:1–2:24
   B. The fall of man, 3:1–24
   C. The spread of man and the beginnings of civilization, 4:1–26
   D. An experiment in judgment, 5:1—9:28
   E. Further growth of civilization and its problems, 10:1—11:9
   F. Singling out Abraham, 11:10–32
II. Promise of redemption for man and civilization, chapters 12–50
   A. The family of Abraham, chapters 12–25
   B. The family of Isaac, chapters 26–36
   C. The family of Jacob, especially Joseph, chapters 37–50

MAIN THEMES

In the foregoing outline we discern the main themes of the book. They are:

1. *Creation.* The whole universe has its beginning in the will and deed of God. It is good. Man, who is placed in the midst of it, is to be more than a creature among creatures; he is to be a creative creature who has dominion. Like all creation, he is basically good; but unlike the rest of creation, he is endowed to a special degree with God's likeness. The stamp of his creator is on him.

2. *The fall.* God's image in man makes sin all the more tragic, but at the same time it makes sin possible. For it is creativity gone wrong, imagination put to evil purposes that is at the root of it. The creative creature vaunts himself to become the rival of his Creator. He rebels and separates himself from his God, introducing fear and hate and greed into the world.

3. *Civilization.* Civilization is man writ large, and it bears the marks at one and the same time of his divine origin and of his deviation from the divine purpose. On the evil side, it is marked by pride and by division. Its tragedy is one of broken community; man is set against God and stands at odds with man. This is by no means the whole story of civilization, for there is much nobility to tell about. But, passing by this nobility, the Tower of Babel draws our attention to the problems of civilization: pride and strife.

4. *Judgment.* This appears as God's provisional answer to the problem of human perversity. It is found in the story of the Flood and again in the confusion of tongues at the Tower of Babel. But judgment as the final solution is unacceptable to God. Why? Because God loves this world which he has made; the clean, surgical solutions of judgment are denied by the claims of love.

5. *Promised redemption.* God's redemptive purpose is as wide as all humanity, but he determines to achieve it through a special people whom he chooses for himself from among the whole of mankind. It is impossible for the human eye to detect special virtues in this people which make them worthy of this choice. They are much like other men. But the choice is there and the promise is made. Through this tiny, inadequate people God will bring redemption to all his children.

KEY VERSE

". . . by you all the families of the earth will bless themselves" (Gen. 12:3).

II. PREPARING YOUR BOOK SERMON

CARDINAL IDEA

Confronted by the problem of human evil in the good which he created, God yearns for the redemption of mankind and determines to seek it through the services of a special people whom he will call to serve him.

SHAPING A PREACHING OUTLINE

There are, of course, many sermons that may be preached *about* Genesis, but we are here interested in the sermon *of* Genesis. This means cleaving to the cardinal idea of the book as clearly expressed in one declarative sentence—if not the statement above, then one of your own making. The purpose is not to tell history but to use it as the means of revealing the need and the means of God's redemptive work in his created world.

One rather obvious approach to outline is through the main themes of the book as stated above. An elaboration of each of the themes with appropriate modern applications should serve very well, provided all of these themes are seen as parts of a connected whole. They are not concepts; they are acts in a divine-human drama: Man's glory, his predicament, his works, his hope; God's creation, his disappointment, his judgment, his proposal for redemption.

Another approach to outline could be made through the use of the outline of Genesis itself, as it appears on page 12. Care should be taken, of course, to put flesh on such a skeleton and to make these bones live through the use of narrative and human interest material, in which Genesis abounds. But one caution needs to be sounded: Do not try to crowd too many people and too much action into a single sermon. Be selective.

A judicious selection of passages from the book—resulting in a condensed edition of Genesis—would produce a sermon entirely in the words of Scripture. The sublimity of the language, particularly in the first eleven chapters, would justify such a method.

A synopsis of the book in one's own words, giving the whole sweep of it in twenty or twenty-five minutes, ought also to be an impressive way of making the message into a sermon. The approach

would be not unlike that under the heading "God's Prologue" earlier
in this chapter.

A MODERN TITLE

Some imp of memory recalls Roark Bradford's title, "Ol' Man
Adam an' His Chillun." It is hard to lay aside. Archbishop Temple's
book on the philosophy of religion is at an opposite literary pole, but
it deals with the same subject as that of Genesis: "Man, Nature, and
God." We might revamp it slightly to read, "Man, Civilization, and
God." The first words of a literal translation of the Bible into
English could not be improved upon in any title: "In the Beginning
of God's Creating."

3

GOD'S PEOPLE

Exodus

PROVINCIAL pride is the common possession of all peoples. We refer to our home region, half playfully, as "God's Country." We are convinced that our native land is the finest nation on earth. We exalt our race or our class by finding some way in which it is superior to all others—it is the richest, or the wisest, or the most virtuous, or the most powerful. "We are the greatest people, the greatest nation. Nothing like us ever was." Such is the meaning that we naturally read into the phrase "The Chosen People."

The Bible takes this natural provincialism and revolutionizes it. God brings down the mighty from their seat and exalts them of low degree. He who would be first must learn how to be last. The aspiring lord of all must learn to be servant of all. God's "Chosen People" are elected not to the role of princes and potentates but to the lowly station of servant. And they serve not for their own glory but to advance God's work of redemption.

It is only in this latter sense that Israel was the Chosen People, and only for that reason that God called them out of Egypt.

I. WORKING YOUR WAY INTO THE BOOK

KEY TO FAITH

Deliverance from Egyptian bondage was to the Israelites what the crucifixion and resurrection of Christ are to Christians—a translation of God's love into historical fact, a demonstration in power of God's redeeming grace. Israel's faith begins not in a philosophical abstraction but in an event. Granted that this event is seen in the light of faith, it nonetheless anchors the religion of Israel not in man's speculations or aspirations but in God's action. It also supplies perspective both for law and cultus, for God does not first appear marching out upon man with heavy demands that he be obeyed and worshiped. He first appears as Deliverer. In fact, that is how Israel *defined* God: "I am the Lord your God, who brought you up out of the land of Egypt" (Ps. 81:10). Law and cultus, properly understood, are seen from the human side as man's grateful response to God's act of mercy, and from the divine perspective as God's disciplining and nurturing of a crowd of former slaves to make of them a nation, a holy nation, worthy to serve as priest to all mankind.

The table of Commandments begins: "I am the Lord your God, who brought you out of the land of Egypt, . . ." (Exod. 20:2). Deliverance before demand, grace before law! The law finds its root in God's redeeming mercy, but that is not the end of the matter; it must find its fruit in the special service of the people who are thus delivered from bondage and disciplined by law and cultus to become God's servant to the nations. Redemption precedes law; and law leads into priesthood. The complete thought connecting redemption, law, and priesthood is contained in a single passage: "You have seen what I did to the Egyptians, and how I bore you on eagles' wings and brought you to myself. Now therefore, if you will obey my voice and keep my covenant, you shall be my own possession among all peoples; for all the earth is mine, and you shall be to me a kingdom of priests and a holy nation" (Exod. 19:4–6).

From the foregoing it can be seen that Exodus occupies a key position in the drama of the Old Testament. The whole action of the entire drama looks back to it; it is the hinge of Israel's history. The first chapter in Israel's faith bears the title "Out of Bondage." This idea is expressed again and again in book upon book throughout the whole Hebrew Bible. For tenderness and depth, no expression surpasses that of Hosea: "When Israel was a child, I loved him, and out of Egypt I called my son" (Hos. 11:1).

SALVATION-HISTORY

The critical literary and historical questions confronting a modern student of Exodus are as numerous and as tangled as those of Genesis.

It is clear that several documents passing through several revisions and from various historical periods have been woven into a single fabric to form our present book. The picture of the Tabernacle which occupies the final third of Exodus, for example, seems to be a highly idealized presentation of a rather primitive Tent of Meeting; the idealization comes from a priestly scribe during or after the Exile, who is looking back upon the past in the light of Solomon's Temple and picturing the Tent in the image of the Temple. Similarly, it is hard to tell just how much of the legal code in Exodus comes from the period of Moses and how much of it must be assigned to a later time.

It is entirely legitimate to subject Exodus to critical analysis to answer these and other questions of factual history, of sociology, of jurisprudence, and of anthropology. So studied, with modern literary and historical techniques, Exodus is a mine of fabulous wealth to the industrious digger. Nevertheless, these modern interests lie outside the purpose of the original writers. They were not concerned to record bare facts in chronological sequence and to give us a book of scientific history. They were writing a testament of faith; this faith was firmly anchored in certain pivotal events, but it was not tied to them in any slavish or literalistic manner. The concerns of the biblical writers go deeper and touch the springs of human action in response to the will and purpose of God.

Once delivered from the necessity of proving the literal historicity of every episode, the reader is free to read Exodus in all its original simplicity and to see it in terms of its own values—a book with the living God shining through every page, a loving God acting in deliverance and discipline to fulfill the promise to Abraham in Genesis 12:3. Although it is occupied with Israel alone, we must not suppose that the purpose of Exodus is nationalistic; Israel is delivered from bondage and called by God into covenant obligation to him, not for its own pleasures but for the sake of all mankind. In a word: Israel is redeemed in order to redeem. Exodus is the story of Israel's calling and of the beginning of her training for this staggering role.

THE UNFOLDING STORY

More than four hundred years had elapsed since the time of Joseph. Israel by the thirteenth century B.C. had multiplied to several thousand, and these, to implement the Pharaoh's vast program of public works, were turned into state slaves. Ironically, Pharaoh held these slaves in absolute bondage, but he also feared them; and because of this fear of rebellion and sedition he exploited them the more. Soon they had nothing to lose but their chains.

Meantime an Egyptian prince—the adopted son of Pharaoh's daughter—learned his Hebrew identity, and sided with the Hebrew slaves against the Egyptians. His new role of champion to the underdog was suspect among the Hebrews, and treason to the Egyptians. So it came about that Moses, a man without a people or a country, was driven into the land of Midian; but there he met a priest and later at Sinai he met the God of the priest, who disclosed himself to Moses and called him to return to Egypt to emancipate his people from slavery.

Fighting his own reluctance, and depending upon his brother, Aaron, for moral support, Moses returned. His first efforts succeeded only in making the slavery of the Hebrews more galling, so that Moses was soon opposed not only by his own fears and by the power of a hostile throne but by the doubts and hostilities of his own kinsmen. With the aid of God, Moses finally overcame all opposition and led Israel victoriously through the Red Sea (actually, the Reed Sea) out of the grasp of the Egyptian masters.

The children of Israel came out of Egypt little more than a mob, far from ready for the assault upon Canaan. They had to be brought under law. This was the work undertaken at Sinai. The instruction of Israel was never easy. The people never ceased their grumbling. *Read Exodus* 14:10–12; 15:23–25; 16:2–3; 17:2, 3.

They preferred the security of Egypt, even though it meant slavery, to their new freedom, for freedom meant hardship and struggle. Nevertheless, reluctant and grumbling as they were and only half grateful, Israel bound itself to God in solemn covenant and promised him obedience in all areas of civil, personal, and religious life.

As God had led his people out of bondage and as he had given them the law at Sinai, he also desired to live in their midst (Exod. 25:8). This led to the making of the Ark of the Covenant (to house the law)[1] and of a Tent of Meeting to house the Ark. Thus pro-

---

[1] The Ark also contained Aaron's blossoming rod and a pot of manna.

vision was made for the continual worship of God, the Deliverer and the Lawgiver.

But, as there had been resistance to the Exodus, there was rebellion toward the law and apostasy from the worship. This is perfectly symbolized in Exodus 32 by the golden calf. God's mercy is met with ingratitude, his leading by stubbornness, his law by rebellion, his presence by idolatry—all of which emphasizes a truth so well summarized in the words: "You did not choose me, but I chose you." The call of Israel lies not in human merit but in the divine goodness. The steadfast love of God for this unworthy people, which he planned to make into a holy nation, is symbolized throughout the book by the pillar of fire and the pillar of cloud. It is on this note of the indwelling majesty and patience of God that the book closes. The time span of Exodus—from Egypt to Sinai—is two years. Thirty-eight years in the Wilderness remained to Israel; in this period a crowd of slaves was turned into a nation.

OUTLINE OF EXODUS

I.   God delivers his people, chapters 1–18
    A. Bondage, chapter 1
    B. The birth and call of Moses, chapters 2–4
    C. The contest with Pharaoh, chapters 5–11
    D. The Passover feast, chapters 12–13
    E. The escape, chapters 14–15
    F. The passage to Sinai, chapters 16–18
II. The covenant at Sinai—law and discipline, chapters 19–24
    A. God appears, chapter 19
    B. The Ten Commandments, 20:1–17
    C. The people's fear, 20:18–20
    D. The laws: civil, moral, and ritual, 20:21—23:33
    E. Ratification of the covenant, chapter 24
III. The cultus—God among his people, chapters 25–40
    A. Worship and the priests ordained, chapters 25–31
    B. Idolatry and restoration, chapters 32–34
    C. The cultus goes into effect, chapters 35–40

MAIN THEMES

1. *Bondage.* The book begins with the people of Israel caught in apparently hopeless slavery.

2. *Deliverance.* With the help of Moses, a dedicated prophet and leader, God achieves the deliverance of Israel. In this he shows both his love and his power. But he also delivers Israel because he has a purpose for his people; he plans to use them as priests of all mankind.

3. *Instruction and discipline.* Untaught slaves have a long way to go to become a nation of free men. They must learn the will of God and bow to it in personal and civil life as well as in cultic matters. God reveals himself in law and he gives the law for the good of his people.

4. *Reluctance and rebellion.* Israel co-operates poorly with God in achieving his purpose for the new nation. This emphasizes the fact that the Exodus was not a human achievement; it was truly a divine deliverance.

5. *The abiding Presence.* Yet, withal, God abides among the people he has chosen, and does not abandon his care and oversight.

KEY VERSES

"You have seen what I did to the Egyptians, and how I bore you on eagles' wings and brought you to myself. Now therefore, if you will obey my voice and keep my covenant, you shall be my own possession among all peoples; for all the earth is mine, and you shall be to me a kingdom of priests and a holy nation" (Exod. 19:4–6a).

II. PREPARING YOUR BOOK SERMON

CARDINAL IDEA

God delivered Israel from Egyptian bondage, made covenant with them at Sinai and schooled them in the discipline of the law, so they could be his people to serve as a holy priesthood for the redemption of all peoples.

SHAPING A PREACHING OUTLINE

The events of Exodus apply uniquely to Israel and cannot be applied to any other nation in the same sense. The Exodus was unrepeatable, a historical event which happened once for all time. And it is a key event, in the light of which all history of all peoples finds its meaning.

This is a large claim. Though it may be tested by reason and experience, and must be so tested, we finally accept the claim by faith, and respond to it only through a life of commitment. The Israelites themselves came to view their election as a human absurdity; there was no good human reason for it. Their people were few in number, poor in territory, inconsequential in military might, inconstant in goodness, fickle and wavering in faith. As a wry rhymster put it:

> How odd
> Of God
> To choose
> The Jews!

But the biblical faith says that God did choose them, not to be his pets, but to be his servants. He liberated them from bondage, not to irresponsible freedom, but to law and discipline. The core of Exodus, therefore, lies in the covenant which God made with Israel; by this means they responded to his act of grace in delivering them and calling them. And by this means they became his people.

In following the cardinal idea and the key passage we find the thought of Exodus moving through three phases: (1) deliverance and call; (2) covenant and law; (3) priesthood and service. This is also the outline of the book as we have given it on page 20. It is the most natural outline for the sermon.

But if Exodus applies uniquely to the covenant community of Israel, where do we come in? We come in, not through the nation to which we belong, but through the church. For the church is the New Israel and is in its own right the new covenant community. This was the thought of various New Testament writers. See Paul's thought in the allegory of the wild branch engrafted upon the olive tree (Rom. 11:17–24). See also how our key Scripture finds a clear echo in the Christian Scripture of 1 Peter 2:9–10. Further light on the same idea is contained in the Letter of Paul to the Ephesians, where the destiny of all history is seen as wrapped up with the life of God's covenant community, the church.

Several years ago the philosopher John Macmurray wrote a book, *The Clue to History,*[2] in which he developed a philosophy of his-

---

[2] New York: Harper & Brothers (1939).

tory around the notion that the Jews are still the key to the understanding of world events. This is not the accepted viewpoint of news
commentators in the press or on the air today, but it is close to the
biblical viewpoint and deserves a far more serious consideration
than it has received in modern times.

CARDINAL IDEA UNIVERSALIZED

*When God gives freedom to peoples, he delivers them not to
license but to liberty; that liberty involves the discipline of truth,
and it is squandered unless it is spent in the service of mankind.*

There are implications of Exodus which apply in some degree to
all human societies. All, to some degree, experience God's grace; all
live under the judgment of God's law; all are called to serve.

Since Exodus begins with a deliverance, we may find light here
for the meaning of human freedom. Applied to free peoples, this
idea might be outlined as follows: (1) author of liberty: basically
freedom comes from God, who made us to be free and who writes
the ultimate word of judgment against all tyrannies; (2) freedom
from bondage: freedom's holy light, streaming from God, is broken
prismatically into three primary colors, the first of which, the red
dawn of emancipation from bondage, we see here; this is only the
beginning of freedom, but it is a necessary beginning which makes
all the rest of the work of liberty possible; (3) freedom under law:
liberty and law are not inimical to each other; on the contrary, only
by accepting internal disciplines can a people avoid hopeless anarchy
and eventual dictatorship; so beneath our feet we must have the
green grass of law and discipline; ours must be a responsible freedom; (4) freedom to worship: we now know that absolute atheism is
not a live option; men who do not believe in God make lesser powers
into gods, and a nation becomes like its gods. True worship of the
true God is the blue sky of freedom. It is not enough that we are
free to worship; we *must* worship, and that worship must be di-
rected toward him whose name is Truth, for only Truth may set us
free. The Mayflower Compact of 1620 is something more than an
echo of Exodus. It breathes the atmosphere of deliverance and covenant. Thus did our nation begin.

There is a ready-made outline for a sermon in the five main
themes of the book as sketched on pp. 20–21. Though these themes

apply in special force to Israel and the Christian Church, the light they shed falls with strong illumination upon all human life, both individual and social.

If one is making application to the life of nations, he will want to call attention to the contrast between Israel and Egypt. Oppressing peoples often oppress to their own undoing. Penalization is one means by which subject peoples are challenged to greatness. Wherever people are in bondage, their cry arises to God, who hears; and God is always summoning some latter-day Moses to go down into Egypt land and "tell ol' Pharaoh, let my people go."

There is a good sermon in the two opposite meanings in the phrase "The Chosen People." Consider it first in its natural, nonbiblical meaning, somewhat after the hints supplied in the introduction to the present chapter. Then consider it in the light of the biblical idea at the heart of Exodus. The Israelites themselves frequently fell out of the biblical idea into the natural one—with disastrous results. The implications for any people, nation, society, or class are clear: Self-indulgent privilege has no charter from God. His people are his servants, chosen to minister to mankind.

A Modern Title

"God's People" and "Covenant Community" convey the idea ordinarily expressed in "The Chosen People." Any one of these will serve to represent Exodus at center. The name *Exodus* translated means "The Road Out," or "The Way Out." This, of course, is "The Road of Ages." Finally, one thinks of several suggestions from the Negro spiritual about the Exodus, "Go Down, Moses."

4

WHOLENESS AND HOLINESS

Leviticus

A RENOWNED teacher of literature once remarked that Leviticus
was a dust heap containing a single pearl. The pearl, of course,
is Leviticus 19:18b: ". . . you shall love your neighbor as yourself. . . ." This pearl is a precious one; Jesus quoted it as the second
part of his summary of the law and the prophets, and Paul quoted it
as the whole law in miniature. But when we turn to the rest of the
book—to the so-called dust heap—what do we find? We find detailed
instructions for Temple sacrifices, for the ordination and installation
of priests, for the ritual of purification from ceremonial defilement;
we find the ceremony of the ancient Day of Atonement when a
scapegoat, laden with the sins of the whole nation, was driven into
the wilderness; we find folkways and taboos—together with no less
than ten or twelve offenses punishable by death; and we find some
few regulations of a moral nature. What has all of this to do with us?

Christians will say that this whole legal system is dead as far as they
are concerned. Paul speaks for us when he says that God has for-
given our sins by grace rather than by law, ". . . having canceled
the bond which stood against us with its legal demands; this he set
aside, nailing it to the cross" (Col. 2:14). But the regulations of
Leviticus are scarcely less applicable to modern Jews; insofar as the
laws were for the Temple and its ritual, they perished from Jewish
national life with the destruction of the Jerusalem Temple in A.D. 70
when the Romans razed it. It seems highly unlikely that Judaism will
ever again slaughter lambs and bulls and goats, and burn parts of
these animals on altars as offerings to God. The symbolisms of the
synagogue seem to have displaced permanently the cruder symbols
of the Temple altar.

What religious value, then, does Leviticus have for the modern Bible reader? Or does it have any?

I. WORKING YOUR WAY INTO THE BOOK

The student of the religious past of Judaism and Christianity will find a mine of riches in Leviticus. The book will go a long way in helping him to reconstruct a picture of the Temple cultus. If he is a careful student, armed with the instruments of literary and historical analysis, he will be able to trace the development of Jewish ritual through many phases, from the earliest days of the nation up through the Persian period, following the Babylonian Exile.

The Temple of Jerusalem really came into its own in the Persian period. Jewish national life could no longer center in the throne; the monarchy was never restored. Therefore, the life of Israel came to be centered in the Temple; and the rituals of the Temple interfused all of the cherished sentiments and emotions which ordinarily attach to patriotism and religion. Take all our national holidays with their parades and bands, our national anthem, our unfurling of the colors, and our salute to the flag; take all of these and add to them the traditions of Valley Forge and Gettysburg and Plymouth Rock. These stand for patriotism. Now take the sacred associations of baptisms and church weddings and Holy Communions and stirring anthems and choir processionals and Christmas celebrations and Easter festivals. These stand for religion. Now roll patriotism and religion together and think of the way in which they tug at our heartstrings, how they grip and inspire us. Ritual and ceremony are the language of action by which a people gives expression to its corporate soul. As meaningful parts of the living present they are integral to our culture; by them we lift ourselves above the beasts into the realm of purpose and meaning. But, of course, as relics of the past, the dusty flags and symbols of yesterday molder among the bones of dead civilizations, and we have great difficulty in resurrecting them in our imagination to their rightful significance.

The ceremonies of Leviticus point to a colorful past, once living at the heart of Jewish national life. They are the mechanical instructions for priests and laymen in certain ritual observances. By themselves they are uninteresting. To appreciate the full meaning of

Leviticus we need to think of Temple worship as a whole—Temple worship with its processionals and symbolic dances, its orchestras and massed choirs, its antiphonal songs. It has been suggested that Leviticus should be read in company with the Psalms; Leviticus gives the mechanics of Temple worship, but Psalms discloses its soul.

Read (in this order) Psalms 42:4; 68:24–25; 149:1–3; 150:3–5; 84:10.

A KINGDOM OF PRIESTS

Israel's call, as we have seen from our previous studies in Genesis and Exodus, was a call to minister to the whole of humanity in the service of God. Israel was to be the world's priest, and its Temple. See Exodus 19:6, for example: ". . . you shall be to me a kingdom of priests and a holy nation."

It is but a step from this role to a searching imperative. A nation which is to serve the world as its priest must be set aside for its office; it must be consecrated and holy. To lead the world in worship, the Chosen People must be especially diligent in worship. To be the Temple of the world, this people must have a Temple at the center of its own life. It is instructive, for instance, that the high priest began the ceremonies of the Day of Atonement with a sin offering for himself and his house. Only after such purification could he make atonement for the sins of the people.

Read Leviticus 16:6.

The role of worship, therefore, is central to the redemptive mission of the people of God. Worship can become dead ritual, or it can become a superstitious sacerdotalism, drying up the springs of private devotion and ethical sensitivity; but at its best, worship is a free-flowing artesian well of life and inspiration, nourishing the whole life of culture. The central institutions of any culture are the religious ones. Who would care to see our churches, our synagogues, and our cathedrals fall into total disuse and ruin? Who would want to see all vestiges of organized religion vanish from our national life?

Apply this insight to our Western culture. It takes only a little reflection to see that the cultus of worship is really at the center, and that nearly all social institutions are the daughters of the church. This is perfectly symbolized in the physical setting of the New

England town in which I served as minister during my days at Yale Divinity School. At the center of the town was "the green," and on the green stood the most prominent building in the whole town, the white church with its tall spire. Near the church stood the town hall, symbol of direct rule by the people, an absolute democracy. Not far distant was the public school, symbol of the democracy of the mind. In the church lives the faith—"You will know the truth, and the truth will make you free"—the faith which is the fountain-source of political democracy and universal education. Cut off democracy and education from their source and they will live on for a while, like cut flowers; but ultimately they will die for want of roots and the nourishment that only roots can give. If a nation is to be God's people, it must worship!

Outline of Leviticus

For all its confusing multiplicity of laws and penalties, Leviticus falls neatly into five main divisions plus an appendix, as follows:

   I. Worship, 1:1—7:38
      A. Regulations for the five main kinds of offerings, 1:1—6:7
      B. Instructions to the priests, 6:8—7:36
      C. Conclusion, 7:37–38
  II. Ministry, 8:1—10:20
      A. Ordination, 8:1–36
      B. Installation, 9:1–24
      C. Warning—the peril of profaning the priesthood, 10:1–20
 III. Laws of purification—national consecration, 11:1—15:33
      A. Clean and unclean animals, 11:1–47
      B. Women after childbirth, 12:1–8
      C. Leprosy, 13:1—14:57
      D. Sex, 15:1–33
 IV. Yearly Day of Atonement, 16:1–34
  V. The Holiness Code, 17:1—26:46
      A. Sacrifices and food, 17:1–16
      B. Sexual relations, 18:1–30
      C. Social behavior, 19:1–37
      D. Penalties, 20:1–27
      E. Sacrifices and priests, 21:1—22:33
      F. The annual festivals, 23:1–44

Taking the five main topics of Leviticus, we may universalize them sufficiently to see that they bear upon public worship, the clergy, the dedication of folkways to God, atonement for sin, and holiness. Let us look briefly at each.

MAIN THEMES

1. *Worship.* As presented in Leviticus, worship is practiced through the ritual of a now outmoded sacrificial system. Probably we shall never discover the full secret of these rituals. Why did the mind of man think to serve God in this fashion? But we can see some factors which emerge as authentic notes of worship in any time: (*a*) Sacrifice was visible, unarticulated prayer. It was a way of communion with God. (*b*) Sacrifice was restitution, symbolic not literal. In this connection it is instructive to observe that literal restitution, together with a fine, had to be paid to the wronged person; and in addition an offering had to be brought to God (Lev. 6:2–7). This is a recognition that fraud against men is, in its deepest sense, an offense against God. (*c*) Sacrifice was a means to communion and fellowship. Many sacrifices were partially consumed by fire on the altar; the larger part of the sacrificial animal was then eaten at a sacred meal by the worshipers. The function of this meal was like that of the Holy Communion in Christian worship; it was a dual communion, with God and with man. (*d*) Sacrifice was frequently thanksgiving. Not all offerings were expiation of guilt; many were for blessings received. (*e*) Sacrifice was homage to God—the paying of honor to God. Thus, dimly at some times and more vividly at others, we see shining through the ancient practices of sacrifice the main themes of worship in all ages.

2. *Ministry.* Although all Israelites were a part of the priesthood, there was need for a special clergy. Priests were set aside in special ceremonies for their lifework, and they were required to hold to an exalted standard of personal excellence both in ritual and in morals.

While it is unkind of laymen to require their ministers to live better lives than they are willing to lead, it is proper and right that ministers should require this of themselves. To live a profane life is always unworthy, but to offer profane fire at the altar is blasphemous.

3. *National consecration.* Details of folkways differ from age to age. Certainly there are few of the Jewish practices which we would care to adopt literally. But the main point still remains valid. The faith of a nation should express itself in a thousand little items of daily life. Many of these have no obvious explanation. They are rituals, like "hello" and "good-by" and shaking hands, but they are all important parts of the folkways which spell out in detail the total atmosphere and attitude of a people. In all our ways let us seek to acknowledge him, not alone when we are in the Temple.

4. *Atonement.* This annual renewal of life through confession of sins may be the secret of Jewish survival. While it is normal to other nations to boast and to blame, it is the genius of the Jews that their most important national holiday is the Day of Atonement. Through confession and forgiveness it is possible for a people to begin again. This time of humiliation is also a time of renewal. Here is a lesson other nations need to learn. We Americans, for instance, are quick to confess the sins of Russia, but slow to see our own.

5. *Holiness.* Holiness has come to mean moral purity. This meaning is derived from the idea of separation. The people whom God calls are to separate themselves from the ways of idolatry and the pagan practices of other peoples. A holy people is one given wholly to the Lord. The key idea is found in a verse like the following: "And you shall not walk in the customs of the nation which I am casting out before you . . ." (20:23). But that is the negative side of the matter; the positive side reads: "Consecrate yourselves therefore, and be holy; for I am the Lord your God" (20:7). In modern times, we are more impressed with the moral aspects of this holiness, and as we read Leviticus we find its most inspiring verses in the elevated ethical code of chapter 19:

Read Leviticus 19:9–18, 33–37.

KEY VERSE

"Say to all the congregation of the people of Israel, You shall be holy; for I the Lord your God am holy" (Lev. 19:2).

II. PREPARING YOUR BOOK SERMON

CARDINAL IDEA

Priest and Temple, administering ritual and moral law, exist to train Israel as God's people, to purify and sanctify their whole life, and to join them to him in fellowship and devotion.

Applied to the church, the New Israel, this idea may be universalized somewhat as follows: *The cultus and the ministry, guiding the church in worship and moral instruction, exist to train the church as God's own people, to purify them, to permeate their common life, and to join them to him in fellowship and devotion.*

SHAPING A PREACHING OUTLINE

We can scarcely offer a better approach to a sermon on Leviticus than the outline which is implicit in the previous discussion of the five main themes of the book. Such an outline has the merit of beginning at the altar and of leading out of the house of worship to the house of our neighbor. It first makes religion inspiringly real, and then it makes it realistically relevant to daily life.

The suggestion that Leviticus should be read side by side with the Psalms may stir someone to construct a table of relationships in which the five main themes of Leviticus are illustrated by appropriate quotations from the Psalter. The idea sounds attractive and should be rewarding.

A much simpler outline is suggested by some Jewish commentators who see Leviticus as built around two main themes: (1) sacrifice and purification, and (2) holiness. The first deals with confession, restitution, and forgiveness for sin; it culminates in the Day of Atonement (Lev. 16). The second deals with the consecration of the common life, imparting sacramental meaning even to ordinary acts such as the cooking and eating of meals. While Jewish dietary laws are alien to us, their meaning is not difficult to see; Paul conveyed this meaning when he wrote to the Corinthians: "So, whether you eat or drink, or whatever you do, do all to the glory of God" (1 Cor. 10:31). Under the first heading in this outline, that of sacrifice and purification, one should note that there were different kinds of sacrifices: whole burnt offerings, symbolizing the surrender of the whole self to God; sin offerings, symbolizing repentance; peace offerings, symbolizing gratitude to God for his bounties; and congregational offerings, part of which were eaten at a sacramental meal by the worshipers as a body, symbolizing human brotherhood devoted to the service of God. Under the second heading of this same outline, the heading of holiness, the consecration of the common life rises to its highest level for the Christian in Leviticus 19:18, which our Lord quoted as half of his summary of the law.

A Modern Title

"Wholeness and Holiness" seems to come closest to the central thrust of the book, especially as we have outlined it in the preceding paragraph. Other possible titles are: "The Lord in His Holy Temple," "Faith Permeates Life," "The Call to Holiness," and "Worship Acceptable to God."

5

HALFWAY TO THE PROMISED LAND

Numbers

THE English name of this book, derived through the Latin and Greek versions, refers to the numbering, or census of the Israelites described in the early chapters. Since the book itself is more concerned with other themes, this English title tells us little about the contents of the book. The Hebrew Bible is much more helpful; the title there, taken from the first words of the book, is "In the Wilderness." Numbers is about God's discipline of Israel through the forty years of Wilderness wanderings. In other words, it deals with the transition from bondage to full national freedom.

Freedom is something more than simple emancipation. In Exodus and Leviticus, we learn that freedom needs law and faith. In Numbers, stress is laid on the necessity of discipline.

I. WORKING YOUR WAY INTO THE BOOK

OUTLINE OF NUMBERS

Numbers covers approximately forty years, the whole period that Israel spent in the Wilderness between the time of its encampment at Sinai and its entrance into Canaan. Considered in terms of the wanderings, the book falls naturally into three divisions:

I. At Sinai, 1:1—10:10
II. Wanderings, from Sinai to Moab, 10:11—22:1
III. On the plains of Moab, 22:2—36:13

But the book as it now stands does not make for easy, continuous reading. This is because of the census lists and the laws and priestly regulations which consume most of the first ten chapters. The casual reader is firmly discouraged at the very start. These same interests in census and priestly regulations (especially the latter) consume other portions of the book, notably chapters 15, 17–19, 26–30, and 33. With the temporary omission of these chapters it is possible to get at the narrative heart of the book, which then emerges as an absorbing story.

Therefore, in your reading of Numbers do not begin at the beginning. Begin, instead, with the tenth chapter and go on as follows:

Read Numbers 10:11–14:45; 16:1–17:13; 20:1–24:25; 27:12–23; 31:1–54.

Having read these selections in a single sitting, one is then free to go back and read the more technical material. Meanwhile, the over-all meaning will inform the more detailed study.

Rabble in Arms

The undisciplined crowd of onetime slaves whom Moses led out of Egypt were far from being a nation. They had been ruled for so long that they had forgotten the meaning of self-rule. And they had experienced the benefits of security for so long that they were utterly inexperienced in matters of freedom. Therefore, Moses did not lead an army that surged forward with the eagerness of pioneers. He led a rabble composed in unequal proportion of three classes of people, as John Haynes Holmes pointed out a number of years ago: (1) the people of yesterday, those who longed to return to Egypt, to whom security—even though it was security within slavery— meant more than freedom; (2) the people of today, those who took their manna and their water where they found it and who complained bitterly about their present lot; lost in the immediate, seeing neither backward nor forward; (3) the people of tomorrow, that small minority who saw the vision of the Promised Land and who stretched toward it in eagerness. Caleb was one of these; Joshua was another.

Consider, for example, the constant complaining with which Moses had to contend:

Read Numbers 11:1, 4; 14:1–4; 20:2–5.

Jealousy broke out among the leaders and came even into the family of Moses:

Read Numbers 12:1, 2.

Among the leaders, jealousy of Moses' authority developed until it became a rebellion:

Read Numbers 16:3.

This complaining band of former slaves also lacked the courage for the work that was before them. Notice, for example, the majority report of the spies who returned from their inspection of Canaan:

Read Numbers 13:31–33.

MOSES

Moses was a magnificent leader. Though at times he chafed against his demanding role, he accepted the responsibility of being the father of his people:

Read Numbers 11:11–12.

It was through Moses that God reached his people to teach and discipline them. It was through Moses that the sense of the living God in the midst of his people was kept alive throughout the long years of discouragement. Moses stood before his people as the representative of both the goodness and the severity of God.

But that is not all. As Moses interceded with his people on behalf of God, he likewise interceded with God on behalf of his people. His was the heart of a true shepherd:

Read Numbers 14:13–19.

GOD IN THE MIDST

But God is in the midst of his people. The foremost symbol of this presence is the Tabernacle with its sacred Ark of the Covenant. There was also the pillar of cloud by day and of fire by night. These speak at one and the same time of the nearness and the majesty of God. God leads his people when they are on the way, and he dwells with them when they are in camp, but he holds them at arm's length. He is not their servant, but their God.

THE SENSE OF MIRACLE

Looking at the undisciplined rabble with which they started and at the small beginnings, our most natural reaction is a question:

"How did they ever make it?" The sense of miracle was strong also in those writers who looked back upon this early time from the vantage point of a later century. For this reason they laid stress upon the multitude, the sheer growth of the population from the tiny beginnings in Joseph's day—hence the preoccupation with census. For this reason, too, they stressed God's provision for the physical needs of Israel: the manna, the quail, the water at oases. Likewise, there was gratitude for victory over disease and human enemies. For a summary of this sense of miracle one may read the delightful, humorous tale of Balaam, a Mesopotamian prophet imported by the king of Moab to pronounce a curse on Israel, who ended by blessing them.

Folk Songs

The poetic sections of the book are undoubtedly very ancient. They preserve a glimpse of the celebrations in song and dance over progress in the journey, at the digging of a well, and at a military victory:

Read Numbers 21:14–15, 17–18, 27–30.

A little historical imagination will bring these songs to life out of the storied past which created them; and it will also bind us in sympathy with this people on their way to nationhood.

The oracles of Balaam in chapters 23 and 24 also offer a high degree of inspiration.

A Quick Summary

For a quick summary of events from Exodus through Numbers and Judges:

Read Psalm 106:1–3, 6–48.

These verses leave little doubt that it was God who was at work in the disciplining and making of a nation. Rebellion, jealousy, complaint, unfaithfulness, were steadily met by the love of God through his judgment and through his deliverance. The load of freedom is a heavy burden for man to carry, but it is even heavier for God. To bring men out of bondage into the glorious liberty of the sons of God is a costly, redeeming task for him and for servants of his like

Moses, who led against great folk resistance toward the call of folk destiny.

II. PREPARING YOUR BOOK SERMON

CARDINAL IDEA

It was God's will that Israel should enter the Promised Land; but until the Israelites could learn to transcend their own selfish desires in loyal, disciplined service to God, they were compelled to wander in the Wilderness.

Properly universalized, this idea has important implications both for individuals and societies. The Wilderness wanderings stood between the bondage of Egypt and a national destiny in Canaan. We can locate Egypt, the Wilderness, and Canaan geographically and chronologically, in which case the story of Numbers is about an ancient people now buried, and reposes in an ancient time now past. On the other hand, we may also locate these three terms psychologically, in the experiences of people everywhere. Egypt then becomes life under duress in some form; Canaan represents coming into one's own; and the Wilderness is the middle ground that lies between. From one side, the Wilderness experience is one of spoiled self-indulgence—the longing for plenty and security, the pouring forth of blame and rebellion. This is freedom without responsibility, liberty degenerated into license. In short, it is not freedom at all, but anarchy. It is not self-determination, but self-destruction. From the other side, the Wilderness experience is the taming of these wild impulses, putting them under discipline to God and man in responsible service.

Apply this to an adolescent just leaving home and learning the disciplines of school and market place. Apply it also to a once-subject people just beginning to tread the hard, dangerous path of self-government. (It is natural to cheat foreign masters, but political graft will kill a democracy; a people who would govern themselves must learn to tame their greed.) Apply it to individual experiences, such as the breaking of a bad habit; only something positive can take its place. Above all, apply it to the church, which tends to forsake its covenant bond with God and to seek its life on its own terms for its own self-indulgent advantage.

Shaping a Preaching Outline

There is, first, the simple narrative of the Wilderness years suggested by the verses listing the narrative heart of the book. A well-told story may carry its own point. Paul Green's stirring drama[1] about Berea College, which in recent summers has played to more than 150,000 persons, suggests both the title and the mood for such a sermon: "Wilderness Road."

Second, there is the outline by John Haynes Holmes, dividing the wandering Israelites into three groups: (1) the people of yesterday; (2) the people of today; (3) the people of tomorrow. (See the discussion of this idea on p. 34.

A third approach uses the outline of the book itself as the organizing principle of the sermon: (1) the beginning at Sinai; the vision of the people, strong in the sense of God's presence; this foundational reality is symbolized throughout the book by the Tabernacle, by the Ark of the Covenant which was carried at the head of the marching column, and by the pillar of cloud and of fire. This point might be called "The Basis of an Ordered Society." (2) the Wilderness wanderings; the essence of these years is discipline, but the experiences range over a wide realm of human emotion and circumstance—vacillation, uncertainty, rebellion, hardship, defeat, discouragement. This point might be called "The Discipline of a Wandering Society." (3) on the heights of Moab, overlooking the Promised Land; at last they broke through the long ordeal of the desert and stood with the Promised Land before their eyes, and this with the knowledge that God had used them in spite of themselves and had finally made them into a nation. This point might be called "The Promise of a Society on the Threshold."

A Modern Title

"In the Wilderness" is the Hebrew title of this book; it is fairly descriptive of the contents of Numbers and may well serve as the name of the book sermon. "A Blessed Preparation" fits the third sermon idea, outlined in the preceding paragraph. "Pilgrims in the Wilderness," "Wilderness Road," and "Halfway from Slavery to Freedom" are other possibilities.

[1] *Wilderness Road; A Symbolic Outdoor Drama* (New York: Samuel French, Inc., 1956).

6

THIS NATION UNDER GOD

Deuteronomy

THIS book is a collection of sermons that started a national revolution. Never did a sacred writing have a more immediate or a more startling influence upon the life of a people. The title, a transliteration of its name in the Septuagint, means "The Second Law." It really indicates the rebirth of law leading to the rebirth of a nation.

In this book, Israel went back to its pilgrim days and found its roots in the era of Moses, just as Americans may go back to the Pilgrim Fathers and find the key to their national origins and destiny as a people. A great hymn captures the spirit of Deuteronomy as it applies to America:

> O God, beneath Thy guiding hand
> Our exiled fathers crossed the sea;
> And, when they trod the wintry strand,
> With prayer and psalm they worshiped Thee.
>
> Thou heard'st, well pleased, the song, the prayer:
> Thy blessing came; and still its power
> Shall onward, through all ages, bear
> The memory of that holy hour.
>
> Laws, freedom, truth, and faith in God
> Came with those exiles o'er the waves;
> And where their pilgrim feet have trod,
> The God they trusted guards their graves.
>
> And here Thy Name, O God of love,
> Their children's children shall adore,
> Till these eternal hills remove,
> And spring adorns the earth no more.[1]

[1] Leonard Bacon, "The Pilgrim Fathers."

I. WORKING YOUR WAY INTO THE BOOK

Background

As early as the fourth century A.D. Jerome and other church fathers identified Deuteronomy with the book found in the Temple during the reign of Josiah:
Read 2 Kings 22:1–23:30.
The finding of the book and the beginning of Josiah's reform may be dated about 621 B.C. A careful comparison of the account in Kings with that in Deuteronomy makes it clear that the book which sparked that nationwide religious revolution was almost certainly the core of the present book of Deuteronomy. The reforms were sweeping. All elements of foreign worship were purged from Judah and Israel. Shrines outside Jerusalem were destroyed. Worship was centralized in the Temple at Jerusalem. The neglected festivals of Israel were resumed. There was a nationwide return to Israel's ancestral faith.

Deuteronomy came at the right moment in the history of Judah. Through the long, fifty-five-year reign of Manasseh and the two-year reign of his son, Amon, plus the first eighteen years of Josiah when the kingdom was under a regent until Josiah should come of age—through these seventy-five years Judah had been in the grip of religious apostasy:
Read 2 Kings 21:1–9, 16–18.
The key to this apostasy was the attempt of Judah's rulers to appease Assyria and the surrounding states by adopting their culture and their cultus. The picture of religious crudities practiced in this period is not a pretty one, for it includes sacred prostitution and human sacrifice.

Judah was ripe and ready for reform. It was time for the pendulum to swing. Moreover, political conditions in the Fertile Crescent were ready. Assyria was in eclipse, on the brink of final extinction. No longer could this ruthless empire impose her way of life upon her former victims. New destinies were in the making. There was always the hope that this would mean a new and brighter day for the Jews. In this time between the times, at the end of one epoch and just before the beginning of another, the hour of the book struck, and a nation took heroic measures to recapture its ancestral faith.

Almost a century had passed since the preaching and writing of the prophetic "Big Four"—Amos, Hosea, Isaiah, Micah. In its own time their work had failed. But now the spirit of their labor rose and effected what they could not do in their own lifetimes. For the reforms of Josiah—in keeping with Deuteronomy, which inspired them—were in the best tradition of the prophets.

FORM AND STYLE

Deuteronomy is cast in the form of three sermons delivered to the nation of Israel by Moses in the last days of the fortieth year of the Wilderness sojourn. The book opens on the first day of the eleventh month of the final year "in the Wilderness," and ends before the Israelites crossed the Jordan in their invasion of Canaan for the first day of the new year:

Read Deuteronomy 1:3; 34:8; *Joshua* 4:19.

At this point, when the Israelites are on the threshold of entering their Promised Land, Moses pauses to recall their national history up to that point, to show his hearers how all this roots in the covenant love of God, demonstrated in his deliverance of Israel from the bondage of Egypt. Then Moses goes on to spell out what it means for a nation to respond to such steadfast love. Such a nation must love God with its whole being. It must worship no foreign gods; it must allow no admixture of foreign influences in its worship. It must remain loyal to the ancestral faith and its simple, disciplined way of life. Moreover, justice and humane mercy must characterize the human relations of such a nation, for these are the people who once were slaves and whom God rescued; having obtained mercy, an Israelite must dispense mercy. Not only is such covenant love toward God the root of the nation, it is also the life of the nation. Let Israel remain loyal and it will prosper; but let it stray from its God and it will perish. Therefore, in the hour when it is entering a new, untried era, let Israel renew its covenant with God! Such is the burden of the three sermons.

Now, to look at the sermons individually. The first sermon is found in Deuteronomy 1:6–4:40. Its burden is a review of history during the previous thirty-eight years in the Wilderness, which have ended in several military victories. These victories augur well for the future. The sermon ends with a stirring appeal to Israel to obey the law because of the love and power of God shown at Mt. Horeb.

The second sermon, a long one, is found in Deuteronomy 5:1-28: 68. It falls naturally into three divisions: (1) introduction (chaps. 5-11), stressing the obedience Israel owes to God in response to his mighty acts: choosing them, delivering them, instructing them, and disciplining them as his own people; (2) exposition (chaps. 12-26), a rather detailed account of what the covenant demands of Israel by way of cultic purity and morality; (3) conclusion (chaps. 27-28), a table of blessings for those who keep the law and of curses for those who break it.

The third sermon (Deut. 29:1-30:20) has a very simple, direct appeal to covenant loyalty: Israel must remain true to God, for apostasy will bring disaster. The choice before her is a choice between life and death.

There are a few sections of the book not included in these three sermons of Moses. The largest of these is an appendix, which gives us the Farewell of Moses (31:1-33:29) and the Death of Moses (34:1-12). The Farewell of Moses, in particular, bears a liturgical stamp; here are corporate acts of worship. In chapter 4 there is a brief narrative interlude which tells of the founding of three cities of refuge in the Transjordan (4:41-43) and which introduces the giving of the law in Moab (4:44-49). There is also the introduction to the whole book in 1:1-5.

We may say that Deuteronomy, therefore, is the prophetic preaching of the covenant. A simple division of the book, for the moment ignoring the organization around three sermons, might break into three main parts, with an introduction and an appendix, as outlined below.

OUTLINE OF DEUTERONOMY

    I. Introduction: Moses speaks to all Israel, 1:1-5
   II. The covenant in history: its meaning, 1:6—11:32
  III. The demands of the covenant
       A. Religious institutions, 12:1—17:7
       B. Those in authority, 17:8—18:22
       C. Various laws: crime, war, property, family, 19:1—25:19
       D. Two orders of worship, 26:1-15
  IV. The blessing and the curse, 27:1—30:20

V. Appendix: the farewell and death of Moses, 31:1—34:12

Deuteronomy is written in a flowing oratorical style. Throughout, it makes a constant appeal to motives and emotions. It is meant to *move* its readers and its hearers.

MAIN THEMES

1. The unity, majesty, and goodness of God.
2. The love of God for his people, expressed in his mighty acts of choosing them, giving them the revelation of his law, delivering them from bondage, and bringing them to a homeland.
3. Israel, a holy people, with its origin and its meaning to be found only in response to God's covenant love. This means unswerving loyalty to God alone, with severe penalties for apostasy; it also means justice and generosity in human relations. Largely as a measure to cleanse the nation from tendencies toward apostasy, worship is centralized in one Temple.
4. National prosperity and adversity are related to the people's faithfulness or unfaithfulness to God in their worship, service, and ethical behavior.

Shocking to us may be the number of offenses which carry the death penalty: murder (19:11–13); sexual promiscuity (22:20–22); selling an Israelite as a slave (24:7); worshiping an idol (13:6–11); and persistently disobeying one's parents (21:18–21). These all center in the sterling importance of absolute loyalty to God and the consequent solidarity and purity of social life. Deuteronomy is a book calling for a burning love of, and loyalty to, God at the center of national life.

KEY VERSES

What passage could serve better than the famous Shema, which to this day is the morning and evening call to prayer for all pious Jews? Thus we nominate Deuteronomy 6:4. But by itself this verse does not supply the motivation; we must see the love commanded as a response to the love of God already poured out upon Israel. Thus we add a section on God's election and deliverance of Israel: Deuteronomy 7:6–11.

Another passage, particularly appealing because of the inwardness of the loyalty it evokes, is Deuteronomy 30:11–14. The Apostle Paul found this much to his liking (see Rom. 10:6–8).

II. PREPARING YOUR BOOK SERMON

CARDINAL IDEA

The life of Israel centers in God, first in terms of what God has done and is doing for Israel, then in terms of an answering love for, and reverent obedience to, God on the part of his people, and finally in terms of a just and humane standard of human relations; when a people loses such a religious center it is in peril.

SHAPING A PREACHING OUTLINE

The universalization of the cardinal idea will apply most readily to the church, the New Israel. It will apply less readily to a nation. Nevertheless, there is in the Pilgrim heritage a good deal that enables Americans to read their history in terms of Christian faith and commitment. Perhaps it may be put this way: The message of Deuteronomy represents the religious ideal of a nation; as citizens we Christians will naturally hold to some such ideal. With that modification and in the spirit of Leonard Bacon's hymn, quoted early in the present chapter, the light of Deuteronomy may shine upon America.

The structure of the book itself will serve quite readily as an outline for a sermon. All one needs to do is to universalize the main points slightly. Then one will get something like the following: (1) what God has done for America: its beginnings in deliverance from bondage, in solemn covenant, and in the disciplines of its early history; this may be traced out in a kind of parallel, showing how deliverance, covenant, and discipline worked for Israel and how those same factors worked for America, or for other nations; (2) what the nation owes to God: reverent loyalty and social justice; (3) the importance of all this: the choice of life and death that lies before us.

A second approach may be based upon the actual words of the book. For example, the second sermon of Moses could be condensed into a twenty-five-minute sermon. (In its present form it is at least an hour long.) Modern relevance will be implicit. The sermon may conclude with a brief application to America today.

A third sermon may be based upon the background of Deuteronomy in 2 Kings 22-23. It will show the effect of taking the Bible seriously in national life. This sermon will sketch the perils and dangers of Judah from 700 to 621 B.C., showing how that nation gradually lost its national character through expediency and through religious and cultural absorption into contemporary paganism. Judah was at the end of an epoch, and at the beginning of a new, uncertain time. It is easy to see the parallels between such a time-between-the-times and our own era. We are a people with a religious heritage, and our hope lies, as did Judah's, in recovering a burning allegiance to this ancestral faith. This we can do if we can repair the temple and recover the book—not as a dead letter but as a living Spirit, a response of love and loyalty in gratitude for all that God has done for us.

As applied to the church, the implications of Deuteronomy are fairly obvious. The force of a single loyalty to one God has special relevance. It means destroying the outlying shrines, obliterating our lingering polytheism of rival gods and substitute gods, whom we worship so easily. The church can make such a rival deity of itself; or it may worship at the market shrine of business success, or at the political shrine of power, or in the drawing rooms of shallow politeness and pseudo culture.

Whatever application we make, there is one point at which Christian insight will probably part company with the message of Deuteronomy. This is at the point of the gospel of material prosperity. A righteous life may tend to health and wealth; there is much to show that it often does. But frequently it leads also to suffering, even to martyrdom. The welfare of God's people, as measured by the Christian gospel, is not registered at the bank. Its treasures are elsewhere, where moth and rust do not corrupt.

A Modern Title

"This Nation Under God," or "Law Grounded in Love," or "Hear, O America, the Lord Your God is One," or "Laws, Freedom, Truth, and Faith in God." The last of these titles is suggested by the hymn, "O God, Beneath Thy Guiding Hand," which is in itself a good title. Another hymn, "God of Our Fathers, Whose Almighty Hand," gives us another very good title: "In This Free Land." The words are from the second stanza, which is fully in keeping with the spirit and message of Deuteronomy:

> Thy love divine hath led us in the past;
> In this free land by Thee our lot is cast;
> Be Thou our Ruler, Guardian, Guide, and Stay,
> Thy Word our law, Thy paths our chosen way.[2]

[2] Daniel C. Roberts.

7

A SAVIOR WITH A SWORD

The Book of Joshua

JOSHUA was the soldier-statesman who led the Israelites as they invaded Canaan in the thirteenth century B.C. and set out upon their war of conquest. The story that the book tells is simple and stirring. It is "full of blood and thunder" and should appeal to audiences fed so consistently by a television diet of gunsmoke and frontier violence from the settlement of the American West. In fact, the book has many parallels to the frontier period of our own national history and can best be understood when we recall our own national origins—invading a new land, pitting ourselves against its thick wilderness, fighting its inhabitants, learning to tame the soil and settle down as citizens.

The story told in Joshua is simple and straightforward, but it plunges us into great perplexities. It does this because the moral standards in the book clash with the moral ideals of the twentieth-century Western world. In Joshua, war is presented as holy; God himself commands military conquest; Joshua, the hero, has a name which means quite literally "Yahweh is Salvation"; hence, Joshua is a savior with a sword! The very concept seems to us a contradiction in terms. How can a leader in a war of aggression be a savior? How can he possibly be doing the will of God? There are other crudities in the book: the wholesale slaughter of noncombatants including women and children, the wanton destruction of cities, the acceptance of the blood feud as an instrument of justice. We are perfectly willing to accept a story like this as an account of the "dark and bloody ground" over which our ancestors marched to bring us the heritage of civilization, but to interpret such inhumane actions as the

47

will of God offends our moral sensibilities. We can see it as history, but to see it from the viewpoint of its original authors and editors as "salvation-history" is very difficult. The Joshua of the Old Testament with his sword seems to us wholly inconsistent with the Joshua of the New Testament with his cross. (*Jesus* is the Greek form of the same Jewish name, Joshua, meaning *Yahweh is Salvation.*) The Savior with a cross seems to demand our eternal repudiation of the savior with a sword. Purely as a book of adventure Joshua is thrilling; but as a book of faith Joshua is perplexing. How shall we understand it or preach its message?

I. WORKING YOUR WAY INTO THE BOOK

THE EDITOR'S STANDPOINT

Joshua is sometimes referred to as the sixth book of the Hexateuch; it does follow chronologically after the story of Deuteronomy, beginning "After the death of Moses" (Josh. 1:1). But for that matter, it would be possible to speak of Genesis through Joshua, plus Judges, 1 and 2 Samuel, and 1 and 2 Kings as one continuous history from Creation to the Babylonian Exile. The Jews themselves, who wrote this history, prefer to group the books as follows: the five books of Moses, the Pentateuch or the Torah, in one collection; the remaining six books of history, the Former Prophets, in a second collection. We moderns do not think of this second collection as prophetic, preferring to call it "history," but the Jews did so think of it. This should throw light on their interpretation; Joshua and the other books of "history" are *interpreted* history, seen in the light of faith. In particular, Joshua was written long after the events, probably in the prophetic surge of the seventh and eighth centuries, viewing the coming of the Hebrew pioneers into Canaan in the light of Israel's covenant with God.

From a literary standpoint Joshua offers a tangled problem to scholars. Seemingly it was edited out of many literary strands. One of these is specifically identified as the Book of Jashar:
    Read Joshua 10:12–13.
Another book which is specifically named as a source in Numbers

may well have served Joshua. This was the Book of the Wars of the Lord:

Read Numbers 21:14, 15.

Besides these books which are named, there were undoubtedly many which are not named but are nonetheless drawn upon. Scholars are not agreed as to what these sources were precisely; but they are agreed that the final editor was "Deuteronomic," or prophetic in spirit. He thus interpreted Israelite national disaster as an outgrowth of disloyalty to Yahweh, and national success and prosperity as the result of religious loyalty. The keeping or breaking of the covenant between God and Israel is the key to Israel's history; that is the editor's standpoint. This standpoint finds its clearest expression in the opening chapter and in Joshua's farewell address:

Read Joshua 1:6–8; 23:4–13.

OUTLINE OF THE BOOK OF JOSHUA

Since the book has its own high story of adventure, there is no better way to enjoy it than to read it as a connected whole from beginning to end. That story falls into four clearly defined parts, constituting the outline of the book:

I. Preparations for invasion and the Jordan crossing, chapters 1–5
II. Conquest and occupation of Canaan, chapters 6–13
III. Allocations of land to the tribes, chapters 14–22
IV. Joshua's farewell and death, chapters 23–24

We need to comment briefly upon an apparent contradiction concerning the speed and thoroughness of the conquest. The book of Joshua as a whole gives the impression that all of Canaan was completely conquered and subjugated in the short space of seven years:

Read Joshua 10:40–43; 11:16–20, 23; 21:43–45.

The first chapter of Judges gives a sharply contrasting account:

Read Judges 1:19, 21, 27–36.

A careful reading of certain passages in Joshua reveals this same piecemeal kind of conquest. We need not suppose that it is entirely inconsistent with Joshua's first, lightning thrust into Canaan. Archaeological evidence points unmistakably to the destruction of several Canaanite towns in the thirteenth century—Bethel, Lachish, Beth-

shemesh, and Debir underwent complete destruction. Because of an inscription found in the ruins, the destruction of Lachish can be dated with great precision soon after 1220 B.C. Archaeological evidence for the destruction of Jericho and Ai in the very same period is more confused but is not contradictory to the view that the Israelites came into Canaan not as a slow infiltration of migrating clans but as a united army of invaders.[1] It is well known, of course, that the fierce unity of war often breaks down in the aftermath. It is one thing to win a war; it is another and longer battle to win a peace:
Read Joshua 13:13; 15:14, 63; 16:10; 17:12–18; 23:4, 5, 12, 13.

SOME SOURCES OF PERPLEXITY

The Ban

Our story presents us with the ancient antithesis to the modern Geneva Protocol against war. This is *the ban* (*hērem* in Hebrew) or *the devoted thing*. For a specific instance of its application:
Read Joshua 6:16–19.

The notion is that a conquered city, its property and its inhabitants, is to be regarded not as booty but as an offering to God. The humane alternatives of taking war prisoners, of respecting their dignity and their rights, and of granting them eventual freedom did not seem to enter the picture as live options. The alternatives of this crude time were two: (1) taking booty of war and capturing slaves or (2) unselfishly devoting it all to God, as an immense burnt offering and sacrifice.

Achan, who violated the ban, did so from no humanitarian motives but purely for selfish reasons. In so doing he elevated his own private interests above those of Israel; and he also cared more for gain than for the service of God. An event has to be understood in terms of its own dynamics. A prevalence of the Achan attitude and its spread to all the invading troops would have sabotaged the strength of Joshua's army.
Read Joshua 7.

There is no humanitarianism here. There is barbarous cruelty,

---

[1] Archaeologists believe that the capture of Jericho was much exaggerated in later memory or that the taking of Jericho was confused with the taking of a different site.

both in the slaughter of innocents and in the imputing of guilt to Achan's family and even to his livestock! But there is a noble side. There is the inhibition of selfish, predatory aims; and there is self-denying devotion to a cause without expectation of private gain. We are caught here, as in all actual events of a social nature, in the relativities of history.

The Blood Feud

The Book of Joshua presupposes an acceptance of the blood feud as a means of social justice. Instead of abrogating this cruel custom, Joshua merely regulated it, so as to offer asylum for those guilty of manslaughter (accidental killing):

Read Joshua 20:1–6.

The main thing to see in this regulation is that it was a restriction upon unlimited revenge. As such it was a step in the direction of individual responsibility and equal justice.

MAIN THEMES

1. Covenant loyalty as the key to national success and prosperity.

2. Reverence for the national heritage. In this connection read Joshua 4:6–7. As we have said before, the whole story was told long after the event to remind readers with what a price of blood and suffering their national heritage had come to them. Someone put the contrast between the inheritors and the pioneers this way: "We are the 'resolutionary' sons of revolutionary grandfathers."

3. The pioneering spirit. This involves a willingness to strike out on untried paths, "for you have not passed this way before" (Josh. 3:4). It also involves unswerving, single-minded devotion to an ideal (Josh. 24:15) and the willingness to accept hardships, like Caleb's request for the hardest places (Josh. 14:12).

4. The corporate consequences of private wrong (Josh. 22:20).

KEY VERSES

There are at least three passages which come close to summarizing the thrust of the whole book. They are Joshua 1:6–9; 23:3b–11; and

24:14–15. We also like another, not because it is a good summary, but because it is so close to the central fire of loyalty which made the invasion of Canaan a success: "One man of you puts to flight a thousand, since it is the Lord your God who fights for you . . ." (Josh. 23:10).

II. PREPARING YOUR BOOK SERMON

CARDINAL IDEA

To enter the Promised Land, the Hebrews had to conquer it; and to conquer it required sacrificial courage and covenant faithfulness. Standing within the covenant community which is successor and heir to the old covenant community of Israel, we as members of the Christian Church need to see the Hebrew pioneers as our own spiritual forefathers. They labored, and we have entered into their inheritance. They fought and suffered and sacrificed and died, and we eat the fruits of their struggle. There is historical depth to our faith, and our debt and responsibility are correspondingly great. The New Testament corollary to this cardinal idea is in Hebrews 11:4–40. And it touches us precisely at the point of Hebrews 11:39–40. Such was the standpoint of the book, looking back from a later century upon the events of the thirteenth century. The addition of centuries only increases our inheritance and deepens our debt.

The message of Joshua to its own time, and to every period and circumstance like that time, is not that of cherishing a heritage but that of creating one. It is that of crossing over new Jordans, entering new Canaans, subduing new enemies, enduring new hardships, resisting new temptations to plunder, remaining faithful against great odds. To carve out a heritage in any new realm requires self-sacrifice, self-transcending loyalty to some ideal; and it depends upon courage and fidelity. This is true whether the new land be America in its pioneer days or a new, creative venture in an individual life, especially a venture undertaken in response to the call of God. And it is equally true of the creative mission of a family or a church.

Applied to the nation, the standpoint of the final editor of Joshua is ours—within a national heritage, looking back to the beginnings. The mood is one of reverent reminiscence encompassed by courageous devotion to the one God. His desire is that the single-minded, pioneering spirit which started it all may not die out among the descendants. It is therefore not hard for us to identify ourselves with the standpoint of the book. Whatever we may say about future wars of aggression, Americans won their land, at least in part, by armed conquest. First it belonged to the Indians. I write these words on the soil of Kentucky, which was known in frontier days as "that dark and bloody ground" because of the blood of Indians and whites spilled here. If injustices and cruelties were committed in those times —not unlike the wholesale destructions and slaughter of whole cities by Joshua—we have inherited advantages thus paid for in blood, and we owe corresponding responsibilities. The past will not lie docile upon the printed page. It rises to grasp us by the elbow and propel us forward in duty and faith. There is such a thing as the genius that gave us birth as a people; our continued history depends upon a pioneering spirit of loyalty to that same dynamic principle.

SHAPING A PREACHING OUTLINE

Several approaches to outline are possible. Selected verses furnish pegs for the various attitudes found within the invading force: (1) there were the fainthearted, who wanted to turn back at the first sign of hardship: "Would that we had been content to dwell beyond the Jordan!" (Josh. 7:7); (2) there was Achan, who saw the campaign as a private looting party (Josh. 7:1); (3) there was Caleb, who asked for the hardest assignment of all (Josh. 14:12); (4) there was Joshua, who kept calling the whole people back to a controlling loyalty to God (Josh. 24:14-15).

A key command of the book is contained in the words "Be strong and of good courage." Following these words are associated ideas which may be used as a skeleton for the ruling points made by the book. For example: (1) the task, claiming a new heritage: "Be strong and of good courage; for you shall cause this people to inherit the land which I swore to their fathers to give them" (1:6); (2) the commitment, self-transcending loyalty being the condition for claiming an inheritance: "Only be strong and very courageous, being careful to do according to all the law which Moses my servant commanded you; . . ." (1:7); (3) the assurance and the fulfillment: "Be strong and of good courage; be not frightened, neither be dismayed; for the Lord your God is with you wherever you go" (1:9). A complete census of all passages containing the words "Be strong and of good courage" may prove quite illuminating.

Our discussion of the cardinal idea in Joshua leads to a still different outline, with two main points: (1) receiving and cherishing our heritage—the standpoint of the authors and readers of the book; (2) pioneering a new heritage—the standpoint of the original pioneers who first entered Canaan, that is, the standpoint within the book. The two emphases belong together, for to do nothing but look back to the revolutionary deeds of our forefathers makes us unrevolutionary conservatives and reactionaries. But to dash into novelty without listening to the lessons of the past is to run a fool's errand that leads nowhere. To capture this same idea in an illustration used by Jesus, we must be like the scribe who brings forth from his treasures things old and things new. This is the recipe for creative pioneering.

Joshua 3:3–4 provides a picture of a frontier land with God as the leading Pioneer. Such a passage may well serve as a text for a sermon on the whole book. Any society, nation, or church begins in spiritual pioneering, and to grow, it must continue in the same spirit.

A Modern Title

Among the possibilities that offer themselves, these seem to be the most appropriate: "Pioneers in a New Land," "Possessing Our Heritage," "Men to Match Our Mountains," and the title chosen for this chapter, "Savior with a Sword."

8

MEN WHO PUT ARMIES TO FLIGHT

The Book of Judges

THE closest approach most of us can make to the social and political situation pictured in the Book of Judges is through the American history of the Old West. Of the period of the judges, the editor wrote, "In those days there was no king in Israel; every man did what was right in his own eyes" (Judg. 17:6). How very like the Old West! A lawless time, groping toward law and order and the emerging destiny of a new nation. The judges of Israel were not unlike the ideal sheriff or United States marshal on the American frontier. These judges were strong men, physically and spiritually superior to their fellows, men who subordinated their own advantage to the common good and who tamed the selfish passions of the people under law. As it was with the pioneers, so it had been with Israel: this staggering transition depended upon men of unusual caliber, men who in both the literal and the figurative sense could put armies to flight.

I. WORKING YOUR WAY INTO THE BOOK

A PERIOD OF TRANSITION

Historically, the period of the judges marks the transition from the Hebrew invasion of Canaan to the beginning of the monarchy. It was a period of approximately two hundred years, from 1200 to 1000 B.C. "Judges" were men who arose from among the people in times of emergency to be military leaders and who continued in the afterglow of their victories to exert some kind of civil leadership in their respective spheres.

The Israelites were not politically united during this period; only by the pressure of necessity were various combinations of tribes driven into coalition from time to time to resist enemies. In fact, the work of the judges may be defined in terms of the differing enemies against whom they fought: Othniel's enemy was Cushan-rishathaim of Mesopotamia (3:8); Ehud's was Moab (3:12); Shamgar's was the Philistines (3:31); Deborah's was the Canaanites (4:2, 3); Gideon's was the Midianites (6:1), etc.

Except for the Canaanites and the Philistines, these national threats from enemies were sporadic; therefore, the political unification of the Hebrews was not uniformly urgent throughout the period. As for the Canaanites, the Israelites captured them peacefully for the most part, by intermarrying with them. And as for the Philistines, their competition for the conquest and control of Canaan did not become a real threat to the Hebrews until the latter part of the period, when Samuel came on the scene, to be followed by Saul.

There were many kinds of transitions during this period besides the political changes we have just noted. The Israelites entered Canaan as nomads; they became farmers. Living in the hills and in the open country between cities—the cities for the most part being walled towns—they looked on the cities with covetous eyes. Especially, they resented the walls and towers of fortification.

Read Judges 8:9; 9:45, 51.

In time the Israelites captured the cities, but for the most part this conquest was a peaceful penetration by trade and marriage. Intermarriage with the Canaanites brought with it the threat of religious and social corruption. The Israelites were soon worshiping idols:

Read Judges 6:25–27; 8:27; 17:4, 5; 18:18–20.

The picture we get from these verses is not one of complete apostasy; it is not that Yahweh had been deserted, but rather that elements of Israelite and Canaanite religion had been fused into an amalgam of some sort and that Yahweh was served through idolatry.

Baalism was a fertility religion. Cultic practices, by standards of the Mosaic law, were flagrantly immoral. Therefore the mixing of Israelites and Canaanites had a demoralizing effect upon Hebrew sexual standards. One will go a long way to read a more sordid tale than that of the Levite's concubine!

Read Judges 19:1–30.

It was a raw and lusty time. Morally there was little about it to elevate or inspire. But idolatry and sexual immorality were not the worst of it. There was also human sacrifice:

Read Judges 11:30–31, 34–40.

We can, in fact, say that the period of the Judges was in many respects a time of anarchy. Fortunately it was not the twilight of national history but the chaotic dawning.

Read Judges 17:6; 21:25.

This was anarchy, but it was the anarchy of a nation coming into being rather than the anarchy of disintegration. There was in Israel the elemental force of creative energy, and somehow in the midst of the frontier rawness there was the enthusiasm and the contagion of a robust religious faith:

Read Judges 6:34; 11:29; 13:24–25; 14:6, 19.

Forces were alive which would lead Israel out of crudity and lawlessness into the discipline of an ordered state and a unified people. And the greatest of these forces was the ancestral faith which Israel brought from Sinai.

MAIN THEMES

The final editors of our book combined history with instruction. Looking back upon a past long since transcended, they nonetheless gloried in their heritage—much as modern Americans glory in the days of the "Golden West" celebrated so fulsomely in the "Westerns" on television and motion-picture screens. But it was not enough for these editors to contemplate the formative period of Israel's history in Palestine; they felt compelled to study its lessons so that their contemporaries, looking back, would have the benefit of these lessons for the living of their own days of destiny.

This instruction takes the form of a philosophy of history which is fully expressed in the second chapter:

Read Judges 2:11–23.

Fragments of this same interpretive philosophy are found throughout the book, as the work of each judge is introduced by it:

Read Judges 3:7–9; 12–15, etc.

In a judge we have a "charismatic leader," a person whose own personality has weight; he embodies both the urgency of his times and the constructive answer to its emergencies. There is no generally recognized law throughout the land; he is the law incarnate. There is no cohesive national will; he is the will of the people. There is no self-transcending loyalty; he galvanizes that loyalty in the name of God, and harnesses it to folk purposes. Lacking political unity or accepted political organs, God unified a people through its religious faith, around a leader who symbolized that faith in its most dynamic character.

The interpretive pattern is quite simple: (1) Israel's unfaithfulness to Yahweh, bringing on its own inherent judgment through the oppression of the Israelites by one or more of their national enemies; (2) the rise of the judge who calls the people in self-transcending loyalty into a kind of league to beat back the enemy and to purge religion; (3) the coming of a period of peace and attendant prosperity. This is the pattern which is repeated for each judge throughout the whole time of the transition.

OUTLINE OF THE BOOK OF JUDGES

I.   The final stages of the invasion, 1:1—2:10
    A. Completing Joshua's conquest, 1:1–36
    B. The passing of Joshua, 2:1–10
II. The judges and their exploits, 2:11—16:31
    A. Introduction: a philosophy of history, 2:11–23
    B. Stories of the judges, 3:1—16:31
III. Appendix, chapters 17–21
    A. The migration of the tribe of Dan, 17:1—18:31
    B. Benjaminite crimes at Gibeah, 19:1—21:25

The stories of Samson stand out both by their greater length and by virtue of their legendary treatment as distinct and different from the stories of the other judges. Above all else they express the roistering, conquering strength of a new people in a new land, sweeping on to victory as long as faith and self-discipline prevail, but despoiled by the softness and corruption of civilization, which is fittingly symbolized as a beautiful but unscrupulous woman. Americans should be able to understand the Samson quality in a people. It is expressed in the legends of Paul Bunyan and Davy Crockett. It is this spirit that led United States Army engineers to boast, "The difficult we do at once; the impossible takes a little longer." It is a great thing to see the young vigor of fresh, new people living in the spirit of the frontier. But it is saddening to contemplate that same people grown timid and morally flabby, not because they have been overwhelmed by enemies in Nature or among nations, but because they have been seduced into softness by their own carnal appetites. Who will say that the story of Samson is an ancient legend with no relevance to the modern world? If anything brings Western culture to disaster it will not be hostile nature or plotting enemies; it will be nothing more frightening than an excessive desire for a good juicy steak, an entertaining show, a satisfying alcoholic beverage, and plenty of girls with easy morals. If we fail, it will be from an indifference to more enduring values and a loss of spiritual and moral integrity. So does Samson speak out of his long past to our contemporary situation.

KEY VERSES

The fundamental pattern of the book is stated most clearly and comprehensively in Judges 2:11–23. It is repeated in detail for each of the judges. This pattern, as we have seen, moved through three stages: apostasy, punishment, deliverance by a judge whom God raised up.

II. PREPARING YOUR BOOK SERMON

CARDINAL IDEA

In the time of transition between Joshua and King Saul, when Israel again and again fell prey to her enemies because of flagging loyalty to Yahweh, the nation was saved by judges, emergency leaders who arose to recall the people to their covenant loyalty and to defeat the nation's enemies.

To what extent is it permissible to universalize this cardinal idea? Stated without reference to any one nation or people, it may look something like this: *If any society is to survive and grow through times of chaotic transition, it must have leaders who will rise in the strength of great faith and integrity to call the people above self-indulgence to loyal, self-transcending service to the common good.*

If we ask, "What are the credentials of such a leader?" we get no clear answer. For it is possible for a leader to "fool all the people some of the time." But in the end, his credentials are his reality or integrity, his devotion to the common good, his qualities that pass the tests of reason and experience applied by those he leads. There has been much blind following of bad leaders; no time has suffered more from it than ours. But, on the other side, there has also been much greatness in our time. It is hard to say where we would be in international law without Woodrow Wilson, in science without Einstein, in social progress without Gandhi. . . . In the springtimes of history, when the solid structures of a long winter break up in the thaw of new life, we are dependent, whether we like it or not, upon the creative minority who sense the need of the times and the hunger of the masses and who articulate and fuse these two forces in new and creative ways. Every nation, every community, every social group, every church, and every family needs men who will not wait for everybody else but who will be the first to step out along the path of duty and service.

Shaping a Preaching Outline

Since the same basic outline applies to each of the stories of the judges, it would be possible to drive home the lesson of the whole book by selecting the story of a single judge. Probably those that appeal most are the exploits of Gideon and Samson. Either story will be easy to universalize. There is the external danger to be faced—the Midianites or the Philistines. There is the internal weakness to be overcome—the lack of discipline in Gideon's followers, the defection to Baal; Samson's weakness for women. There is the faith of the judge, eventually triumphant, and the final defeat of the enemy. The interest-catching power of the narrative should be used. Tell the story; then drive home the lessons—ancient and modern.

There is an approach to outline by way of the three major divisions of Judges: (1) entering a new land; (2) the vigorous, somewhat lawless frontier period, with great sins but with great powers of repentance and moral renewal; (3) the degenerate compromises and indulgence of the sordid ending of the book. How can any people keep its history from following this pattern? How can we change the third division? The answer lies in finding the saving powers within men who rise above their times. If there is no king in the land, not everyone will do that which is right only in their own eyes; some will do what is right in the eyes of God, and will devote themselves to something greater than their own pleasures.

There is a good sermon which emphasizes the role of the exceptional man. We in the twentieth century have learned to distrust exceptional men; they have turned out so often to be men of diabolical genius—a Hitler or a Stalin, or their lesser shadows Mussolini, Perón, Batista. Is the alternative to the demonic leader, then, nothing but the democratic mass? Or is there a place for the man of integrity who will take the great risks of leadership and who will rise by his own moral might to meet the challenges of disturbing times? Perhaps we have overstressed the cult of the common man; perhaps we have become such conformists, such organization men, that we have no patience any more to encourage the unique talents of individual genius. Nevertheless, there are times when the human race is lost unless it has human leaders, men who tower above the commonality of men, and who see farther than most of us. When Jeremiah ran through the streets of Jerusalem looking for a single man who was manly through and through, he was looking for the earth's highest treasure. Else why do we honor our Schweitzers, our Kagawas, our Lincolns, and our Gandhis? These men have insights that cannot be arrived at in a committee meeting!

Any sermon on Judges will do well to stay rather close to the central statement of purpose in Judges 2:11–23, which may be taken as the text of the whole book. The various movements of thought within that brief passage are the major movements of the book, and so may constitute the essential outline of the sermon.

A MODERN TITLE

Hebrews 11:32–34 contains a number of phrases descriptive in the main of the judges; from this fruitful section one may glean a number of suggestions: "Men Who Put Armies to Flight," "Faith to Conquer Kingdoms," and "Winning Strength out of Weakness."

9

YOUR PEOPLE SHALL BE MY PEOPLE

The Book of Ruth

THE paradox of human community is that it is at once inclusive and exclusive. When I reach out my arms to encircle my fellows I confront all who are not thus encircled with the back of my hand. Those whom I do not draw to me I tend to thrust away. Instead of saying with Ruth, "Your people shall be my people," it is much easier and more natural for me to say, "Your people are not my people."

The Book of Ruth addresses itself to this problem.

I. WORKING YOUR WAY INTO THE BOOK

The placing of Ruth in the Old Testament canon is our first significant key to interpreting it. In our Christian Bibles it occupies a place between Judges and 1 Samuel, for this is the period of life it reflects—about 1075 B.C. But in the Hebrew Bible it belongs among the Writings (*kĕthūbhīm*) because it was written in the period after the Exile. It is, in fact, one of the five rolls read in Jewish services at festival times; the other rolls are: Song of Solomon, Ecclesiastes, Lamentations, and Esther. Ruth is read at the Feast of Weeks.

The book deals with the custom of drawing off a shoe to bind a contract as though it were an ancient custom long since out of use and, therefore, needing explanation:

Read Ruth 4:7.

We begin to suspect, then, that we have here a writing in the vein of a historical novel, written in one period about a much earlier time. There are two additional reasons for dating the book after the Exile. The first of these is a matter for technical scholars, but we are told by students of Aramaic and Hebrew that the book contains Hebrew words found only in a late period and that it also contains a number of Aramaisms, a definite mark of later date.

HISTORICAL SITUATION

The final indication of postexilic date is the main point of the book, which directs us to a definite historical situation. That main point registers clearly for anyone who reads the book at one sitting. Ruth is presented as a Moabitess, a foreigner:

Read Ruth 1:22; 2:2, 6, 21; 4:5, 10.

The fact that Ruth is a foreigner is stressed through repetition. Nevertheless, this foreign woman was the great-grandmother of David, king of Israel:

Read Ruth 4:13, 17.

The attachment of this Moabitess for her Jewish mother-in-law is only one part of the picture setting her forth in a favorable light. Orpah does what one would expect foreigners to do—stay in their own land, adhere to their own people. But Ruth clings to Naomi with a love that breaks through national barriers. This love gives us one of the most lyrical passages of the Bible:

Read Ruth 1:16–17.

A story like this has universal appeal, as does any story that overcomes human conventions of various sorts. But this emphasis upon foreigners and especially upon Jewish marriage with a foreigner had also a peculiar timeliness. To begin with, marriages between Jews and Moabites were expressly forbidden in the Deuteronomic law:

Read Deuteronomy 23:3–4, 7–8.

Notice that the descendants of Jewish-Moabite marriages were excluded from the congregation of Israel for ten generations (longer than the United States of America has been a nation). In contrast to that, the offspring of a Jewish-Edomite or of a Jewish-Egyptian marriage could be considered Israelites after the third generation. The Moabites (along with the Ammonites) were marked out for special hatred. And yet, Ruth, the great-grandmother of David, was a Moabitess.

There was a period of time following the Exile when intermarriage between Jews and foreigners came in for special attack. This was during the Ezra-Nehemiah period:

Read Ezra 9–10; Nehemiah 13:23–27.

Several features of these accounts strike us. The number of inter-marriages seems to have been quite large. Ezra and Nehemiah prosecuted the ancient Deuteronomic law with great vehemence: threatening confiscation of property and excommunication from the congregation of Israel, even using physical torture. Not only were additional foreign marriages forbidden, but existing marriages were broken up, even when there were children.

There is one feature of the story that may be overlooked. It appears in Ezra 10:15. A small minority of leaders opposed the ruthless purism of Ezra. Would that we might hear a spokesman for this small minority! What were they thinking? What were their reasons for standing out against the crushing majority? Did they oppose the majority out of selfishness or upon a widening religious principle?

Fortunately we do have a spokesman. Whether he is one of the men named we cannot know. But he is a person who took his stand with them. This author shares the broad human sympathy with all peoples displayed by the Book of Jonah and by Second Isaiah:

Read Isaiah 49:5–6; 56:1–6.

Here we have a repudiation of the narrow, nationalistic particularism which became the main Jewish tradition following the Exile. This particularism came to its fullest expression in the Pharisaism of the New Testament. Second Isaiah, Ruth, and Jonah were unheeded voices lifted in support of a missionary-minded universalism. The day was carried by the majority who followed Ezra.

But these minority voices from the Old Testament did not die. In the New Testament period, their song was taken up and became a swelling chorus. Jew and Gentile came at last to worship together and to be members of a single household of faith:

Read Acts 10:34–35; *Galatians* 3:28; *Colossians* 3:11.

The minority report of the Old Testament became the majority report of the New Testament. The early Christians who thus widened their fellowship believed that they were only carrying out the mandate of God to his people. God does not build walls; he makes boulevards.

ADDED BACKGROUND

With the historical circumstances to which the book was ad-

dressed, we have given the principal elements of background necessary to an understanding of the Book of Ruth. But there are two
elements that may be added for the sake of further clarity. One is
the law of levirate marriage; the other is the law of gleaning.
Read Deuteronomy 25:5–10.

With this as background we have no difficulty in understanding
Ruth 4:1–12. The law was, of course, an expression of the Hebrew
solidarity and also a product of their high evaluation of the family.
Read Deuteronomy 24:19–21.

This law is expressive of Hebrew solidarity and social conscious-
ness. Jews cared for their own poor and unfortunate. In the day of
agriculture, the law of gleaning was one of the ways in which they
made such provision.

OUTLINE OF THE BOOK OF RUTH

Since Ruth is a short story, it is best to think of it as unfolding
through episodes:

I. Moab, 1:1–18
   A. Naomi, Ruth, and Orpah widowed in Moab
   B. Naomi decides to return to Israel but tries to persuade Ruth
      and Orpah to remain among their own people in Moab
   C. Orpah remains, but Ruth clings to Naomi
II. The return, 1:19–22
   A. Naomi and Ruth arrive in Bethlehem during the barley harvest
III. Gleaning, 2:1–23
   A. Naomi induces Ruth to glean in the field of Boaz, who takes
      notice of her and provides for her safety and protection
IV. The threshing floor, 3:1–18
   A. Naomi, knowing the Jewish law of levirate marriage and trust-
      ing the integrity of Boaz, sends Ruth to him at night to claim
      his protection in marriage
   B. Boaz is willing, but he has a kinsman whose legal right has
      precedence
V. The meeting at the city gate, 4:1–12
   A. The nearest kinsman agrees to secede his legal right to Boaz,
      and the contract is made
VI. The marriage, 4:13–17
   A. Ruth and Boaz marry and become the parents of King David's

grandfather, Obed, and Naomi finds her bereavement assuaged by the coming of a grandchild

Main Theme

There is only one: human love breaking national barriers. This is seen on one plane as Ruth leaves her native Moab to cleave to Naomi; on a second plane, as Boaz loves Ruth the Moabitess; and on a third plane, as Ruth, the Moabitess, becomes the great-grandmother of King David.

Key Verses

The most lyrical passage of the Book of Ruth is, without question, 1:16–17; but it is not the key to understanding the main purpose of the book. The key to the story is found in 4:13–17; a Moabitess (ordinarily hated by Jews and excluded from the congregation of Israel for ten generations) was the great-grandmother of the foremost Israelite. Such is the biting irony that lies at the heart of this crusading idyl.

II. PREPARING YOUR BOOK SERMON

Cardinal Idea

When human love breaks through the barriers of nationality, it can be a blessed and holy thing and should be so received by God's people.

Shaping a Preaching Outline

We have no difficulty in seeing the relevance of the Book of Ruth to the time of Ezra and Nehemiah. It was a powerful protest against chauvinistic hatred of foreigners and against the exclusion of those foreigners from the congregation of Israel. We do not so easily see the relevance of the book to our own time.

And yet there is a great deal of current history that fits the situation precisely. Soldiers, sailors, and airmen have been to the four corners of the earth. A good number of them have brought back foreign wives—from Japan, from Germany, from the islands and continents of the world. What is the godly attitude toward these marriages? To pretend they did not happen? To regret that they happened? To ostracize the GI's and their brides? To break up these marriages? Or can we construct a way of life that will reach out and include them, making them genuinely at home in this land of many peoples? We begin to see that we are more like Ezra and Nehemiah than we had imagined! This is a difficult assignment. It meets us among our deepest feelings and demands more than we have been willing to grant.

The answer of the Book of Ruth is not to think of it as a social problem or to face it on legalistic terms, but to think of it in terms of the *persons* who are involved. Ruth's portraits of persons is vivid; the people of the book are alive. Once we will let Ruth be a person and not simply a member of a hated foreign nation we have no difficulty falling in love with her as both Naomi and Boaz did. The key to these vexing social questions is to stop looking at stereotypes and really to see persons as persons and to grant them the dignity and worth that persons deserve.

Such, in brief, is a sermon-starter that begins with the basic problems with which the Book of Ruth grapples. There are, of course, many kinds of barriers that divide people into hostile and exclusive camps. All come under the searching judgment of the universal vision of Ruth. Perhaps the only adequate New Testament commentary upon them is found in a text like Colossians 3:11: "Here there cannot be Greek and Jew, circumcised and uncircumcised, barbarian, Scythian, slave, free man, but Christ is all, and in all."

A second approach to the sermon could be the reverse of this. Begin by sketching the historical background of Ezra's and Nehemiah's time. Add the law against foreign marriages from Deuteronomy. Then present the story of the Book of Ruth in your own words as briefly as possible. Finally, emphasize the point of the story and apply it to comparable contemporary situations. The main features, then, would be: (1) the law against intermarriage, and the severe enforcement of that law; (2) the story of an intermarriage that not only worked but without which Israel would have been deprived of her greatest king; (3) the point and application of the story in the light of intermarriages in the twentieth century.

Here is one sermon that justifies a full manuscript. (And the script is already provided!) It may be set up in the following order: (1) read Deuteronomy 23:3–4; 7–8; (2) read Ezra 9:1–10:17, 19, 44; (3) read the Book of Ruth as a whole; (4) do nothing more; let the reading carry its own implications and do its own work. It goes without saying that this public reading of the Bible must be prepared and rehearsed with great thoroughness.[1]

Still another way of organizing the sermon is to develop it around personalities. There are five of these: Naomi, Ruth, Orpah, the unnamed kinsman of Ruth 3:12, and Boaz. Naomi represents the moving force of wide, international sympathy and love. She has lived in Moab; she married her sons to Moabitesses. She is attached by great cords of affection to a foreigner. Ruth and Orpah are opposites: Orpah is caught in the web of narrow nationalism and cannot escape it. But Ruth breaks through the barriers; her love for Naomi is strong enough to crash these barriers. In the same way, Boaz and his kinsman are opposites. The kinsman takes the safe, traditional way; but Boaz follows his heart and challenges the conventions in the name of a love that transcends them. The appeal of the sermon rests upon the natural tendency of your hearers to seek identity with the most attractive of the five persons.

A Modern Title

"Love Breaks Down Barriers" is a title suggested by members of a class in Old Testament at the author's seminary. It is obviously a strong one. "Your People Shall Be My People" has the advantage of being a direct quotation from the favorite passage in the book (1:16–17). Titles taken from current church school lessons on this book are: "A Home Made Happy," "No Stranger with God," and "Friendliness for Newcomers." This last title finds its point of contact with the contemporary situation in the influx of displaced persons into America. My colleague William L. Reed once preached a book sermon on Ruth using the title, "Making the World More Homelike."

---

[1] For suggestions on reading the Bible aloud *see* Dwight E. Stevenson and Charles F. Diehl, *Reaching People from the Pulpit* (New York: Harper & Brothers, 1958), chap. viii.

10

NO KING BUT GOD

The Books of Samuel and Kings

THOMAS HOBBES somewhere in his writings speaks of the state as a mortal god. And a modern author has written a book about nationalism, denominating it *Man's Other Religion*.[1] Political order is necessary, but political loyalties have a way of competing with religious loyalties. The mortal god does not want to submit to the God Immortal.

Lord Acton spoke of the same tendency in another way when he framed his famous epigram, "Power always corrupts, but absolute power corrupts absolutely." This is an observation appropriate not only to kings—the kings of Israel included—but to all political government whatsoever.

Sovereign power is to be trusted only when it is consciously exercised under loyalty to a sovereign God. This thesis, so relevant and so modern, is also the thesis of the Old Testament writings known to us as the Books of Samuel and Kings.

I. WORKING YOUR WAY INTO THE BOOKS

In Hebrew, the Books of Samuel and Kings are not four but two. The Greek Septuagint treats them under one topic, "The Kingdoms," as four volumes of one work. We shall follow the lead of the Septuagint and deal with all four as one.

Anyone writing on a body of Scripture as vast as that contained in the four books of the Old Testament which we have here chosen to treat as one must do one of two things. He must either write a

---

[1] Edward Shillito, *Nationalism: Man's Other Religion* (Chicago: Willett, Clark & Company, 1933).

very long and complex treatise or be exceedingly brief. We choose to be brief.

The reason for this decision lies in two facts: (1) Few parts of the Bible are better known than the absorbing narrative which sweeps the eager reader along from the birth of Samuel more than a thousand years before Christ to the Babylonian Exile of Jehoiachin five centuries later. (2) But the point of this exciting story—though the editors are at pains to repeat and underscore it—is frequently lost on the modern reader. In what follows, laying aside the detailed examination of narrative and its many sources together with its critical questions of history and its anthropological treasures, we shall confine ourselves to a discussion of the editors' purpose. *Why was this history written?*

PURPOSE

Conditioned by our own schooling in the writing and reading of history, we naturally suppose that these biblical books were composed as a matter of simple record. We assume that they were meant to preserve the story of past events for posterity, and nothing more.

Two facts force us to reconsider our assumption. The Jews themselves never classified this Scripture as history. These four books, together with Judges, were known to them as "The Former Prophets." The books tell a history, but not so much for the purpose of *informing* as *reforming* the reader. Although recording the past, they use it as an instrument of religious instruction and discipline. They retell history not for its facts but for its lessons.

The second fact challenging our assumption is the lack of chronological balance in the narrative of the books. The story of David, covering little more than forty years out of a story of many centuries, dominates 1 and 2 Samuel; and the story of Ahab and Jezebel, with the attendant account of Elijah and Elisha, gets a similarly expanded treatment in 1 and 2 Kings. Had the editors' purpose been to give a connected and representative history, they would surely have resisted this obvious chronological distortion.

The final editors select and organize their materials to make a case. They state frankly their own evaluation of the history passing under their hands. There is, for example, the obvious and often repeated device of passing summary judgment upon the entire reign of a king under the formula "and——did what was right in the eyes of the Lord." Or "and——did what was evil in the sight of the Lord." A tracing of this formula through the record is instructive; notice a few instances of it:

Read 1 *Kings* 11:6; 15:1–5, 11, 31–32, 33–34; 16:25; 22:41–44; 2 *Kings* 8:16–18, 25–27; 21:1–2.

By this reckoning there were few good kings and many bad ones. The monarchs of the Northern Kingdom were judged uniformly bad. In the South, there were a number of good ones, but among these David stands out above all the rest as the king after God's heart. After reading the intimate account of David's reign and private life, the modern reader may wonder at this approval. He seems to have been guilty of most of the sins in the book: murder, adultery, theft. He was an unwise, indulgent father whose sons turned out badly; he could not rule his own household. But still he was a king after God's own heart. Why? Because he never tried to put himself in the place of God. He was devoid of arrogant pride. He was quick to acknowledge his mistakes. And he was loyal to God from beginning to end. In contrast to Saul, who arrogantly offered sacrifice rather than wait for an authorized priest, and to Solomon, who followed his foreign wives into their foreign religions, David remained both humble and loyal. He was human, all too human, but God could use him because his life was open to divine guidance and correction.

Nevertheless, the verdict of the whole history is not favorable to kings and kingdoms. According to this view the monarchy arose in the first place because Israel was not intense enough in its loyalty to God. A truly fervent religion would have made a king unnecessary, and Israel would have been spared this indignity of being "like other nations."

Read 1 *Samuel* 8.

This unfavorable verdict upon kings is largely substantiated by the record. Few kings were worthy. Many were a curse to those they ruled. And in the end, largely through the intrigues and arrogant mistakes of kings, the bright hopes of Israel's early years were shrouded in the night of exile. Whereas at the beginning they had a land, a kingdom, and a Temple, they ended by losing all three.

We shall have to say, just the same, that the monarchy had the grudging endorsement of God—as a necessary second best. But it also had its conditions and its sanctions:

Read 1 *Samuel* 12:19–25.

This is the Deuteronomist's philosophy of history, applied to the monarchy. Since Israel will not persist in the first best—a theocracy under a prophetic priesthood—let it proceed under a king; but let it know that the prosperity of the nation will depend not upon kingly power but upon the faithfulness of both people and king. And let it know that the king himself lives under God, the King Immortal.

Israel and their kings did not often remember this, and because of their faithlessness they suffered many troubles and three calamities. The first was the dividing of the kingdom and an unresolved state of civil war between Judah and the North. The second was the captivity of the Northern Kingdom at the destruction of Samaria in 722 B.C. The third was a like fate for Judah in 587 B.C. as it entered Babylonian Exile.

The great goods to be sought in the life of Israel were the unity of Israel and covenant love toward God. The great evils were disunity, social injustice, arrogant disobedience, and serving foreign gods. A good text for the whole Deuteronomic history, from Judges through 2 Kings could be: "Not by might, nor by power, but by my Spirit, says the Lord of hosts" (Zech. 4:6).

Outline of the Books of Samuel and Kings

I.   Samuel and Saul; the emergence of the monarch, 1 Samuel 1–14
II. Saul gives way to David, 1 Samuel 15–31
III. The reign of David, 2 Samuel 1–24
IV. Solomon's rise, reign, and decline, 1 Kings 1–11
V.   The divided kingdoms, 1 Kings 12—2 Kings 17:6
VI. Judah until the Exile, 2 Kings 17:6—25:27

Subordinate Themes

1. The story of the Ark of the Covenant and of the Temple. In a way, this is the key to everything else. The loss of the Ark to the Philistines near the beginning, the building of the Temple to house the Ark, and the eventual destruction of that Temple form a thread upon which one may construct the whole story.

2. Social justice. Covenant loyalty to God is not indifferent to, or

inimical of, the social welfare of the people. On the contrary, as is shown in Nathan's rebuke of David in the matchless parable of the One Little Ewe Lamb and in Elijah's judgment of Ahab upon his confiscation of Naboth's vineyard, covenant loyalty demands social justice.

3. The threat of foreign entanglements and of apostate religions. The two go hand in hand, and both are injurious to Israel's national health. They show lack of true faith in God.

KEY VERSES

There are many which could serve as quick summaries of the central purpose of the books under study, but none does it more vividly than 1 Samuel 12:19–25.

II. PREPARING YOUR BOOK SERMON

CARDINAL IDEA

Well-developed political institutions have a tendency to obscure a nation's primary reliance upon God; but no national power can ever afford to ignore or defy the sovereignty of God.

SHAPING A PREACHING OUTLINE

No sermon on Samuel and Kings can hope to represent the internal complexity of the books. That sermon will be successful which is both selective and specific, and which thereby adheres to the narrative simplicity so characteristic of the books themselves.

One good plan would be to state the cardinal idea, to embody it in the key passage, and then to illustrate it episodically by drawing on a single brief narrative from stories of each of four or five kings: Saul, grown melancholy and mad, jealous of David his young rival; David submitting to Nathan's censure, showing himself submissive to the ultimate kingship of God; Solomon seduced by wealth and women; Rehoboam, absolutely corrupted by absolute power, keeping up his pathetic parade of brass shields after the golden ones had been stolen by the Pharaoh Shishak; Ahab and Jezebel, under the lash of Elijah's tongue for crushing the right of Naboth and for serving foreign gods.

Another approach would be to begin as before by stating the cardinal idea and the key passage, but to illustrate it from the life of one king. Because the sources are most abundant for only a few kings, the choice will naturally fall upon one of the following: Saul, David, Solomon, Ahab-Jezebel. Alternatively, avoiding kings altogether, one could approach the whole message through Elijah, "the troubler of kings." The main thing is to drive home the lesson of the books by using narrative material. There is no excuse for an abstract, generalized sermon on books like these.

A third approach, after stating cardinal idea and key passage, would rely wholly upon whetting the appetite of the hearers for further reading by reading them a connected narrative out of the heart of the history. This reading would occupy the sermon time. By way of specific suggestion, we offer the following passages from the reigns of Solomon and Rehoboam:

Read 1 *Kings* 4:20–28; 5:13–18; 7:1–12; 10:14–11:13, 41–43; 12:1–20.

After such a reading, the obvious conclusion of the "sermon" is the advice to go home and read Samuel and Kings. An individual could accomplish this in two sittings of two hours each; or a family could do it in two weeks, a half hour or more to a sitting, reading aloud.

A MODERN TITLE

"Of God and King," "The Sovereign State and a Sovereign God," "No King but God," "A King after God's Heart," and "A Mortal God under the God Immortal" are possible titles.

11

HISTORY AS SEEN FROM THE ALTAR
Chronicles-Ezra-Nehemiah

W HEN a priest or a minister writes history from his own point of view we may expect special pleading. We get much the same thing from the businessman when he says, "Business pays the freight," thus making business central to every cultural advance. And from the educator we hear the same tune, though the words may be a little different; education is the secret of everything. The truth is that no single human activity is the key to all other phases of our complex life; but if our lives are not to be divided into watertight compartments they must have some kind of center. To the minister it seems not unreasonable that that center is the Living God. Therefore, when he tries to view history in proper perspective, he insists that the only place to stand is not in the countinghouse, the theater, or the playground, but at the altar.

That is where the Chronicler took his stand as he surveyed Hebrew history. Like all men, he saw some things clearly and truly; he saw other things more dimly. But what he saw at his best is valid now as it was then.

I. WORKING YOUR WAY INTO THE "BOOK"

A Four-Volume Work

Jerome named Chronicles when he translated the two books for the Latin Vulgate. He called their connected story "a chronicle of the whole sacred history" from Adam to Cyrus. His name still obtains in our English-language Bibles. It is evident to any reader that the two books of Chronicles are but a single work. They are continuous; their style and point of view are identical.

Ezra and Nehemiah are also a unity. The oldest Talmudic tradition so regarded them. The Masoretic indication of the middle of the book, located in Nehemiah 3:32, would be off center if they were not. Their division into two books in a Hebrew text was not known until the Bomberg edition of A.D. 1525. While the continuous nature of Ezra-Nehemiah is not quite so obvious as that of Chronicles, it is easily evident to any careful reader.

We have now reduced four books to two. Under closer scrutiny these become one:

Read 2 Chronicles 36:22–23; Ezra 1:1–3.

At the end of Chronicles, the editor-author of the connected history breaks off the edict of Cyrus in the middle. Then he takes it up, repeats and completes it at the beginning of Ezra. Were this overlapping of material the only evidence for the fundamental unity of the four books, it would perhaps fail to convince us completely; but we have to assert of the whole work what we have already asserted of 1 and 2 Chronicles: the editorial interest and the style are the same throughout.

While there are disadvantages in working with a "book" as long as this, there are certain values of perspective which make it highly advisable to approach Chronicles-Ezra-Nehemiah in this way before considering them separately.

PURPOSE

If the Chronicler had written only Ezra-Nehemiah, we might have concluded that his purpose was to complete the history interrupted by the Exile, carrying on the story through the return of the exiles and the restoration of Judah. But the fact that he found it necessary to rewrite Samuel and Kings, picking his way among his sources in a very sure-footed manner, leads us to realize that he had other motives in addition to the obvious one of completing the history. The special interests of the Chronicler become much clearer in 1 and 2 Chronicles by virtue of the fact that we have the same history in Samuel and Kings, but written from an entirely different point of view. As we compare the two works, Samuel-Kings on the one hand with Chronicles on the other, noting the Chronicler's omissions and additions, these interests emerge clearly. The Northern Kingdom is almost entirely omitted; when it is mentioned it is treated as a heretical schism from the true Israel. David is the one towering king of all Israel, before whom all the others are pygmies; and David is the source not only of the monarchy but, even more important, of the Temple and of its ritual. While David did not build the Temple, he provided for it by collecting all the materials, by drawing up the plans, and by instructing Solomon in detail just how it was to be done. In the ritual sections, great attention is given to Levitical functions, including choirs and musical instruments.

All of this leads us to conclude that Chronicles-Ezra-Nehemiah was written from the theocratic point of view of an Ezekiel. The editor-author saw the Temple as the natural heir to the Davidic throne, and wrote his history from the point of view of a Levitical priest who deeply and sincerely believed that the true center of Jewish life and its destiny was to be found in Temple worship. Thus Chronicles-Ezra-Nehemiah is a sacerdotal work showing the direction that post-exilic Judaism actually did take as it developed toward the kind of Jewish society which lies in the background of the New Testament.

Date and Historical Setting

We are sufficiently familiar with the historical background of Chronicles that we need not repeat it here, but for the Ezra-Nehemiah period a few background dates are very much in order:

539–530 B.C. Cyrus the first Persian monarch
538 B.C. The decree of Cyrus permitting the Jews to return to Judah
520–515 B.C. The rebuilding of the Jerusalem Temple
464–424 B.C. The reign of Artaxerxes I of Persia
404–358 B.C. The reign of Artaxerxes II of Persia

Against this background we may read the rather exact dates in Ezra-Nehemiah:

Read Ezra 1:1; 7:1–7; *Nehemiah* 2:1.

Quite clearly the Chronicler envisioned three stages of return and restoration, in this order: (1) under Shesh-bazar, which resulted in the rebuilding of the Temple; (2) under Ezra, which established the authority of the law; (3) under Nehemiah, who rebuilt the wall. Even so, it is difficult to date the work of Ezra and Nehemiah because we do not know which Artaxerxes was ruler when each returned. Thus, Ezra may have returned in the seventh year of either ruler; i.e., his return may have been in 457 B.C. or 397 B.C. And Nehemiah's return, by the same kind of reckoning, may have been in 444 B.C. or 384 B.C. (For an impressive argument for dating Nehemiah's return 444 B.C. and Ezra's return 397 B.C. see *The Interpreter's Bible*, Vol. III, pp. 562–63.) W. F. Albright places Ezra's return in the thirty-seventh year of Artaxerxes I, that is, in 427 B.C.[1] He also offers a slight reconstruction of the text of Nehemiah 8:9 and 12:36, bringing them into harmony with his theory.

What about the Chronicler's own dates? This haziness about Ezra and Nehemiah indicates that the Chronicler worked at a still later date. There are a few clues. In 1 Chronicles 3:12–24 there is a genealogy extending to the sixth generation beyond Zerubbabel. If we date Zerubbabel about 520 B.C. and allow thirty years to a generation, we date the sixth generation about 350 B.C. In Nehemiah 12:10–11, we have a list of successive high priests, including Jonathan, the father of Jaddua; and from the Jewish historian Josephus we learn that Jaddua was high priest at the time of Alexander the Great (336–323 B.C.). These bits of evidence seem to push the work of the Chronicler well toward or even into the Greek period. Scholars have also argued that style, vocabulary, and the special interests of the Chronicler argue for a date between 300 and 250 B.C. By this time the Samaritans would have built their own Temple on Mt. Gerizim and the force of Hellenistic culture would have begun to exert its influence in Jewish life. All the more reason, then, to emphasize absolute loyalty to the Jerusalem Temple and the kind of Jewish particularism which Ezra 9–10 and Nehemiah 13 so clearly exemplify. In the battle with schism and apostasy Judaism needed to assert its claims strongly, which is precisely the aim of the Chronicler.

There is one other argument for a late date. Chronicles-Ezra-Nehemiah appears in the Writings—the third division of Jewish Scripture—not in the Law or the Prophets. Samuel and Kings, in contrast, are among the Prophets.

SOURCES

The Chronicler mentions about twenty books which he had used as sources of his history:

[1] *The Interpreter's Bible* (Nashville: Abingdon Press, 1956), Vol. III, p. 554.

Read 1 *Chronicles* 29:29; 2 *Chronicles* 9:29; 13:22; 24:27; 26:22; 27:7; 33:18; *Nehemiah* 7:5; 12:23.

In addition to those named, we know that he also used the Pentateuch (for the long lists of names in 1 Chronicles 1-9) and Samuel-Kings. Quite obviously he had the memoirs of Nehemiah, written in the first person, and he appears to have had firsthand accounts from Ezra in the first person (Ezra 7:27-28; 8:1-34), though this is hard to determine because the style of the Ezra memoirs, so called, is identical with that of the Chronicler himself. This fact has led W. F. Albright to argue that Ezra was himself the Chronicler; but many other scholars find this position untenable. The Chronicler also had Haggai and Zechariah available (see Ezra 5:1-2). Linguistic study shows a special source in Aramaic for Ezra 4:8-6:18; 7:12-26.

From all of this we learn that the Chronicler showed great respect for his sources. He quoted them almost unchanged. He achieved his special purpose by extensive omissions and additions. He omitted all history before David, except as it was represented by nine chapters of genealogy. He also omitted nearly the whole of the history of the Northern Kingdom. He greatly expanded sections dealing with the Temple, its rituals, and the Levites, doing all of this so as to underscore his own conviction that David's kingdom and the Temple, the true heir to the Davidic kingdom, were the genuine source of God's will for his people.

AUTHOR

Aside from the suggestion made by W. F. Albright and already alluded to, we are led by internal evidence to conclude that the author-editor of Chronicles-Ezra-Nehemiah was a Levite in the Temple, whose special work was that of a musician, possibly in the guild of Asaph. In any case, he was a priest who believed fervently in the Temple and its ministry as central to Israel's mission and destiny.

OUTLINE OF CHRONICLES-EZRA-NEHEMIAH

I. Prelude to David's reign, genealogies, 1 Chronicles 1-9
II. David's reign, Israel's glorious morning, 1 Chronicles 10-29

III. Solomon's reign, the fulfillment of David's plans for the Temple, 2 Chronicles 1–9
IV. The kings of Judah, alternate light and shadow, culminating in exile, which in turn ended with Cyrus, 2 Chronicles 10–36
V. Shesh-bazzar's return and the rebuilding of the Temple, Ezra 1–6
VI. Ezra's return and the establishment of the law, Ezra 7–10; Nehemiah 7:73b—8:18
VII. Nehemiah's return and the rebuilding of the wall, Nehemiah 1—7:73a; 9:1—13:31

The effect of Chronicles is to establish David as the true prototype of all Judean kings, by which standard all later kings are judged, and to make of him the towering, ideal figure symbolizing all Israel. It is, further, to make David in turn the architect of the Temple and to place the Temple, as the true Davidic successor, at the center of Jewish life. By rebuilding the Temple, reading the law, and rebuilding the wall, Ezra-Nehemiah sought to re-establish what David had wrought.

Scholars have noticed that the pattern of each of the three returns discernible in Ezra-Nehemiah is much the same: (1) a Persian ruler issues a decree commissioning a particular Jew to return from exile leading certain Jewish followers; (2) each band of exiles returns and sets to work upon its own special commission; (3) opposition develops, always from foreign sources; (4) the Jews nevertheless complete the task; (5) then a great celebration is held and a great festival is observed.

Main Themes

Two themes emerge as the predominant ones: (1) tight Jewish community with the Temple and the law at the center; (2) strong repudiation of all foreigners and foreign influences. The symbol of the whole work of the Chronicler could be the wall, which at once drew those on the inside together and excluded those on the outside. The Chronicler sees the Jews of the postexilic period as "a united, self-conscious people, avoiding all foreign contamination and maintaining a fierce loyalty to the law of their God."[2] Circles have two sides, an inside and an outside. They are friendly to those who are taken in but cruel to those who are shut out. It is hard, even for

[2] *The Interpreter's Bible*, Vol. III, p. 566.

religious people, to draw the circle as wide as God himself would draw it.

There are a number of subordinate themes. Among these are the normative nature of the Davidic kingdom, return from exile, the restoration of national life, the rebuilding of the Temple, the establishment of the law, and the rebuilding of the wall of Jerusalem.

Nevertheless, the Chronicler's account is a view of history as seen from what he regards as its center—the altar. And it is an altar which he jealously guards from all non-Jews.

II. PREPARING YOUR BOOK SERMON

The problem of universalizing the message of the Chronicler and of applying it to our day lies in the fact that we both approve and disapprove of it in the light of later Christian insights, and even in the light of insights from books like Jonah, Ruth, and Second Isaiah. It seems probable that the Jews could have preserved their national and religious identity only by the course that they actually did take in the postexilic period. That was a combined course of fervent loyalty to law and Temple and of narrow and even hostile particularism. And yet all human loyalties which have so far emerged in history are of this nature: they are circles that shut out more people than they include. There is a sense in which every human solidarity must exclude those outside if that solidarity is to mean anything. A family, a local church, a luncheon club, a university, a nation—all must have a membership which is not coterminous with the membership of the whole human race. The difficulty is how to be loyal to the family without being hostile toward those outside it, how to be in a denomination without becoming parochial, how to belong to a nation without becoming nationalistic and chauvinistic.

This is simply to say that the Chronicler's view of history has both its strengths and its dangers. But, when sifted down to its essential, the position of the Chronicler is really that of any conscientious minister. He believes that God is the Lord of history and that his earthly headquarters are in the church; therefore, the right kind of churchmanship is not only good religion, it is also indispensable to good economics, good politics, good education, and everything else. But, just as the right kind of churchmanship can be very close to the heart of God, a wrong or misguided kind of churchmanship can be inimical to the very purpose of God, and almost endlessly harmful to society.

CARDINAL IDEA

God, the Lord of history, has his earthly throne in the Jerusalem Temple; and he requires his people to stand united, separate from all foreigners, and to maintain a fierce loyalty to the law.

Universalized, this idea says not only that the worship of God stands at the center of our common life, but that to worship God truly we must maintain a flintheaded exclusiveness toward those who do not follow the truth as we see it. This was the point of view which actually did prevail in postexilic Judaism. We call it *particularism*. The Old Testament at its best, in Jonah, Ruth, and Second Isaiah, repudiates particularism. The New Testament as a whole repudiates it. Here is one instance in which one part of the Bible must not be read narrowly, out of context with the whole. We must allow the nobler vision to lead us to higher ground.

But from a particularistic writing such as this we may be alerted to this tendency within ourselves. We not only worship God; we also deify the particular institutions through which we worship him. We worship God and our own denomination; God and our own liturgical tradition; God and our own race; God and our own nation. What is more, we tend to make the proper service of God dependent upon the elevation of that particular denomination, race, or nation. The truth is that we often use our highest moments of inspiration as rallying points for our deepest prejudices; we gain sanction for those prejudices by assigning them to God. The temptation to which Judaism succumbed when it embraced particularism is not far from any one of us.

SHAPING A PREACHING OUTLINE

A sermon on this four-volume work will accept the tension that is in the work itself. The worship of God stands at the center of all other concerns and enterprises. But the worship of God cannot be "in general." It has to be in a place—in our own particular Jerusalem. It takes refuge behind its own walls: forms, rituals, membership requirements. And there is always the danger that worship, the most universal of human aspirations, shall turn into an instrument of human division and hostility. The contrast within the Chronicler is also ours: fervent loyalty to the one true God, on the one hand; our own security and self-elevation, on the other. It is easy to build up hostile feelings toward those who have our faith but do not express it according to our cultus; they are our Samaritans. It is equally easy to lose the spirit of this faith in rigid legalism and in the zealous suppression of all differences. We are tempted, too, to take a pigeonhole view of religion as one human activity among others, albeit the most important activity. It is, after all, not human worship or human faith which is at the center of human life; it is God himself who is at the center. And all our systems are judged by the extent to which they point to him.

A second approach, with much the same message, is through the use of the wall as a symbol. Ephesians 2:14 characterized the division between Jews and Gentiles as a middle wall of partition. The rabbis sometimes symbolized the law as a fence. And the Temple had its well-known wall between the Court of the Gentiles and the Inner Court, with an engraved warning to foreigners that trespass meant death. Thus law, Temple and city wall may all be subsumed under this figure. Each produced solidarity, and each tended to become a basis for exclusion. This particular sermon could use "Mending Wall," the poem by Robert Frost. There would be two main divisions: (1) protection, Nehemiah 2:17; 6:15–16; (2) exclusion, Nehemiah 13:3. In such a sermon no preacher will be able to resist using the dialogue between Frost and his neighbor in a part of the poem. To the dogma of the neighbor, "Good fences make good neighbors," Frost replies:

> There where it is we do not need the wall:
> He is all pine and I am apple-orchard.
> My apple trees will never get across
> And eat the cones under his pines, I tell him.
> He only says, "Good fences make good neighbors."
> Spring is the mischief in me, and I wonder
> If I could put a notion in his head:
> "*Why* do they make good neighbors? Isn't it
> Where there are cows? But here there are no cows.
> Before I built a wall I'd ask to know
> What I was walling in or walling out,

And to whom I was like to give offense.
Something there is that doesn't love a wall,
That wants it down!" . . .[3]

Other sermons on something less than the whole of the four-volume work will occur in abundance to most ministers. Under the section "Outline of Chronicles-Ezra-Nehemiah" (pp. 79–80), we drew attention to the five stages of each return-restoration. This would make a good outline for a sermon dealing with the two-volume work of Ezra-Nehemiah. Universalization and modern application are fairly straightforward. Using this pattern, it would be possible, of course, to deal with all three return-restorations (Temple, law, and wall) or with any one of them.

Another way of presenting the three topics is to select psalms which celebrate each of them, or psalms which focus, like Chronicles-Ezra-Nehemiah itself, upon the Temple. There are psalms aplenty on Jerusalem, the Temple, and the law. These three topics are not ancient history, for every people needs a place—a homeland—and a law and a cultus.

The significance of the law can scarcely be overemphasized. For this was perhaps the beginning of the Jewish canon of Scripture. The Bible came into its revered place in Jewish life quickly there-after—at any rate, those two divisions of it known as the Law and the Prophets. The German poet Heine has called the Bible a "portable fatherland of the Jews." May not the Christian find something of the same thing in his Bible?

A MODERN TITLE

"Mending Wall," "The Lord is in His Holy Temple," "A Minister's View of History," "History as Seen from the Altar" are possible titles.

---

[3] "Mending Wall" from *The Complete Poems of Robert Frost* (New York: Henry Holt & Co., 1930).

12

AS DYING, AND BEHOLD WE LIVE

The Book of Esther

THE Book of Esther centers in one of the ugliest facts of human history—anti-Semitism. No century has been free of it. Age after age has seen the Jews hated and persecuted. Driven over the face of the earth, exiled and killed, they have never known when the terror would break out afresh, nor from what quarter. And the end is not yet. In modern times and in a civilized European state, a mad dictator set out systematically to exterminate the Jews; he forced them to wear the star of David, manufactured tales of their crimes, confiscated their property, herded them into concentration camps, and in the gas chambers and incinerators of Buchenwald and Dachau killed and burned six million of them.

How have the Jews reacted to this recurring horror? The principal fact is that they have survived; and they have survived not simply to exist. They have survived triumphantly and vibrantly, to create. Their touch is felt in the realms of music, drama, art, literature, science, law, and finance. We are all in their debt in countless ways. They have lived on.

The Jews have lived on to outlast their persecutors. It is this fact that the Book of Esther celebrates.

I. WORKING YOUR WAY INTO THE BOOK

Esther culminates in the celebration of the Feast of Purim (the Feast of Lots). This, in fact, seems to be the principal purpose of the book. The role of the *pūr*, or the lot, is the key to the story. *Read Esther* 3:1–11.

Here we have a story of a major persecution of Jews planned by Haman, grand vizier of Persia. His motivations are instructive: (1) his hatred for an individual Jew, Mordecai, which is then extended to all Jews; (2) his hatred of them because they have their own culture and do not readily assimilate into other cultures. These have remained the reasons for persecuting the Jews down the centuries.

Haman—that Persian Hitler before Hitler—plotted the extermination of the Jews. To set the day of slaughter, he cast a die, or a lot. It fell on the 13th of Adar, the twelfth Jewish month, corresponding roughly to our February-March:
Read Esther 3:12-15.

But the plot of Haman failed. With genius and with a kind of ultimate courage, Mordecai and his kinswoman Esther, the queen of Persia, succeeded in turning the tables on Haman and in getting the order reversed:
Read Esther 8:3-17; 9:1-3, 16-26.

And so the Feast of Purim came into being. It is kept by the Jews to this day. Through the centuries it has been observed by feasting, drinking, noisemaking, masquerading, exchanging of gifts, and giving of alms to the poor. In the synagogues, the Book of Esther is read on the eve of the Feast; when the name of Haman occurs it is greeted with hisses and the stamping of feet.

Esther is a late Old Testament book. Just how late is not certain, but it is after the Persian period. Some scholars place it as late as 125 B.C. during the Maccabean struggles. There seems little doubt that it rose out of a time of intense anti-Semitism. And it seems just as clear that it is a piece of historical fiction—a parable with a purpose. Since that purpose is related to the celebration of Jewish survival despite persecution, the book has a timeless relevance; it is not necessary to date it precisely nor to settle the question of how much actual history may lie at the core of the story.

With the background we have given, the book tells its own story, and a superb story it is:
Read the Book of Esther.

REACTIONS

Anti-Semitism and the Jews' reaction to it; that is the gist of the matter. The Jewish response is twofold: (1) gratitude and joy over the astonishing fact of survival; (2) vindictiveness. There is just cause for celebration, for Jewish survival is a kind of historical miracle. Israel was contemporary to ancient Egypt, Assyria, Babylon, Greece, Persia, Rome; and still Israel lives on while the sand drifts over the ruins of the proud peoples who were once their masters and their persecutors. But there is the unlovely aspect—vindictiveness—that troubles many readers of the book. It is a minority note, but it is present. On the 13th of Adar the Jews throughout Persia rose against their enemies and slew 75,500 of them in a single day. We read this rightly as a wish rather than as a fact, a suppressed wish. There are other facets of the same spirit in the Old Testament, notably among the imprecatory psalms. The Bible is realistic in reporting this most natural, human reaction to unjust oppression. In fairness we shall have to admit, however, that vindictiveness is not the dominant note of the book. Celebration in joy and gratitude is the leading note. "To the Jew the book teaches the indestructibility of Israel 'the eternal miracle of Jewish survival.' "[1]

The reaction of readers has divided sharply. The Jews have loved the book through the centuries, and still love it. The medieval Jewish philosopher Maimonides said that when the rest of the Old Testament passed away in the messianic age, the Torah and Esther would remain. And certain Talmudic rabbis even placed Esther above the Torah. In contrast to this, Christian reaction has tended to follow Martin Luther's point of view. He said, "I am so hostile to this book that I wish it did not exist; for it Judaizes too much and has too much heathen naughtiness."[2]

It is to be expected that the Jewish view of this book will differ from the non-Jewish view. And though it must be admitted that Esther is not particularly religious—the name of God does not occur in it—and that we are far beneath the lofty ethical insights of a book like Ruth or Hosea, yet the Book of Esther deserves serious attention. From the Jewish standpoint, the Feast of Purim is certainly no more nationalistic than the Fourth of July or Bastille Day; it is perhaps less so, and it has all the positive values of those national holidays. But from the Christian standpoint, the subject matter of the

[1] Bernhard W. Anderson, "Esther," in *The Interpreter's Bible,* Vol. III, p. 830.
[2] Madeleine S. and J. Lane Miller, *Harper's Bible Dictionary* (6th ed.; New York: Harper & Brothers, 1959), p. 174.

book is doubly important because it confronts us with our part in the ancient crime of anti-Semitism.

The thing that should give the Christian pause as he reads the Book of Esther is his own guilt for sharing in and perpetuating prejudice and persecution against the Jews. If we look for our place in this story we do not find ourselves among the persecuted. Rather, we find ourselves among the persecutors. We have not risked our lives opposing prejudice and discrimination! Let us be honest: We are not the Esthers or the Mordecais of this story; we are Haman or one of the minor court officials or citizens acting on Haman's orders. We may not have been the fanatics of prejudice, but we have shared in its taint, we have relayed its lies; we are the gentle people of prejudice—the ones who keep it alive and make it work.

II. PREPARING YOUR BOOK SERMON

CARDINAL IDEA

For Jews: *Let us celebrate the miracle of Jewish survival in spite of persecution.*

For non-Jews: *Let us likewise give thanks for the miraculous survival of the Jews, but let us also repent of our own role in persecuting them.*

SHAPING A PREACHING OUTLINE

Many sermons have been preached on Esther 4:14, 16: "And who knows whether you have not come to the kingdom for such a time as this?" (Mordecai's question, challenging Esther). ". . . if I perish, I perish" (the courageous response of Esther, risking her life for her people). These are great texts and they point to the great theme of Jewish national loyalty. When presented to Christian audiences, however, they tend not to convey the central, narrower message of the whole book. They become discussions of loyalty and courage in general. The book has a more limited subject: the survival of the Jews in spite of anti-Semitism. Loyalty and courage in the face of persecution certainly play their role, but it is not loyalty and courage as general traits that we must talk about; it is loyalty and courage as applied to the social phenomenon of Jewish persecution. This means that the Jew will approach the Book of Esther from the standpoint of a courageous Mordecai or Esther, but that a non-Jew must approach it from the standpoint of a repentant Haman. Jews need the courage to face and outwit persecution. Non-Jews need the courage to admit the fact of persecution and to repent of it.

One approach to outline is built around the personalities of the book. Sketch the story briefly in your own words, then discuss the personalities. There are two large, opposing groups of people who enter the story en masse; these are the Jewish victims of persecution scattered throughout the empire, on the one hand, and the citizens—petty court officials, couriers, soldiers, and others—who represent the persecuting majority, on the other hand. Then there is Haman, the instigator, the arch Jew-baiter. There is the king, his pliable regent; he becomes an agent of persecution, not because he harbors ill will toward the Jews, but because he is preoccupied with other matters and just isn't interested. The matter doesn't concern him, so he co-operates more by default than by design. Over against Haman and Ahasu-erus stand Mordecai and Esther; they have the ingenuity and the courage to stand up to persecution, to do something about it, to outwit it and outlast it. The listener is simply asked to cast himself, to find his role in this story. Using modern examples, this sermon can live in contemporary terms; it can be made a truly relevant and challenging experience.

A topical presentation may be less dramatic, but it can be effective. Some of the topics are these: (1) the fact of anti-Semitism and its extent; (2) the causes of anti-Semitism; (3) the agents of anti-Semitism; (4) the miraculous survival of the Jews; (5) our reaction and our duty.

Although it is not a usual practice to involve more than one person in delivering a sermon, the Book of Esther presents an opportunity that is hard to resist. It is a superb story and will make its best impact when it is presented in its own terms. This can be done in the format of a play reading, with several persons. Let the cast sit as a group about a table, and after a brief introduction of the main problem and purpose of the book in a five-minute talk by the pastor, let them simply read the story. It is possible to condense it slightly and to make it more pronounceable by eliminating some sections, such as the lists of cities in 9:7–10a; but for the most part the story will stand as it is. This type of presentation requires eight voices: Narrator; King Ahasu-erus; Memucan (1:16; he can also double as spokesman for the king's servants, in 2:2); Mordecai; Esther; Haman; Zeresh, the wife of Haman; Harbona, a eunuch (7:9). Since the roles of Memucan and Harbona are so minor, they could be absorbed by the Narrator without much loss to the dramatic force of the reading. The reading of the book in this manner might then be followed by a forum on anti-Semitism.

A MODERN TITLE

The Psalms deals frequently with anti-Semitic persecutions, and in so doing presents a number of suggestive phrases that might serve as titles for the Book of Esther. Psalm 44 yields these, among others: "A Byword among the Nations" (44:14), "Slain All the Day Long" (44:22). Psalm 35 suggests: "Hatred without Cause" (35:19). A good deal could be said in favor of a simple, descriptive title: "Anti-Semitism."

13

WHEN TROUBLE COMES TO GOOD PEOPLE

The Book of Job

DO YOU want to know what a man really feels about himself, about his fellows, and about his God? Watch him when the pressure is on, when he is in deep trouble. The hidden man will out.

But that is not all, the man who comes out of hiding will stand before his God, and as he stands there in the unaccustomed candor and deep searching of trouble, he may cast himself on God and undergo a rebirth. That was what happened to Job.

I. WORKING YOUR WAY INTO THE BOOK

The Book of Job is a long poem, with a prologue (1:1–2:13) and an epilogue (42:1–17) in prose. The prose section is a dramatic narrative which could be cast and presented as a play. The poetic section could be called a dramatic dialogue; although the speeches are too long for the normal give and take of conversation, and there is almost no stage action, this section, too, could be cast and presented in dramatic form. It is best read in that frame of mind.

The prologue introduces us to Job, his sudden misfortunes, and his three friends, Eliphaz, Bildad and Zophar, who come to comfort him. Then follows a long poetic discussion of Job's tragedies and their religious meaning; this discussion takes the form of three cycles of speeches: each friend speaks in turn and Job answers each, until the discussion has gone around the circle three times (3:1–31:40). At this point there is an interruption in the person of the brash, young, dogmatic Elihu, who breaks into the discussion to rebuke Job in a long-winded speech, and then vanishes without notice, as he had appeared (32:1–37:24). The drama comes to a climax when God himself appears in the midst of a whirlwind and speaks directly to Job, questioning and challenging him (38:1–41:34). Job, now suddenly contrite, answers in a very short but highly significant speech (42:1–6), bringing the poetic discussion to a close. The prose epilogue returns us to God, who rebukes the friends of Job for doubting him and who then restores Job's prosperity.

Scholars feel that this poetic drama may be based upon an Edomite folk story from patriarchal days, and was shaped into its present form in Israel's postexilic period. The poetry is wisdom literature, that classification which also includes Ecclesiastes and Proverbs. But the actual dating of the writing is not a crucial matter for the modern reader; Job deals with a timeless and universal theme—a man's basic relation to God as that relation is emphasized by suffering. Job's problem is the problem of every man. And the discussion is as timely now as it was when it first appeared.

Derived from different sources, perhaps even from different ages, the prose and poetry of Job are often studied separately, and assigned separate messages. For our present purpose we shall let them stand together in one book; and we shall assume that this book has a single message, whose theme is the question of Satan in the prologue: "Does Job fear God for nought?" (1:9). It is Satan's contention that Job has found it profitable to be loyal to God, that his religion is essentially utilitarian, and that he has no deep, abiding, disinterested faith in God:

Read Job 1:6–12.

All the sufferings and misfortunes that befall Job constitute the test to answer Satan's question. What is Job's real relation to God? Is he as righteous as he appears, and as he himself had thought? Is his faith as stanch, his integrity as unassailable?

This basic concern of the Book of Job is firmly rooted in the psychology of religious experience. Trial, suffering, temptation test a man; they bring out the best in him, and the worst. They bring his hidden character into the light. What a man is under stress, he secretly is in quiet times.

The reader is "in on" this basic secret of the book, but the characters are not. In the nature of the case they cannot be. It is the fact of his affliction that Job faces; the why of it is hid from him. And Job's friends, in spite of pious pretensions, have no more light on the matter than he has. They are all confronted with a hard, evil fact, and are compelled by that confrontation to resolve it somehow in the light of their religious faith.

In the course of their long stormy discussion they address themselves to the questions, "Why do the righteous suffer?" and "Why do men suffer?" And they give all the answers available to men except the last two in the following list:

1. Suffering is punishment for sin.

2. Suffering can be disciplinary—purifying.

3. Suffering sometimes seems arbitrary, unreasonable.

4. Suffering may be probationary—God's way of testing genuineness.

5. Life after death will level out the apparent injustices of earthly existence through rewards to the righteous and punishments to the wicked.

6. Suffering, when it is voluntary and vicarious, is redemptive.

Nevertheless, these questions and their answers are nothing but instruments of the deeper concern. The book does not set out to give, and does not give, a philosophical solution to the problem of suffering. Instead, it asks, "What will a truly religious man *do* with the fact of suffering? How will his suffering affect his relation to his God?" The richest treasures of the Book of Job, therefore, are not to be found in its intellectual answers to philosophical questions. They will be found, instead, beneath the surface, in the emotional response to the unpleasant, brute facts of human existence on its darker side. You will read this book most instructively if you approach it as a personal counselor who has learned to listen not to what people are saying but to what they are feeling. For it is in this emotional realm that estrangement from God and man takes place; it is there that encounter and reconciliation occur.

Job at first responds to his troubles with a storm of emotions. He laments the fact that he was born (3:1–10). He wishes to die (6:8–13). He pronounces life futile (7:1–6). He lashes out at his friends in anger and resentment (6:14–20; 13:1–12; 16:1–5). He accuses God of being unjust and arbitrary (9:8–12; 19:1–6); he even finds God guilty of laughing at men and mocking them (9:20–24). He defies God (7:12–16; 10:20–22), summons God to a trial (13:20–27), dissolves into bewilderment (7:17–21). And he pridefully maintains his own goodness (27:1–12). There are still other emotions in Job's stormy response to God and men in the face of his troubles.

The book is great for the honesty of its emotional portrait. Job's first, startled, angry reaction to his plight may be summarized as a deepening *estrangement* from God and men. God seems to hide; he will not answer Job's prayers. God seems cruel; he will give no reasons for Job's troubles. And man, too, fades away; even close friends become miserable comforters. The first effect of suffering is a fearful spiritual isolation, a terrible, futile loneliness.

The reaction of Job's friends to his troubles may be summarized in New Testament words. He asked them for a loaf and they gave him a stone. They were never able to get inside his troubles, to feel them as their own. They met his needs with dogmatic opinions and arguments. They made an idol of their theology and served it in place of God; and they rejected their friend because he could not subscribe to their neatly packaged theology.

But Job has a second reaction to his troubles. They force upon him an awareness that one so easily forgets in times of prosperity. God is infinite; man is finite. Man is dependent, a child in learning, in power, and in goodness. Man meets God as God; he confronts God and is confronted in a terrible, cosmic meeting. This is the basic meaning of those exalted words out of the whirlwind (38:1—41:32).

A third reaction quickly follows. We see Job re-evaluating his own prideful righteousness, repenting of his resentment and rebellion, acknowledging himself to be but a man after all, and freely surrendering himself in trust and obedience to his God. And it is this brief, final response that is really the key to the whole book:

Read Job 42:1–6.

One is now ready to read the book as a whole. By eliminating the long speeches of Elihu (32:1—37:24) and the third cycle of speeches between Job and his three friends (22:1—27:23) one may get the gist of the argument quickly. Then he may go back to enlarge his impressions by reading the omitted sections.

II. PREPARING YOUR BOOK SERMON

CARDINAL IDEA

Under the revealing pressure of suffering, man discovers his true relationship to God; and if he is mature he will move from a tradi-

*tional, secondhand faith through pride and rebellion to a genuine
face-to-face meeting with God.*

SHAPING A PREACHING OUTLINE

As described above, Job's reactions to affliction passed through
three main phases: (1) deepening estrangement from God and man
through his pride and rebellious resentment; (2) a new experience
of the power and majesty of God, in contrast to his own finiteness
and dependence; (3) a meeting of reconciliation and submission.
Thus, for a development of the stages of Job's growth through affliction, one may note three stages, represented by three words: estrangement, encounter, and reconciliation.

The key passage of the book (42:1–6) may be taken as a text, in
which case the sermon may develop around the contrast between an
inherited and a face-to-face religion. Job does not have a face-
to-face experience until his prideful self-righteousness is shattered
and he gets *himself* out of the center of the universe. There is a
genuine dislodgment from a certain point of view which Job held
throughout most of the book—a point of view which is irreligious in
the name of religion. Not until he is routed from that fortress is he
ready truly to meet God and know him in person.

One of my former students, Newton Fowler, developed a book
sermon on Job around the contrast between inherited religion and
relevant faith. It unfolded somewhat as follows:

1. Inheriting a religion and substituting it for a relevant faith in
   God (1:1, 8; 2:3, 9a; 1:5; 20–21; 2:10b)
2. The failure of inherited religion as a substitute for relevant faith
   a) Confronted with suffering and tragedy, inherited religion
   has little to offer (7:1–6; 6:11)
   b) Its hope that a man might achieve his own destiny is a
   false one (7:20, 21a; 13:20–23)
3. The matrix of relevant faith
   a) Encounter (chaps. 38–41)
   b) Surrender (42:1–6)

Another student sermon, this one by Donald Steffy, is suggestive.
Working from the title "When Adversity Visits a Righteous Man,"
it unfolds through three points: (1) adversity travels an unpredict-
able course; (2) adversity is met by an unexpected dismay, involving

both men and God; (3) adversity is properly received in the spirit of graciousness, through love, insight, and faith.

The Introduction to the Book of Job in *The Interpreter's Bible*[1] suggests a sermon built around the main themes of the book:

1. Adversity against integrity
   - *a*) Job's integrity (1:1; 1:5)
   - *b*) His initial fortitude (1:20–22; 2:10)
   - *c*) His eventual disintegration (3:1)
2. Job's controversy with God
   - *a*) His innocence as a claim upon God (10:7; 27:6)
   - *b*) His judgment of his Creator (9:18–29)
   - *c*) His inconsistent expectation of acquittal (23:3–7)
   - *d*) His claim that God is avoiding him (23:8–10)
3. Job's controversy with his friends[2]
4. Meeting God face to face
   - *a*) God's power and majesty; man's finiteness (chaps. 28, 37–41)
   - *b*) Job's change from self-vindication to his search for grace (31:35 versus 42:6)

A condensation of the book can be made, permitting it to be cast and presented as a play reading. Select seven persons for the following roles: Narrator, Eliphaz (gentle), Bildad (dogmatic), Zophar (vindictive, sarcastic), Elihu (authoritarian), God, and Job. In making the book condensation, eliminate most of the speeches of Elihu and most of the third cycle; select carefully the few telling verses needed from the final chapters.

A MODERN TITLE

Possible titles are: "When Adversity Visits a Righteous Man," "Seeing God through Our Tears," "Hearsay Religion at Wit's End," "Why Do the Righteous Suffer?" and "Born to Trouble."

---

[1] Samuel Terrien, "Job," in *The Interpreter's Bible*, Vol. III, pp. 899–900.
[2] For right and wrong views of these friends, see *The Interpreter's Bible*, Vol. III, pp. 899–900.

14

DEEP WRIT UPON THE HUMAN HEART

The Psalms

I N INTIMACY and in emotional power no book in the Bible com-
pares with the anthology of prayers and hymns which make up
the collection we now study. This book, as no other, bears witness
to the flowing, surging spirit of the living God touching the inmost
recesses of the human soul, "deep writ upon the human heart," as
Daniel Ben Judah so majestically wrote six centuries ago.

I. WORKING YOUR WAY INTO THE BOOK

TREASURED IN MEMORY

The first place to look for a psalm is in the human memory. Few
people, even the most cursory churchgoers, have failed to learn at
least a psalm or two, perhaps even without intending it. First in the
heart of the people, undoubtedly, is Psalm 23, but there are others
that also ring in the memory. We shall not attempt to list them here,
but a casual leafing through the Psalter will show any reader at once
those songs with which he is already familiar. Much of the Psalter
lies not merely in the Bible outside of us; it lies within us, treasured
in memory, quickening the heart.

THE HYMNAL

The next place to look for a psalm is in the Christian hymnal.
From the earliest times Christians sang psalms as a part of their
corporate worship:

Read Colossians 3:16; *Ephesians* 5:18b–19.

In more recent times some denominations have sung nothing but psalms, metrical versions of which have been provided in profusion ever since the Reformation. England and Scotland alone have had 326 such hymnals. For an example of a metrical version of Psalm 23, consult a hymnal for the hymn written by James Montgomery. The first stanza reads:

> The Lord is my Shepherd, no want shall I know;
> I feed in green pastures, safe-folded I rest;
> He leadeth my soul where the still waters flow,
> Restores me when wand'ring, redeems when oppressed.

Older hymnals, especially, carry many such hymns.

The presence of psalms in the hymnal may not be quite so obvious in more recent times, but they are there nonetheless. Numerous hymns have been written with psalms as their inspiration and chief source of ideas. Take, for example, the stately hymn by John Milton, found in most hymnals:

> Let us with a gladsome mind
> Praise the Lord, for He is kind;
> For His mercies aye endure,
> Ever faithful, ever sure.

After reading all the stanzas of this hymn, read Psalm 136, which served as its inspiration. There are others, even more familiar. We simply list a few of them:

Thomas Ken's "Doxology" and Isaac Watts's "From All that Dwell below the Skies" (Ps. 100); the anonymous "Praise the Lord, Ye Heavens, Adore Him" (Ps. 148); Harriet Beecher Stowe's "Still, Still with Thee" (Ps. 139); Joseph Addison's "The Spacious Firmament on High" (Ps. 19); Martin Luther's "A Mighty Fortress is Our God" (Ps. 46); Isaac Watts's "O God, Our Help in Ages Past" (Ps. 90).

Anthems in great number also owe their inspiration to the Psalter, not a few of them relying generously upon the exact wording of psalms for many phrases.

Thus, because of the treasures of memory and of the Christian hymnal, most people begin from within the Psalter and know more about it than they at first realize.

OUTLINE OF THE PSALMS

The reader who examines the Psalms as a whole will find it divided into five books, each ending with a doxology. This arrangement is very old, having been made before the Septuagint version. It was apparently known to the Chronicler (1 Chron. 16:36; cf. Ps. 106:48). The division into books is as follows:

Book I, Psalms 1–41
Book II, Psalms 42–72
Book III, Psalms 73–89
Book IV, Psalms 90–106
Book V, Psalms 107–150

Consult the end of each book for the doxology. This is a single verse in Books I, III, and IV; two verses in Book II; but it is a whole psalm in Book V—Psalm 150, which serves as the doxology not only to Book V but also to the whole Psalter. In much the same way, Psalm 1 serves as the prelude to all the psalms. The division of the Psalter into five books is apparently a tribute to the five Books of Moses, the eventual arrangement of the Torah into five books, known best to us by the Greek title, Pentateuch.

Examination of the psalms from the standpoint of their collection shows us no less than eight or nine groupings. With the exceptions of Psalms 1, 2, 10, 33, 66, and 67, Books I and II are ascribed to David. One scholar has called these "His Majesty's Hymnbook." This does not mean that David wrote them all, but that they are in some way associated with his name. We have still a third Davidic collection in Psalms 138–145. All told, there are 73 psalms in the three Davidic collections—nearly half of the entire Psalter.

Other collections include: the Sons of Korah (Pss. 42–49, 84–89); Asaph (Ps. 50, 73–83); the Hallel Songs (Pss. 105–107, 111–118, 146–150); Pilgrim Songs (Pss. 120–134); an unnamed collection, Pss. 93, 95–100.

To all appearances, the Sons of Korah, and Asaph were Temple singers. The Pilgrim Songs (or Songs of Ascent) were evidently used as a booklet of devotions by pilgrims going up to Jerusalem annually to the Passover and to the other festivals, as commanded in Deuteronomy 16:16. The Hallel Psalms were probably connected in some way with Temple and synagogue worship; as early as six centuries after Christ we know that synagogue congregations knew all of them by heart; how long they had been using them in that way we can only surmise.

Hymnal and Prayer Book

From what has been said so far it will be seen that the Psalms is not a book at all in the usual sense. It is a book in the sense that an anthology of many poets is called a book. It is a book as a hymnal is a book. Scholars know and refer to it as "The Hymnbook of the Second Temple." Browsing through the Psalter, anyone will quickly see that many of the psalms bear musical notations for tune and accompaniment. There is that interesting, cryptic word "selah," which must have had a liturgical meaning as direction to the choir or congregation. What a stirring thing it would be if we could go back in time to the Temple as it was in the days when the huge antiphonal choirs sang these psalms in the Temple service. We may be assured that the experience was a thrilling, spine-tingling one for anyone fortunate enough to be there when those things happened. Today, we best recapture the mood of many of these psalms only as we participate fervently in corporate worship, led by great choral and congregational singing.

There are some scholars who think that many of the psalms were never set to music and that they were never used in corporate worship. They belong to the library of private devotion. We do know that modern Jewish worship uses only about half of them. At any rate, they run the full range of human feelings and celebrate the whole of life in intimate fashion. Martin Luther long ago said what most needs to be said: through the Psalter we "can look into the heart of all the saints." This does not mean that all the thoughts of the psalms are lofty and exemplary—for among other things there are the maledictions and imprecations against enemies, but these psalms are honest and searching; in them men bring all that they are, good and bad, intimately into the presence of God. To this day they stand as an adequate resource for the expression of the deepest of human emotions, whether of joy or despair, love or hate, confession, thanksgiving, or rededication. One who is rich in the words of the psalms is rich in the language of prayer.

SPECIAL OCCASIONS

The Jews came to associate certain psalms with certain occasions. There were festival psalms, for example: Passover (Pss. 83, 135); the Feast of Weeks and Tabernacles (Ps. 29); Purim (Ps. 7; see also the Book of Esther); the Dedication of the Temple (Ps. 30); the Destruction of the Temple on the 9th of Ab (Ps. 137); various festivals of the New Moon (Pss. 98, 104); the New Year (Pss. 47, 68). There were also psalms for the various days of the week: Sunday (Ps. 24), Monday (Ps. 48), Tuesday (Ps. 82), Wednesday (Ps. 94), Thursday (Ps. 81), Friday (Ps. 93), Saturday (Ps. 92).

MAIN THEMES

The contrasting moods within the Psalms are like the sharp geographical contrasts in the land of Palestine. Notice a few representatives of various moods:

1. *Revenge and imprecation* (Pss. 58, 83, 94, 137). Ancient Jews (and modern, too) have been harassed by the anti-Semitism of other peoples through long centuries. It is only natural that they should harbor some resentments. The teachings of Jesus now make us ashamed of such feelings, but shame is not the answer to them. To root them out we have first to face them.

2. *Despair* (Pss. 22, 42, 43, 88, 102, 142). Jews are not alone in their experiences of the dark night of the soul, but their historical circumstances made them somewhat more intimate with despair over longer periods. No more authentic voices have called out of the depths than the voices of the psalmists.

3. *Joy* (see the Hallel Songs, listed under the section "Outline of the Psalms"). At bottom, the Hebrew religion was one of gratitude for deliverance from bondage and for the special role of Servant which God had conferred upon the Hebrew people. The note of joy springs forth full bodied in the songs of praise.

4. *Confession* (Pss. 51, 139). Nothing so fully fits the mood of prayer and worship as confession. Indeed, there can be no true worship of the living God without it.

5. *Trust* (Pss. 23, 91, 103, 146). Here is the true ground of hope and comfort—the reality of the living God. No shield or defense was like this fortress, no strength so comforting.

6. *Soliloquy* (Pss. 8, 90). Midway between corporate worship and private prayer is the mood of soliloquy when the soul sits quiet and reflects upon life and destiny.

There are psalms appropriate to various circumstances as well:

1. *On a journey* (Ps. 121). This is really a traveler's prayer used by pilgrims on their way to the festivals at Jerusalem. But it is appropriate to any journey: "The Lord will keep your going out and your coming in from this time forth and for evermore."

2. *Home and family* (Pss. 127, 128, 133). The picture of domestic love and of family solidarity which we get from these psalms is strengthening.

3. *In church* (Ps. 84). This lovely psalm is often sung as solo or anthem by church choirs.

4. *Out of doors* (Pss. 19:1–6; 29; 104). Here we celebrate nature, when gentle and when aroused.

5. *After a serious illness* (Ps. 116). "For thou hast delivered my soul from death, my eyes from tears, my feet from stumbling; . . ."

The Psalter is a treasury of moods and circumstances. As you read it you will want to add to the list which we have started.

II. PREPARING YOUR BOOK SERMON

CARDINAL IDEA

Share your whole life with God, withholding no secret chamber of the heart, and pour out all that is within you to the Father of your spirit; acknowledge him in all your ways.

SHAPING A PREACHING OUTLINE

One way of presenting the Psalms would be to draw the whole service of worship on a given Sunday from the Psalter. One such service contains the following stages: (1) call to worship (Ps. 134); (2) adoration (Ps. 145:1–13); (3) confession (Ps. 51); (4) thanksgiving (Ps. 136:1–9, 23–26 read as a litany; to each phrase, as the leader pauses, let all say "for his steadfast love endures forever"); (5) supplication (Ps. 130:1–6); (6) illumination (Ps. 73 or Ps. 84); (7) submission (Ps. 121); (8) benediction (Ps. 67:1–2). Each stage of worship will also have its appropriate hymn or choral response.

A careful selection of hymns and of choral numbers will derive the whole service from the Psalter, a fact which may be announced in advance and also at the time of the service.

A variant upon the foregoing arrangement will include a sermon at the stage of "illumination," the sermon being an expository treatment of the Psalms somewhat in the manner of Part I of the present chapter.

A third approach will treat the Psalter as the book of the heart, showing how it reflects the moods and tensions of the human spirit in the presence of the living God. Such a treatment will have to be highly selective; it cannot hope to be exhaustive. But as many as five major moods may be selected and illustrated directly from the Psalter and from contemporary experience.

A fourth approach is a combination of sermon and anthem. The minister and choirmaster working together could select as many as three anthems drawn from various psalms, each anthem to be sung after its exposition by the minister. Such an approach may succeed better in capturing the spirit of the Psalms than any exposition by itself can ever do, for these psalms are meant to be sung or prayed, or both.

A MODERN TITLE

"Theme Songs of Faith" is suggested by Psalm 45:1. There will be no end to the titles that could be drawn from the poetic phrases of the psalms themselves. "Deep Writ upon the Human Heart," the title of this chapter, is a phrase from Daniel Ben Judah's Hebrew hymn of the fourteenth century: "Praise to the Living God," which is also a good title.

15

ALTERNATIVE TO FOLLY

The Proverbs

Long ago Benjamin Franklin taught Americans to love proverbs. His *Poor Richard's Almanack* is a treasury of prudential wisdom valued by many. Turn its pages and read a few of its gems: "A false friend and a shadow attend only while the sun shines." "Many a man thinks he is buying pleasure when he is merely selling himself a slave to it." "He that falls in love with himself will have no rivals." "Let him who scatters thorns not go barefoot." "He that lieth down with dogs shall rise up with fleas."

Many of *Poor Richard's* sayings exhibit a gentle cynicism: "The tongue offends, and the ears get the cuffing." "Keep your eyes wide open before marriage—half shut afterwards." "The bell calls others to church, but itself never minds the sermon."

How many of us remember learning these and other proverbs from our parents and grandparents? I personally recall several which were repeated by my mother in my childhood until I knew them by heart. As vivid principles of conduct they stayed with me: "If at first you don't succeed, try, try again." "People who live in glass houses should not throw stones." "A bird in the hand is worth two in the bush." "A stitch in time saves nine."

And it is precisely here—in the instruction of the young—that proverbs are meant to function. In a few words a proverb speaks volumes. Because of its vivid figures of speech, its rhythm, and its brevity, it sticks in the memory and is easily passed on. It lives best not in books but in oral tradition. And its purpose is always practical: to bring up a child in the way in which he should go, so that even when he is old he will not depart from it.

I. WORKING YOUR WAY INTO THE BOOK

THE SAGE

Apparently the Hebrews always had their sages, or wise men. They stood among the elders, or "ancient ones" who were presumed through experience to have learned more of life than others, and who were thus competent to instruct the young. But, in the earlier times at least, the sage was always overshadowed by the priest and by the prophet. Only after the Exile did he come into his own. Then, with the priest occupied in liturgy more than in instruction, and with the prophet silent, the sage gained prestige and influence. There is some indication that the sages were from among the scribes—those naturally accustomed to shaping phrases and polishing them.

For what appear to be two pictures of the ideal wise man:
Read Job 29:7–25; *Ecclesiasticus (Apocrypha)* 39:1–11.

These men often gave their instruction in public, the city gate being a natural place of congregation. Instruction was oral, even catechetical, in nature—drilled through repetition.

The sages appear in earlier times to have stood in some disfavor with the prophets:
Read Isaiah 29:13–14; *Jeremiah* 8:9; 9:23–24.

It is easy to understand this. The sages, while being men of piety, were also voices of moderation, whereas the prophets often found it necessary to be zealots and extremists. The sages, too, tended to place primary emphasis upon what man could do for himself, while the prophets were ever conscious of the primary action as God's. Moreover, the sages tended to be rather prudential and even utilitarian in their teachings, whereas the prophets scorned worldly success and followed lost causes with careless disregard for their own safety or popularity.

Nevertheless, the wise men sought to be true to the prophetic spirit. The prophets had spoken to the nation; the sages spoke to individuals, applying the prophetic truth to these individuals. The standard of ethics which they taught was a lofty one, enjoining reverence toward God, industry, chastity, neighborliness, charity, truthfulness, and other marks of personal integrity which we have come to know so well from Judaism at its best, and also from our own Puritan forebears.

These wise men were not philosophers in the Greek sense. Their realm for the most part was not metaphysics but ethics. Their concern was with conduct, for their wisdom was practical and experiential, not speculative. And when they said "instruction" they meant discipline. Their main concern was not the conveying of information or the enlightening of the mind but the shaping of character.

PURPOSE

The purpose of Proverbs is clearly indicated in its opening verses, which serve as a kind of theme for the whole book:
Read Proverbs 1:2–7.
The ethical ordering of daily life through the training and discipline of the young—line on line, precept on precept—that was the program.

SOURCES

Proverbs as we now have it is a collection of wise sayings from many centuries, finally ordered and put into its present form after the Exile. The book itself indicates some of these sources:
Read Proverbs 30:1; 31:1.
The two final chapters, standing in the nature of an appendix, are thus from two different sages by the names of Agur and Lemuel.
But Solomon gets the most credit. On the surface it would appear that the whole book is from him:
Read Proverbs 1:1; 10:1; 25:1.
A closer reading will show that large sections of the book are assigned to anonymous wise men in the plural:
Read Proverbs 22:17; 24:23.
We even know through the study of comparative literature that Proverbs 22:17—24:22 was derived almost entirely from the Egyptian Wisdom of Amen-em-Opet, written sometime between 1000 and 500 B.C. Literature of this type was common to Egypt, Babylon, and Edom. Job, you will recall, was an Edomite rather than a Jew.
Solomon was famed for his wisdom and was credited with the origination of three thousand proverbs:
Read 1 Kings 4:29–34.
It is an irony that a man reputedly so wise should have proved such a misguided ruler. Nevertheless, the legend persisted in spite of

the unwise example. There seems no reason to doubt that many of the proverbs in the book are from Solomon, just as many of the songs in the Psalter are David's, but in the end Proverbs, like Psalms, is the work of a whole people, the product of many centuries.

OUTLINE OF THE PROVERBS

The book falls into six rather clear divisions. Of these, the first is introductory, a tribute to wisdom; and the sixth is appendix, consisting of three fragments (30:1–33; 31:1–9; 31:10–31).

I. Introduction: in praise of wisdom, 1:1—9:18
II. First collection (couplets), 10:1—22:16
III. Second collection (strophes), 22:17—24:22
IV. Third collection, 24:23–34
V. Fourth collection, chapters 25–29
VI. Appendices: chapters 30–31

This outline is geological rather than topical; it shows the strata which entered into the formation of the book, though it does not show the subjects dealt with. In the nature of the case, a topical outline of Proverbs in its present form seems impossible. But the outline given is nevertheless useful; it enables the student to compare and contrast collections. The introductory chapters are much the most systematic. The first collection consists wholly of couplets. Chapter 30 is preoccupied with numbers. A reading of each collection as a unit makes these and other differences obvious.

COUPLETS AND STROPHES

Since we have referred to the terms "couplet" and "strophe," a word of explanation is in order. These are poetic forms. In Hebraic poetry, the couplet presents a complete thought in two lines. The second line does one of three things: (1) it gives the antithesis of the first line; or (2) it repeats the thought of the first line; or (3) it completes it. For examples of these, in the order presented:
Read Proverbs 10:4; 4:14; 6:6.
The strophe is really a stanza of several lines, set up in the same parallel structure and using the same types of parallelism in different combinations. For strophes of varying length:

Read Proverbs 22:17–18, 24–25; 23:29–35.

Since wisdom literature rests heavily upon the contrast between wisdom and folly, its most characteristic form is antithesis in couplet form, known as "antithetical parallelism." Take, for example, Proverbs 22:3:

> A prudent man sees danger and hides himself;
> but the simple go on, and suffer for it.

For this particular proverb. William Jennings Bryan coined a vivid paraphrase:

> A wise man gets an idea in the head;
> The fool gets it in the neck.

Main Themes

In enumerating the main themes of Proverbs we can scarcely do better than quote Fleming James:

The divine plan calls for a society in which people work hard, observe each other's rights, respect each other, treat the less fortunate kindly, have concern for the poor, maintain an atmosphere of general friendliness, enjoy the pleasures of moderation, love their families and homes, are sincere, modest, self-controlled, temperate, reliable, chaste, willing to listen and learn, forgiving, considerate, discreet, kind to animals, sweet-tempered, liberal, yet withal prudent and keeping an eye to their own welfare.[1]

Key Verses

There can hardly be any choice other than Proverbs 1:2–7.

II. PREPARING YOUR BOOK SERMON

Cardinal Idea

The art of living well depends upon a good moral character grounded in a reverent faith in God.

---

[1] G. Henton Davies, Charles L. Wallis, Alan Richardson (eds.), *Twentieth Century Bible Commentary* (New York: Harper & Brothers, 1932, 1955), p. 257.

SHAPING A PREACHING OUTLINE

This will be a difficult sermon, but we can see two rather clear possibilities for it. One will begin by discussing the book and its main features, much as we have done here; then it will go on to give a random sampling of some of the more striking proverbs, and end by inviting the members of the congregation to go home and read the book for themselves. As an aid to such reading, it may be helpful to supply the readers with a copy of the outline, showing the main strata of the book.

The second approach to outline is frankly topical. Since the central contrast of the book is between Wisdom and Folly, let these be the main topics. Work out what seems to you to be the main subtopics under each, and present them in an expository manner, supporting each by direct quotation from the book. A word of caution: Do not quote too many proverbs; they are too concentrated for heavy dosage.

As a tentative example of how this second approach might develop, we would begin with "The Stupid Life," or the way of folly. It includes the unwillingness to listen or to be disciplined, laziness, unchastity, drunkenness, and dishonesty. Browsing through the book, one will quickly find good proverbs applicable to each of these characteristics. In contrast to the stupid life we have "The Enlightened Life," or the way of wisdom. It is a life of reverence, of industry and self-control, lived in close family solidarity and with a sharp sense of social justice and benevolence. Again, browsing through the book will supply appropriate quotations in support of each subtopic. The good life, as Proverbs envisions it, is frankly materialistic, but it is the materialism of men who have integrity and compassion. Though we read,

> A rich man's wealth is his strong city;
> the poverty of the poor is their ruin,
> [Prov. 10:15]

we see this sentiment quickly qualified by such considerations as the following:

> He who trusts in his riches will wither,
> but the righteous will flourish like a green leaf.
> [Prov. 11:28]

> Better is a little with the fear of the Lord
> than great treasure and trouble with it.
>
> [Prov. 15:16]

> Bread gained by deceit is sweet to a man,
> but afterward his mouth will be full of gravel.
>
> [Prov. 20:17]

A MODERN TITLE

Emphasis upon the aspect of child training, which seems so strong in the book, suggests "The Bent Twig." "Alternative to Folly" is a left-handed way of presenting "The Way of the Wise." "A Common-sense Guide to a Good Life" preserves the practical and prudential atmosphere so essential to Proverbs.

16

SECULAR AND PIOUS

Ecclesiastes

W E ARE both secular and pious, you and I. Secularism and piety do battle in our century, not so much between different men as within all men. We live in the church, but we also live in the world; we take a little from both. For these reasons we are not far from the mood and spirit of Ecclesiastes, one of the most secular writings in the Bible.

One of the most beautiful literary works in the world, Ecclesiastes belongs to the class of writings known as wisdom literature. This literature was a late development in Judaism. For the most part it is cosmopolitan in its sympathies, individualistic and practical in its interests. On the theoretical side wisdom literature tends to open inquiry, even to doubt, as in Job, or to disillusionment and pessimism, as in Ecclesiastes. In the Hebrew Bible, Ecclesiastes appears among the Writings, which forms the third part of the Old Testament canon. The book is thought by many to have been written and edited in the third century B.C.

I. WORKING YOUR WAY INTO THE BOOK

Ecclesiastes presents every thoughtful reader with the problem of unity. Scholars have solved this in various ways. One scholar, for example, requires no less than ten authors and editors to account for all the literary strands which he detects in his analysis of the book. Another scholar, equally reputable, argues for a single author— writing at various times and from differing moods, and then collecting and editing his own work. We shall not be able to settle this debate among the experts, but we shall have to take account of the fact occasioning the debate, namely that Ecclesiastes presents us with at least three strands of ideas reflecting at least three differing moods. One strand gives us prudential wisdom like that of Proverbs. A second strand reflects traditional Jewish piety. And the third— which is the bulk of the book—is written in the mood of gentle cynicism from secular premises.

Whatever the original viewpoint of the original writer or writers, we are able to understand the viewpoint of the modern reader without speculation. Of this reader we have to say that if he is an average member of twentieth-century society, he carries within himself in unresolved contradiction all three sets of ideas, all three moods. He is at one and the same time practical, pious, and secular. Perhaps Ecclesiastes stands closer to the mood of the twentieth century than does any other book in the Bible. It meets us in our honest perplexity, caught in conflict, in the midst of a booming workaday world, between lofty faith and searing doubt; and the doubt haunts us about as much as the faith inspires us.

PRUDENTIAL WISDOM

The similarity to the style and spirit of Proverbs is immediately detected in the following verses:

Read Ecclesiastes 4:5, 9–12; 5:3, 7; 6:7; 7:1, 4–12; 8:1; 9:17–18; 10:8–15, 18–19.

You may find it useful to mark these verses in your Bible with colored pencil; then they will be recognized at a glance. They contain the kind of advice that Benjamin Franklin gave the early Americans in *Poor Richard's Almanack.* They extol industry, temperance, patience, self-control, and like virtues.

TRADITIONAL PIETY

Quite different from the expediency of the canny, practical man is the idealistic devotion of the pious:

Read Ecclesiastes 2:26a; 3:14b, 17; 5:1–2, 4–6, 19; 7:26b, 29; 8:11– 13; 11:9b; 12:1a, 13b–14.

If these verses, in turn, are marked in your Bible with a different colored crayon, you will be able to group and compare them at a glance. They enjoin reverence for God, belief in ultimate justice, persevering faith and hope in the face of oppression and temptation, and conscientious observance of religious vows; they assert that moral obedience is the way to religious knowledge, that man was originally upright but is now a sinner, and that such happiness as comes is not man's doing but is the gift of God. In the total bulk of the book these verses, like those reflecting prudential wisdom, are few and slight. Perhaps they are about what we would expect from a man, immersed six days a week in the secular world, who goes to church on Sunday for one hour but who spends little time beyond that reading, reflecting, or talking about religious matters. He is religious; let no one gainsay him! But he is also busy.

GENTLE CYNICISM

For the rest of the book we have the reflections of a disillusioned secular mind, echoed and re-echoed in the refrain "All is vanity and a striving after the wind." This is not the cynicism of a violent, uncouth man; this is the cynicism of a gentle soul, a lover of beauty and culture. It is tinged not with anger but with sadness. We move now to the consideration of this gentle cynic under five headings: his quest, his observations, his conclusions, his advice, and his *summum bonum* or ultimate goal.

The Quest

The quest for deep and lasting satisfactions and for a creative break-through from appearance to reality took *Koheleth*—the Preacher—down five different roads. Like two routes running together over the same stretch of highway, sometimes two or more of these roads coalesce. Here they are: knowledge, pleasure, possessions, hard work, and fame.

Read Ecclesiastes 1:12–18; 2:12–17; 6:10–12; 7:23–25.

Apparently, intelligence cannot give us ultimate knowledge. Immanuel Kant said that pure reason is like a dove; we imagine that because it can fly through the air of practical affairs it can also fly off into the space of metaphysical questions. In the end, man does not by intellect alone soar into the presence of ultimate truth and reality. The more he knows, the more he discovers his remaining ignorance. Reality is deep, very deep; who can fathom it? "The more you know the more you suffer: the more you understand the more you ache" (1:18 MOFFATT). "Headache or heartache?" asks Halford E. Luccock. If headache, then knowledge is a dead-end street; if heartache, then knowledge is a feeder highway pointing beyond itself to the Way, the Truth, and the Life.

Read Ecclesiastes 2:1–11, 18–23.

In these verses it is difficult to disentangle three quests: pleasure, possessions, and hard work. Pleasure is the key. Possessions are sought to the point of luxury for the pleasure they promise. Work is undertaken for the same reason. Evidently Koheleth found what Epicurus had discovered earlier, that the avid quest of pleasure invites so many pains—the kicks of life have so many kickbacks—that one may soon settle for a tranquil existence aimed at avoiding pain. We are reminded here of the harassed man who went into a shoe store to buy a pair of shoes two sizes too small for him. Why? Because his life was so full of grief that he wanted to look forward each day to the pleasure of taking off his shoes! If pleasure is nothing but the absence of pain, the grave is not merely the end but the goal, as Koheleth more than once indicates. Cry at birth; rejoice at death! A peculiar issue of the quest for pleasure, but a logical one!

Read Ecclesiastes 4:13–16; 9:13–15.

Fame is both capricious and fleeting. It is easily confused with notoriety, so seldom matched to merit.

The verdict upon the fivefold quest is: futility. These are roads that lead neither to God nor to human happiness. It should be noticed that they are the normal preoccupations of the secular world, that they are ways of self-salvation.

Observations

In addition to what he himself undertook, Koheleth spent much time observing the world of society and nature around him. Among subjects he remarked upon are:

Oppositions: Read Ecclesiastes 3:1–9, 16:

By a kind of diabolical law of compensation, black and white cancel each other out, leaving a dull gray. Ultimate meanings are lost in relativity. Everything is right in its time and place; nothing is right forever and everywhere.

Mortality: Read Ecclesiastes 3:16, 18–22; 9:2–10:

Death is the great leveler. When it takes the measure of a man, it finds the good man no taller than the bad, and no man above the beast. Curiously, this observed impartiality of Nature came in for comment by Jesus. (see Matt. 5:45). Koheleth and Jesus looked at the same facts; Koheleth saw them as evidence of God's remoteness and indifference, Jesus saw them as an expression of God's impartial grace.

Competition: Read Ecclesiastes 4:4–8:

When life is turned into strife it is not elevated but degraded.

Oppression and Injustice: Read Ecclesiastes 4:1–3; 5:8–9; 7:13; 8:10, 14; 9:11–16; 10:5–7:

The world seems not unlike a huge chicken yard where the pecking order is the rule. Where there is oppression there are injustice and inequity.

Desire: Read Ecclesiastes 5:10–11:

Man's appetite grows by what it feeds upon. The more you give it the more it wants. There is no satisfying it. Modern advertising knows this, and thrives upon it.

Women: Read Ecclesiastes 7:26–28.

Like most men before and after him, Koheleth found women both his fascination and his undoing. "You can't live with them and you can't live without them."

Conclusions

The world Koheleth saw was, like ours, not all outside him; what he saw outside was colored and selected by his own internal world. So even his observations were, in part, conclusions or judgments upon existence. Nevertheless, there are a few conclusions which were Koheleth's judgments, pure and simple.

The Cycle: Read Ecclesiastes 1:2–11; 3:15:

Both Nature and history are judged to move in a cycle which keeps repeating itself. This means, of course, that history is without destiny.

Agnosticism: Read Ecclesiastes 3:11; 7:24; 8:17–9:1; 11:5:

God is remote; man cannot find him or know him. Here we must interpolate the observation that secular roads do not lead to God. God can be found, but not by humanistic means. Attempting to find God by inappropriate means is like trying to observe the planet

Venus by cocking your ear toward her. Or it is like trying to reach Rome by combing your hair. Knowing God is not primarily a matter of reasoning, possessing, doing, or enjoying; it is a matter of obeying —a mode of being.

Relativism: Read Ecclesiastes 3:1–9 *again.* Other passages also bear out the same conclusion.

Nihilism: Read Ecclesiastes 7:1–3; 4:2–4:

This sounds very much like the pessimism of the East. It is better not to be born at all, but if that cannot be avoided, the next best thing is to die. (There is no counsel of suicide here; the death longed for is a natural one.)

Advice

In light of all this, how is a man to conduct his life? Koheleth seems to have four kinds of advice: (1) learn to compromise; (2) do nothing in excess—learn not to expect too much; (3) live spontaneously—act without thinking everything out beforehand; (4) enjoy your youth while you have it.

Read Ecclesiastes 8:1–9:

Learn to compromise. The perfect idealist is a fool. The man who sticks his neck out will get his head chopped off.

Read Ecclesiastes 7:16–17:

Do nothing in excess—be it vice or virtue. This reminds one of the unofficial motto of the drafted soldier: "Don't volunteer for nothin'."

Read Ecclesiastes 11:1–8:

Live spontaneously. Although we cannot know final answers, we are immersed in a world of action. We cannot stand forever pondering; we must act. It is possible to be afflicted with the paralysis of analysis. And the man of action who does what his hand finds to do will get a great deal of satisfaction out of life.

Read Ecclesiastes 11:9–12:7:

Enjoy life. Youth doesn't last long; make the most of it while you have it.

Summum Bonum

Read Ecclesiastes 2:24; 3:10, 12–14, 22; 5:18, 20; 8:15:

To Koheleth, life's highest good is pleasure or happiness. But long-lasting pleasures are unattainable and a general state of happiness, at best, is a gift of God not to be predicted on human terms. So we must fall back upon a revised estimate, a workable second best. This is a mild life of momentary pleasures: eating, drinking, working, and loving one's wife. The eating and drinking in this goal do not seem to involve the hedonism of traditional "wine, women, and song"; rather, they are the normal enjoyment of one's daily meals. These are simple pleasures, but they are the best in the long run.

II. PREPARING YOUR BOOK SERMON

CARDINAL IDEA

Life meets us in our honest perplexity, caught by a practical work-aday world in conflict between lofty faith and searing cynicism; but though faith is a quiet, minority voice in a clamoring world, we cannot shut it out.

SHAPING A PREACHING OUTLINE

The three main strands of literature in Ecclesiastes offer themselves quite naturally as the basis for a three-point sermon, such as that developed by a former student of mine, Eugene Maddox: (1) a word of wisdom; (2) a word of despair; (3) a word of faith. Regarding such an outline, there are two cautionary safeguards that should be mentioned. You should take care to preserve the tension of the book itself between these differing strands or moods, always remembering contemporary relevance to a secularist culture. And you should also keep the subdivisions of the sermon few and simple. Not all that has been discussed in our analysis of the book can be included. The purpose of the sermon will be a double one: to convey the main thrust of this biblical book as it bears on our contemporary situation, and to stimulate your congregation to read the book itself.

Much is to be said for a sermon based upon the quests of Koheleth. It would deal with the five quests he tried, with the disillusioning outcome, and with the untried quest which is barely glimpsed as the book closes (12:13–14). A good text for this sermon would be

Ecclesiastes 7:24: "That which is, is far off, and deep, very deep; who can find it out?"

A somewhat fanciful approach to outline may be made through the idea of going in circles, the idea with which the book opens. The idea is triggered by an incident in a store, related by Halford E. Luccock. A customer approached the clerk with a request for a compass. "Which kind do you want," the clerk asked, "a compass for drawing circles, or one for going places?" Secularism was Koheleth's compass for going in circles, for the futile round of meaningless existence. Religious faith, with its moral disciplines, could have shown him how to get somewhere.

The conflict between secularism and faith is neatly symbolized by the *last word:* Koheleth's last word on life, repeated and re-echoed throughout the book, is: "Vanity of vanities; all is vanity and a striving after the wind." This is man's last word, but not God's. God's last word is at the conclusion of the book: "The end of the matter; all has been heard. Fear God, and keep his commandments; for this is the whole duty of man. For God will bring every deed into judgment, with every secret thing, whether good or evil." All attempts at self-salvation are vain; but God is Redeemer, and he can save if we are willing to turn to him in full obedience.

A Modern Title

The words "under the sun" appear about twenty times in Ecclesiastes; this fact, plus the conflict in the book, suggests the title, "Duel Under the Sun." "The Gentle Cynic" is the title of a good commentary on the book. "Man's Last Word—and God's" is appropriate to the idea sketched in the paragraph preceding this one; "Going in Circles," for the one before that.

17

LOVE AND MARRIAGE

The Song of Solomon

IN TREATING this biblical book we shall set aside our usual pattern.

It is hard to improve on Hugh Thompson Kerr's summation of the Song of Solomon: "The theme of the book is love: pure, sensuous, youthful, passionate love; love that is 'hungry as the sea.' "[1] The conventions and taboos of the ancient Oriental world are not ours. Even American radio programs, saturated as they are night and day with the lyrics of young love, would not tolerate some of the language of this book. Some of its words are too bold, too erotic for modern taste.

To find in the Bible a book so frankly sexual is as disturbing to some readers as it would be to hear a choir render "Chloe" as the morning anthem in a church service. It is perhaps this sense of shock which caused the ancient rabbis to interpret the book as an allegory of the love of God for Israel and of Israel for God. The same sense of shock caused the translators of the King James Version of the Bible to introduce chapter headings interpreting the book as an allegory of the love of Christ for the church.

Modern scholars are now inclined to leave these interpretations behind, but they are by no means unanimous in the alternatives that they suggest. Some say that we have here nothing more nor less than an anthology of secular love songs from an ancient time. Others feel that the text must be a part of a ceremony—a wedding ceremony or a ritual derived from an ancient fertility cult.

Again, even in regard to the literary form of the book there is disagreement. To mention only three divergent analyses: *The Com-*

---

[1] *The Interpreter's Bible*, Vol. V, p. 98.

plete Bible: An American Translation[2] discerns three spokesmen: a youth, a maiden, and a chorus of women. But editor Ernest Sutherland Bates in *The Bible Designed to Be Read as Living Literature*[3] lists four spokesmen: King Solomon, the Shulamite, the brothers, and a chorus of the daughters of Jerusalem. Still others think they discern a love triangle: Solomon, a shepherd, and a maiden—plus the chorus of women.

If the experts cannot agree, what is a mere layman or a parish minister to make of it all? It seems possible for us to make two valid observations:

1. The love of courtship and marriage is a proper concern of religion. These are mighty forces. Rightly channeled, they are like the Colorado River harnessed at Boulder Dam—giving light and power. Neglected, they are like the Ohio on the rampage at floodtide—dealing death and destruction. Love and marriage are not the private preserve of the disc jockeys and the juke boxes; they belong not merely to Hollywood and the advertising boys. They are the deep responsibility of the church. They are vital concerns of religion.

2. Again, the relationship of lovers, and of wives to husbands, teaches us something about the proper relationship of God and man. Belief in God, in the biblical sense, is like a marriage—a commitment of the whole self to another "for better, for worse, for richer, for poorer, in sickness and in health, . . . till death us do part. . . ." The prophets of Israel—Hosea and Jeremiah in particular—used the tender, passionate, and powerful forces of sexual love as the basic analogy in their teachings about the ties that bind man to God. There are deep lessons of religious truth that we can learn from this analogy today.

Meantime, the marks of young love lyricized in the Song of Solomon are universal and timeless. Here we meet love's passionate desire, its blindness, its dreams, its extravagance, its exclusiveness, its pricelessness, its lovesickness, its power. These marks of love would make a good basis for a sermon. If the preacher cared to do a little research among the lyrics of popular, modern love songs he might find a modern parallel for each. Popular music, along with the comic

[2] By J. M. Powis Smith, *et al.*, and Edgar J. Goodspeed (Chicago: University of Chicago Press, 1935).

[3] New York: Simon and Schuster (1937), p. 772.

strips, may be a great untapped reservoir of pulpit illustration. It has captured the fancies of the millions; may it not be used with power by the pulpit?

KEY VERSES

If one is looking for a key passage for the Song of Solomon, he can hardly do better than 8:6–7. This text, in fact, is so good that it may be made the basis of a textual sermon which, in turn, may be presumed to present the essential message of the book.

The critical problems of divergent interpretation have made it inadvisable to present this chapter after the usual patterns of this book. Perhaps these same problems warn us away from a sermon which seeks to present the Song of Solomon as a book sermon. But there is room for a sermon and for many sermons about the main concerns of the Song of Solomon. For these concerns are the main staple of popular music and of modern advertising. The church that neglects them will abandon its hymn of faith for a pagan love song.

18

GOD OVER ALL

The Book of Isaiah: Chapters 1–39

I T has long been customary for scholars to divide the Book of Isaiah into at least two parts: (1) Isaiah, chapters 1–39; (2) Second Isaiah, chapters 40–66. Some scholars posit a Third Isaiah and assign him chapters 56–66. For our study we have chosen the two-fold division, the first part of which now follows. Second Isaiah will occupy our attention in Chapter 19.

Isaiah (by whom we mean the First Isaiah) spoke to a nation living through a cold war and anticipating a hot one. His concern was that the leaders of Judah in the tumult and the shouting of the Great Powers should not lose sight of the power of the Most High. How modern this sounds! The theme of Isaiah is much like that ringing through the "Recessional," which Rudyard Kipling wrote in 1897 for Queen Victoria's Diamond Jubilee. Let the words of one stanza set the mood for our present discussion:

> For heathen heart that puts her trust
> In reeking tube and iron shard,
> All valiant dust that builds on dust,
> And, guarding, calls not Thee to guard,
> For frantic boast and foolish word—
> Thy Mercy on Thy People, Lord![1]

I. WORKING YOUR WAY INTO THE BOOK

THE TIMES OF ISAIAH

From the first verse of the book bearing his name we learn that

[1] *The Five Nations* (New York: Doubleday & Company, 1903).

122

Isaiah's ministry fell within the reign of four of Judah's kings. Uzziah (783–742 B.C.), Jotham (regent 750–742 B.C., king 742–735 B.C.), Ahaz (735–715 B.C.), and Hezekiah (715–687 B.C.). The call of Isaiah, recounted with dramatic fullness in chapter 6, is specifically dated: "In the year the King Uzziah died" (742 B.C.). The last work of the prophet to be recorded in this book seems to be dated 701 B.C., in connection with Sennacherib's siege of Jerusalem, which proved so nearly fatal. Legend has it that Isaiah lived on into the reign of the wicked Manasseh, under whom he was martyred by being sawed in half.

The times of Isaiah were also the times of Amos, Hosea, and Micah. Anyone reading the four books together will find them reflecting the same social situation: prosperity, social injustice, political corruption, apostasy, foreign intrigue. The forty years of Isaiah's active ministry corresponded roughly with the resurgence and vigorous expansion of the Assyrian empire under Tiglath-pileser III (745–727 B.C.), Shalmaneser V (727–722 B.C.), Sargon II (722–705 B.C.), and Sennacherib (705–681 B.C.). The aggressions of Assyria struck terror in the hearts of the rulers and citizens of all the Near Eastern states. Their response to the crisis was a nervous, vacillating one: they banded together to resist; they ran to Egypt for help; they fell apart under attack and made their own humiliating capitulation. Caught in the crosscurrents of these pressures, the state of Northern Israel perished utterly in 722 B.C.

Locked in its mountain home, away from the trade routes and military roads passing through the coastal plains of Sharon and Philistia, Judah could have escaped this devastation by quietly minding her own business. That was Isaiah's advice: Make no entangling foreign alliances. But Rezin of Syria and Pekah of Israel had banded together to resist Assyria, and they were determined to have Judah as an ally—so determined that in 732 B.C. they actually waged war against Ahaz to compel him to join them:

Read Isaiah 7:3–9; 8:5–15.

Ahaz, seized with panic, ran to Assyria for protection, thus making Judah an Assyrian satellite. The price was high, not only in money but in religious and cultural concessions as well:

Read 2 Kings 16:1–20.

Ahaz' disregard of Isaiah's advice and the collaborationism that followed robbed Isaiah of a role throughout the rest of his reign. He seems to have remained silent until Hezekiah ascended Judah's throne in 715 B.C. There was a momentary flurry of anti-Assyrian intrigue in 711 B.C. Isaiah spoke of that, as we shall see later. Isaiah's advice was: Keep your agreements; do not rebel.

But in 705 B.C., Sargon II died, leaving great unrest through the empire. Merodach-baladan emerged from the hinterland to lead a Babylonian assault upon Assyria. To do this he needed allies. Among those he wooed and won to his cause was Judah:

Read Isaiah 39:1–4.

The harvest of that sowing was red—Assyrian vengeance led by Sennacherib, the new Assyrian monarch. Sennacherib's campaign was a crushing blow which devastated Judah by fire and pillage, and almost resulted in the sack of Jerusalem. These blows fell in 701 B.C. Sennacherib's own account has been discovered by archaeologists:

> As to Hezekiah, the Jew, he did not submit to my yoke, I laid siege to 46 of his strong cities, walled forts and to the countless small villages in their vicinity, and conquered (them) by means of well-stamped (earth-) ramps, and battering-rams. . . . I drove out (of them) 200,150 people, young and old, male and female, horses, mules, donkeys, camels, big and small cattle beyond counting, and considered (them) booty. Himself I made a prisoner in Jerusalem, his royal residence, like a bird in a cage. . . . His towns which I had plundered, I took away from his country and gave them (over) to Mitinti, king of Ashdod, Padi, king of Ekron, and Sillibel, king of Gaza. Thus I reduced his country, but I still increased the tribute and the *katrû*-presents (due) to me (as his) overlord which I imposed (later) upon him beyond the former tribute, to be delivered annually. Hezekiah himself, whom the terror-inspiring splendor of my lordship had overwhelmed and whose irregular and elite troops . . . had deserted him, did send me, later, to Nineveh, my lordly city, together with 30 talents of gold, 800 talents of silver, precious stones, antimony, large cuts of red stone, couches (inlaid) with ivory, *nîmedu*-chairs (inlaid) with ivory, elephant-hides, ebony-wood, box-wood (and) all kinds of valuable treasures, his (own) daughters, concubines, male and female musicians. In order to deliver the tribute and to do obeisance as a slave he sent his (personal) messenger.[2]

Read Isaiah 36:1–37:4.

Now Isaiah fell back to a third line of advice: Put your faith in Yahweh and trust him for the outcome. Isaiah, in sharp contrast with

[2] James B. Pritchard (ed.), *The Ancient Near East* (Princeton: Princeton University Press, 1958), pp. 200–201.

Jeremiah a century later, was intuitively certain that neither Jerusalem nor the Temple would be destroyed in this campaign:

Read (in this order) Isaiah 37:33–35; 30:15, 20–21; 31:4–5, 8; 32: 17.

Subsequent events bore Isaiah out. We have three variant accounts of what happened. One is Sennacherib's own account, quoted above. Another is that in the Book of Isaiah 37:5–7, 36–38. A third account, probably earlier than the one now in Isaiah, is found in 2 Kings 18:13–16. These should be read together.

THE MAN ISAIAH

Isaiah was evidently an aristocratic counselor of kings who had direct access to the throne (7:3a), and who appears to have composed a part of the liturgy for the coronation of Hezekiah:

Read Isaiah 9:2–7; 11:1–9.

This suggests a priestly connection. The suggestion is strengthened by the fact that Isaiah received his call at a spot in the Temple where, normally, only priests would be allowed to stand, within the threshold (6:4); and it is further strengthened by Isaiah's request of an affidavit from the priest Uriah (8:2).

Isaiah was married and had two sons:

Read Isaiah 7:3; 8:1–4.

Through the names of these sons he dramatized his teachings, for Shear-jashub means *a remnant shall return;* and Maher-shalal-hash-baz (a really impressive name!) means *swift is booty, speedy is prey.* It is thought that the first son was old enough to walk at the time of the conference with Ahaz in 732 B.C. The second son may have been born about 711 B.C., in the midst of the situation which caused Isaiah to disrobe to his loin cloth and go about Jerusalem in symbolic representation of an Assyrian captive being led into exile:

Read Isaiah 20:1–6.

From chapters 7 and 8 we may conclude that Isaiah became discouraged by Ahaz' defection to Assyria in 732 B.C. and that he closed the first period of his prophecy at that time, committing it to his disciples to be written down:

Read Isaiah 8:16.

We may assume, for the most part, that the preceding chapters are a record of the oracles of Isaiah delivered up to this time. There is no indication of prophetic activity from Isaiah during the rest of Ahaz' reign, but there was evidently a revival under Hezekiah, for whom he composed coronation oracles and with whom he often consulted.

Isaiah again became vocal under Hezekiah:

Read Isaiah 14:28–32.

He appears to have become considerably agitated over pro-Assyrian, pro-Egyptian intrigues in the year 711 B.C., as we have seen from the naming of his second son and from his lone dramatization of captivity:

Read Isaiah 18:1–7; 22:12–25.

When the revolt of 705–701 B.C. came, Isaiah had more to say about the folly of relying on Egypt:

Read Isaiah 30:1–5; 31:1–3.

He taught now, as perhaps at other times, that Assyria was God's chosen "rod" to chastize sinful Judah, but went on to indicate that Assyria itself would finally come under God's judgment:

Read Isaiah 10:5–16.

Putting Isaiah 8:16 and 30:8 together, we get a glimpse of various stages in the collection and recording of Isaiah's preaching over a long period, perhaps even beyond the lifetime of Isaiah himself.

LITERARY STRANDS

As it now stands Isaiah 1–39 gives us several kinds of literature; it is, in fact, a kind of anthology: Oracles, scraps of autobiography and biography, psalms, parables, proverbs, and liturgies.

The oracles predominate. They are brief, polished public sayings of eight to ten verses in length, such as those that comprise the bulk of chapters 1–12. For an example, which, incidentally, shows Isaiah's agreement with the thought of the prophet Amos:

Read Isaiah 1:10–17.

For an item of autobiography which Isaiah alone could have told, read the magnificent sixth chapter. And the seventh chapter falls easily into the class of biography, narrated in the third person by one who was, perhaps, one of Isaiah's disciples.

The twelfth chapter gives us what is quite obviously a psalm. Something very like a parable or an allegory may be read in 5:1–7 or 28:23–29. Isaiah 32:1–8 sounds distinctly like an echo from Proverbs, for these verses give us the same kind of proverbial wisdom. We have already noticed the liturgical songs which Isaiah may have prepared for the coronation of Hezekiah. In reading the Book of Isaiah (chaps. 1–39) the reader will find it instructive to distinguish these literary forms as he goes along.

OUTLINE OF THE BOOK OF ISAIAH: CHAPTERS 1–39

I. Early oracles and narratives, 1:2—10:4
II. Oracles on Assyria and the Messiah, 10:5—12:6
III. The doom of foreign nations, 13:1—23:18
IV. Judah's ultimate triumph: psalms and prophecies, 24:1—27:13
V. Various prayers and poems, 33:1—35:10
VI. Historical appendix, 705–701 B.C., 36:1—39:8

In reading this portion of Isaiah there may be some advantage in skipping chapters 13–28, reserving them to be read at the completion of chapter 39. Thus the reader will be able, at one sitting, to acquaint himself with the main import of the book and to keep closest to the narrative thread and the most important oracles.

MAIN THEMES

1. God is Lord of all history. He uses even the Assyrian, who does not acknowledge him, as an instrument of his divine purpose; and in the same way he judges the Assyrian. He condemns social injustice and political expediency.

2. God is high and holy. He is not only exalted over all the earth in power, high and transcendent above all that man can ask or think; he is also a moral force, demanding purity and social justice among men. Where there are apostasy and injustice, this means judgment.

3. Faith in God is man's surest strength. "If you will not believe, surely you shall not be established" (7:9). "In returning and rest you shall be saved; in quietness and in trust shall be your strength" (30:15).

4. A remnant of truly converted people, faithful to God, will survive catastrophe to continue the covenant role of the people of God. It is not merely that a minority will return from exile, but also that this minority will turn to God.

5. God's Messiah will come to usher in an ideal age of justice and peace.

Key Verses

No single verse of Scripture seems quite to capture in capsule the rich thought of Isaiah. Various ones have been suggested. Chapter 6, the call of Isaiah, does furnish a central light, illuminating the whole of the book; and yet it neglects the themes of hope—those of the remnant and the messianic kingdom. Chapter 5:18–20 and chapter 1:18–20 commend themselves in much the same way, with like limitations. Perhaps no single verse comes as close to a summary of the whole positive force of the book as Isaiah 30:15: "In returning and rest you shall be saved; in quietness and in trust shall be your strength."

II. PREPARING YOUR BOOK SERMON

Cardinal Idea

Trust in God and commit your ways to him, for he is Lord of history, bringing down arrogant and unjust peoples and vindicating the faithful as the seed of his future kingdom.

Shaping a Preaching Outline

Before outlining the sermon, make sure that you have a firm grasp upon the situation to which the message of Isaiah is addressed. In ancient terms, we may see it somewhat as follows: With the death of Uzziah and the rise of Tiglath-pileser III, a long period of peace and prosperity was shattered, and Judah, in crisis, was thrust back upon ultimate resources. As a military power, Judah knew herself to be a mere pygmy confronting a ruthless giant; nevertheless, she chose to play out the dangerous game of power politics. With survival alone as her aim, she abandoned principle and surrendered her fate to fickle expediency. Under the shifting fortunes of the power struggle, Judah's foreign policy wavered and vacillated with every wind. Isolationism; collaboration, now with Assyria, now with Babylon; intrigue with predatory Egypt or with the frightened sister-states of Palestine; rebellion—these were the stormy forces at work sweeping Judah on to disaster.

It was a desperate and discouraging struggle for survival. Few saw it at a deeper level. But one who did was Isaiah. He saw some things clearly that others appeared not to see at all: There is a Higher Power in history than the Great Powers; any policy which takes account of the Great Powers but ignores the Power of the Most High is doomed to disappointment. Deeper than the struggle for survival is the courage to be, to stand up for principle, to respond to the will of God, to do the right because it is right. Not to count stockpiles of weapons but to take inventory of moral resources; not to court survival but to love justice; not to follow the majority who live for the moment but to stand with the minority who live for God in the light of the years and centuries—it is in this high dedication to principle, and in this alone, that man can find strength and inner reality by which to rise above the pressures.

Now look at the modern parallel. We, too, live in a period of crisis and danger; cold war verges on hot war, and flashes out here and there in sporadic flame. We, who brought forth a new nation conceived in liberty and dedicated to the proposition that all men are created equal, seem to be more concerned about security than liberty, more committed to comfort than equality. We turn the high adventure of justice into the dogged struggle for survival. We hate Franco, but make treaties with him. We declare our disbelief in imperialism, but prop Europe's tottering colonialism all over the world. We behave as though God were dead. We do not ask, "Is it right?" Instead, we want to know, "Will it work? Will it keep us safe?" Why not submit our values to a higher tribunal? For power, substitute justice. For security, courage. For survival, integrity. For faith in the most explosive weapon, faith in God the Most High. We have sometimes bowed to these higher principles, as in the Marshall Plan and in the rebuke to France and Britain during the Suez crisis; but we have done it seldom, and even then our action has been tainted with self-interest.

The more we consider the moral and spiritual alternative to the politics of power, the more we see how searching it is, for it judges us; it demands our repentance and the renewal of our humane concern for the underprivileged and the downtrodden; this is the concern which is the real light that shines from the torch of Liberty.

And now let us consider a few possible approaches to outline. One may be derived from a combination of the text, Isaiah 30:15, with the cardinal ideas of the book. The text becomes the proposition, the truth of which is supported by the minor propositions in the cardinal ideas. These may be combined and rephrased somewhat as follows: (1) the Great Powers stand under the Power of the Most High; (2) within the state the greatest moral force resides not with man's majorities but with God's faithful minorities; (3) the norm for the future is not Mars but the Prince of Peace.

Taking Isaiah 6 as a clue to the whole, treat it as the prophet's summons to an unpopular cause. Contemplating Uzziah's death, Isaiah could have said, "The king is dead. Long live the King of kings." Only in some such allegiance could he see hope for his war-threatened nation. But to give allegiance to the King of kings meant something much more searching than a drain on the treasury of Judah and the pocketbooks of its citizens; it meant humility before the Most High, confession of sins, acceptance of his call to serve, dedication to his will without anterior assurance of success.

A book so nobly expressed as Isaiah invites the preacher to build a sermon made up exclusively of excerpts from the book. Thus one may begin with the prophet's call in chapter 6. Then he can move on to two or three selected oracles from the early chapters. This may be followed with narratives from chapters 7 and 20, and these by the great passage, "Ah, Assyria, the rod of my anger," in chapter 10. Then may come the warning against the game of power politics using verses like 30:1-5, to be followed by verses emphasizing the return of the remnant; and ending with the great coronation hymns in chapters 9 and 11.

A MODERN TITLE

As suggested earlier, Kipling's "Recessional" dwells upon Isaiah's central theme. A study of this stirring hymn yields several good titles for the message of Isaiah: "Lord of Our Far-flung Battle Line," "Still Stands Thine Ancient Sacrifice," "If Drunk with Sight of Power," and "All Valiant Dust that Builds on Dust." The holiness of God, so central to Isaiah's thought, is beautifully celebrated in the hymn "Holy, Holy, Holy," which also yields some possible titles: "Lord God Almighty!" "God over All," and "Holy, Holy, Holy, Merciful and Mighty!"

19

THE GOSPEL BEFORE THE GOSPELS

The Book of Isaiah: Chapters 40–66

CAUGHT at home in a culture bent upon neurotic competition, and confronted abroad by a world armed to the teeth on the brink of war, modern man is surely compelled to ask these questions: (1) Why does it have to be this way? Is there not a better way than that of self-interest and the will to power? (2) Moreover, is it not possible that the world beneath the surface is actually organized on a contrary principle? May it not be true, after all, that the mighty do not prevail and that the meek, the terrible meek, do inherit the earth?

The Scripture of Second Isaiah meets us at both levels. On the one hand, it presents us with a vision of the momentous possibility that some nation, or some people, even some church, may yet dare to try the road of sacrificial service rather than the road of self-aggrandizement. On the other hand, it meets us with the mystical assurance that God himself is a God of suffering love whose power is made known through what often passes for weakness. In those inner chambers of the soul where the profoundest annals of man are recorded, he does put down the mighty from their seat and exalt those of low degree. Thus, Second Isaiah both lures us to an ideal and comforts us by a deep spiritual reality. In both of these themes we are close to the Christian gospel; indeed, Second Isaiah is not inappropriately called "The Gospel before the Gospels."

I. WORKING YOUR WAY INTO THE BOOK

HISTORICAL SETTING

The year 539 B.C. is one of the towering watersheds of ancient history, for in that year Cyrus conquered Babylon; the long centuries of Semitic empires yielded for succeeding centuries to the sway of the Indo-European (Aryan) empires: Persia, Greece, Rome. Cyrus first emerged as a conquering monarch when he succeeded in uniting the Persian and Median states in 549 B.C. and in conquering Lydia in 546 B.C. Under Cyrus and his successors, the Persian empire swept on in quick stages to the rule of Asia Minor, including the Greek cities on the eastern coast of the Aegean Sea. The Persian bid for power over the Greek mainland was dashed to earth in the bloody battles of Marathon and Thermopylae; but meanwhile Persia had become overwhelmingly the largest empire of all history up to that time.

What did all of this mean? Who could understand it? Second Isaiah is the answer of an inspired Jewish poet-prophet living in this period. He wrote as Cyrus was striding in conquest across the world, and he or his disciples continued to write after this same Cyrus had released them from their Babylonian captivity and permitted them to return to their homeland, where they pitted their pathetically small band of returning exiles against the ruins of Jerusalem, the hostility of those who had closed in during their long absence to occupy their lands, and the hardships and uncertainties of rehabilitation and rebuilding. Thus we date Isaiah, chapters 40–66, from about 540 to 500 B.C. Chapters 40–55 seem clearly to be set in Babylon, contemporary with the fresh surge of Cyrus' power; chapters 56–66 appear to have a Palestinian setting, early in the period of resettlement.

Cyrus proved to be a liberator of exiles. We have a triple record of this fact—from his own well-known Cyrus Cylinder and from Ezra 1:2–4 and Ezra 6:3–5.

THE JEWISH RESPONSE

Jews could respond to the end of their exile in one of three ways: (1) They could elect to stay in Mesopotamia where many of them prospered as bankers and traders; apparently most of them chose this alternative. (2) They could return to Judah with motives of a narrow Jewish nationalism, provincially concerned for themselves and the purity of their religion, and fenced in from the encroachments of the power and culture of other peoples. For the returning exiles this proved to be the appealing course, and it became the policy of the overwhelming majority.

But there was a third alternative; it was stated by Second Isaiah and seconded by the courageous pens that wrote the Book of Ruth and the Book of Jonah: (3) They could elect to be the agents of a new kind of world-mindedness, a spirit of universal justice and peace of all peoples; they could do this by assuming the role of peaceful, even suffering, servants to the whole of mankind. This would mean neither Puritan withdrawal into their own holy community nor military defensiveness, but the opening of the life of the Jewish people to the world in a mission of teaching and humanitarian service on behalf of the one true, loving God. Israel, the inspired author argued, had been chosen by God himself from among all the nations. Why had their history been a furnace of affliction? To refine away their dross; to make them more precious. And now, why were they suddenly released from their captivity? So they could escape from their affliction to enjoy their own unencumbered happiness? Far from it. All the past sufferings were no emergency, no abnormality from which they could hope to escape and so return to "normal." These were but preparation for the unique role that God meant Israel to play as the special ambassadors of his yearning, suffering love for wayward mankind. "It is too light a thing that you should be my servant to raise up the tribes of Jacob and to restore the preserved of Israel; I will give you as a light to the nations, that my salvation may reach to the end of the earth" (Isa. 49:6). The Lord God Almighty, Sovereign of the whole earth and of the starry immensities, refused to be squeezed into the narrow borders of tiny Judah.

MAIN THEMES

The writing through which the great unknown disciple of Isaiah transmits this noble vision is dramatic poetry in a most exalted mood. In the very reading of the book we are swept, almost unawares, into the surging music and triumphant choruses of Handel's *Messiah*. And as we read the words of Scripture we find ourselves singing them to Handel's music.

The Prophet's Vision: Chapter 40 sets the mood. God appears from heaven before the exiled Jews and their prophet; in voice reminiscent of thunder he promises the end of exile and the opening up of a highway of deliverance (40:1–5). The prophet, perhaps standing a little apart from his people, receives God's call to preach, but finds himself at a loss for a message (40:6–8). God answers him with assurances of his power to be shown in loving care for Judah (40:9–11). Thus answered, the prophet in the mood of soliloquy meditates upon the unrivaled majesty of God (40:12–20); and at last he speaks to the people: God is Lord of history (40:21–24). And God speaks to reconfirm him (40:25–26). But the people, thinking of Jerusalem lying in ruins and of their long exile, complain that God has forgotten them (40:27b). To which the prophet answers that God is Lord everlasting, that those who believe in him shall find their strength renewed, their weariness gone (40:28–31).

After the stage of the cosmic drama of judgment and redemption has been set, we turn in chapter 41 to God's summoning of the nations to assemble before him in a great trial scene. In this chapter most of the important themes of the book appear to be echoed and re-echoed throughout succeeding chapters. God summons the nations to trial (41:1, 5, 6, 21, 22). The gods of the nations are asked to come to the aid of their peoples; but they are dumb idols who can do nothing against the omnipotent God (41:7, 23–24, 29). Having lost their case before the cosmic tribunal, the nations are sentenced to judgment, as God is about to destroy the dominion of human pride (41:2–3, 11–16). In particular, the work of punishing the nations is committed to the hand of an earthly agent, God's anointed one (41:25), who is named in later chapters; he is Cyrus, the first emperor of Persia. The Jews will be restored to their homeland, and a new humanitarian era will begin with all the nations living in a universal kingdom, in justice and in peace; these themes—Jewish restoration, the conversion of the nations, and the coming of God's kingdom on earth—are only faintly suggested in chapter 41, but the hint is unmistakably there (41:17–20). The Jews themselves are to play a unique role in all this; they are not to think alone of themselves and of their security in their own spiritual and political isolation; but they are to be the nonviolent servants of the nations and of the living God (41:8–10; 42:1–4). Thus the Chosen People will take up a role never before assumed by any nation—not that of self-interest but that of the universal good. In this reading of chapter 41 and the first four verses of chapter 42 we get a foretaste of the major themes in the book's unfolding drama: the power of the one true God pitted against the idols of the nations; the judgment of the nations, Cyrus being God's anointed agent to shatter these idolatrous kingdoms; the return of exiles, the restoration of Judah, and conversion of the nations to the worship of God, thus inaugurating a new, universal kingdom; the role of Judah as the Servant.

There are other themes in Second Isaiah, but let us pause to consider those just mentioned by seeking them out through the succeeding chapters. As we do this we discover the thought of the book ascending like a spiral—returning again and again to each theme, but ever rising toward the triumphant consummation.

1. *The power of God pitted against the idols of the nations.* Consider the power and majesty of the one true God:

Read Isaiah 41:4; 42:5; 43:10b–11, 15–17, 20; 44:6–8; 45:5–8, 17–18; 48:12–13, 17–19.

No book in the Bible asserts more vigorously or exultantly the sovereignty of one God. Now place over against this majestic power of God, the impotence of idols:

Read Isaiah 42:17; 44:9–20; 45:16, 20–21; 46:1, 6–7; 57:5–9, 13.

2. *The judgment of the nations.* Judgment is a theme running like a strong current through the book. It is really two currents: the judgment upon the nations to subdue them, and the judgment of Israel to refine her for her role of international service. Most of this judgment of Israel is in the past:

Read Isaiah 42:22–25; 43:27–28; 48:10; 50:1; 51:17–20; 57:17, 20–21; 59:2–3, 9–15; 63:10; 64:5b–6, 10–12; 65:6c–7, 11–12.

Having looked at God's judgment upon Israel, look now to the judgment of foreign nations:

Read Isaiah 42:13, 15; 43:14; 45:9–10; 46:1–47:15; 49:26; 50:10–11; 59:15b–18; 66:14b–17, 24.

3. *Cyrus as God's anointed.* Cyrus, the Persian emperor, is to be God's agent of wrath:

Read Isaiah 45:1–4, 11–13; 48:14–15.

4. *Return and restoration.* The absorbing central excitement of

the book gathers about the prospective return of the exiles and the restoration of Judah:

Read Isaiah 42:16, 18–21; 43:5–7, 19; 46:12–13; 48:20–21; 49:5, 8–21, 25; 50:2b–2c; 51:3–6, 9–16; 52:1–10; 54:1–6, 9, 11–17; 55:12–13; 57:14–15a; 58:8–14; 60:1–9; 61:1–4, 7, 10; 62:10–12; 63:7–9, 11–14; 65:8–10; 66:7–14.

Actually, Second Isaiah's picture of restoration is transmuted into a new creation; a whole new era of world history is in prospect:

Read Isaiah 48:6–8; 55:1–3; 60:17–22; 62:1–5; 65: 17–25; 66:22–23.

5. *The conversion of the nations.* The nations of the world will be converted to the worship of God:

Read Isaiah 45:14, 22–23; 55:5; 56:6–8; 60:3, 10–14; 61:9, 11; 66:18–21.

6. *The Servant.* Israel's role in all of this is not that of the conqueror and despot; it is that of a Suffering Servant:

Read Isaiah 41:8–10; 42:1–4; 43:10; 44:1–2, 21–22; 49:1–7; 50:4–6; 52:13—53:12.

These passages give us the sublimest moral heights and the deepest insights of the Old Testament. Though they were probably written as the ideal of the nation of Israel (the Jews have always so understood them), they are best fulfilled in Jesus of Nazareth, the ideal Israelite. Here we are face to face with the power of redemption in vicarious suffering. Here is the Mount Everest of the Old Testament.

SUBORDINATE THEMES

Having heard the echoing and re-echoing of themes from chapters 40 and 41 throughout the rest of Second Isaiah, we are now ready to review the few remaining themes of the book.

1. *God's forgiveness of the Jews.* This forgiveness is the work of God's grace, not of the Jews' merit:

Read Isaiah 40:2b; 43:25; 44:3–5; 48:9; 51:21–23; 54:7–8, 10; 57:15–16, 18–19; 63:9; 65:1–2, 16c.

2. *A call for repentance.* In the light of all that has gone before, what should Israel do? The answer is, "Repent":

Read Isaiah 55:6–11.

3. *A cry for justice.* In chapters 56–66 the city of justice reminds us of the same emphasis heard so often in chapters 1–39. These later chapters evidently rise out of the period of reconstruction in Pales-

tine. Then the high vision had to fight for its life in the midst of many discouragements and compromises. For the call to justice:
Read Isaiah 56:9–12; 58:1–7; 59:1–15; 61:8.

4. *The idolatry of foreign nations.* The picture of idolatry which we get in third Isaiah is the idolatry of Israel in her homeland, much like that of Hosea's time, whereas in Second Isaiah the writer is concerned mostly with the idolatry of foreign nations:
Read Isaiah 57:1–13.

5. *A whisper of discouragement.* This note, alien to Second Isaiah, is no stranger to Third Isaiah. The Temple lies in ruins; it almost seems that God has brought them back to Palestine only to desert them:
Read Isaiah 63:15—64:12.

6. *A shout of vengeance.* In no part of the book do we find anything quite so violent and vindictive as the celebrated section on the grapes of wrath:
Read Isaiah 63:1–6.

And yet, in spite of all these counterpressures in the struggle to rebuild a shattered nation—in spite of the greed of some, idolatry of others, attacks from hostile neighbors, and the burden of an almost hopeless desolation—the vision lives on. The main themes are there: restoration, the conversion of the nations, God's universal kingdom, God's forgiving mercy. Nothing excels in lyrical brilliance some of the poems of this section. Witness, for example:

> Arise, shine; for your light has come,
>   and the glory of the Lord has risen upon you.
> For behold, darkness shall cover the earth,
>   and thick darkness the peoples;
> But the Lord will arise upon you,
>   and his glory will be seen upon you.
> And nations shall come to your light,
>   and kings to the brightness of your rising.
>   [Isa. 60:1–3]

The pressures were there which turned Judah inward upon herself in narrow nationalism and particularism. We can read that story in Ezra and Nehemiah—and we know it existed with the Pharisees of Jesus' time. But Second Isaiah and his disciples did not yield to these pressures. They remained true to their vision. Notice, for example, a sublime passage enlarging the bounds of Judaism to include foreigners and eunuchs, formerly excluded:

Read *Isaiah* 56:3–8.

Pressures which led to the elevation of Temple ritual made no appeal to these prophets; in this respect they were true to their founder, calling for justice rather than sacrifices, penitent hearts rather than slaughtered animals:

Read *Isaiah* 66:1–4.

The vision of Second Isaiah and his disciples proved too great for men's small hearts. No nation has been able to live up to it. And though it was completely embodied in Jesus of Nazareth and has since come to life in numerous Christlike individuals, it has never been completely embodied even in the Christian Church, the New Israel born under the inspiration of that vision. Nevertheless, the vision lives on to lure and inspire us. It is our one remaining hope in a competing and violent world; for, as George Bernard Shaw reminds us, we crucified Christ on a stick, but he somehow managed to get hold of the better end of it; and we all know that if we were wiser men we would try his plan.

OUTLINE OF THE BOOK OF ISAIAH: CHAPTERS 40–66[1]

I. The imminent coming of God, 40:1—48:22
  A. The coming of the Lord, 40:1–11
  B. Creator of the ends of the earth, 40:12–31
  C. The trial of the nations, 41:1—42:4
  D. The new event of the divine intervention, 42:5–17
  E. The blind and deaf Servant redeemed, 42:18—43:7
  F. Yahweh and Israel, 43:8–13
  G. Redemption by grace, 43:14—44:5
  H. Yahweh glorifies himself in Israel, 44:6–8, 21–23
  J. A satire on the making of idols, 44:9–20
  K. The anointing of Cyrus, 44:24—45:13
  L. The conversion of the nations, 45:14–25
  M. The collapse of the gods, and Yahweh's salvation, 46:1–13
  N. A mocking song on the virgin of Babylon, 47:1–15
  O. History and prophecy, 48:1–22
II. The redemption of Israel, 49:1—55:13

[1] James Muilenburg in *The Interpreter's Bible*, Vol. V, pp. 415–418.

    A. The Servant of the Lord: called, commissioned, and comforted, 49:1–26

    B. An impenitent nation and a confessing Servant, 50:1–11

    C. The coming salvation, 51:1–16

    D. The Lord has become king, 51:17—52:12

    E. The Suffering Servant of the Lord, 52:13—53:12

    F. The consolation of Israel, 54:1–17

    G. Grace abounding, 55:1–13

III. Admonitions and promises, 56:1—66:24

    A. Prophetic instructions, 56:1–8

    B. Blind leaders and corrupt worship, 56:9—57:13

    C. Persisting grace, 57:14–21

    D. The service pleasing to God, 58:1–14

    E. God's intervention, 59:1–21

    F. The coming glory of the Lord, 60:1–22

    G. Glad tidings of salvation to Zion, 61:1–11

    H. The messianic people, 62:1–12

    J. The year of redemption, 63:1–6

    K. A prophet's intercessory prayer, 63:7—64:12

    L. Judgment and salvation, 65:1–25

    M. The new birth of Zion and the fire of judgment, 66:1–16

    N. An eschatological summary, 66:17–24

KEY VERSES

It is too light a thing that you should be my servant
    to raise up the tribes of Jacob
    and to restore the preserved of Israel;

I will give you as a light to the nations,
    that my salvation may reach to the end of the earth.

                        [Isa. 49:6]

II. PREPARING YOUR BOOK SERMON

CARDINAL IDEA

Disciplined by suffering, God's Chosen People are restored to world-wide influence, not to exercise power over men or to gain glory for themselves, but to spend themselves as servants of mankind, taking up the cares of men and nations as their own burden.

Shaping a Preaching Outline

The insight of Second Isaiah is the insight that suffering, when vicarious, can be redemptive. The sovereignty of God's power, when plumbed to its depths, turns into the sovereignty of suffering love. The throne of the universe proves at last to be the cross. By these standards Great Powers among nations and Big Wheels among individuals are ultimately weak. Even the church, falling to the temptations of prestige and influence, tends to become just one more pressure group in a power culture; she forsakes the cross and seeks a throne, thereby deserting her Lord and losing her soul.

We have developed this chapter largely in terms of the main themes of Second Isaiah. These are not separate categories of thought, but actions in a drama of social redemption for war-weary humanity. Therefore, one good approach to outline can be made through the use of these themes. Start with the old order of power among nations and classes, the war of each against all, the exploitation of the weak by the strong. Then move through the successive acts of the drama, perhaps in this fashion: (1) the power of the one God confounding idols and judging the power of nations and of others in the seat of the mighty; (2) the vision of a new kind of world: in place of injustice, justice; in place of conflict, peace and a universal world order; (3) the way to this new world—not through the strategies of power but through the work of a Servant; God seeks a people—a nation, a church, a group, an individual—who will come forward and take upon itself the burdens of the world's woe and bear them as its own; such a Servant must first repent of his own involvement in the corruptions of power and self-aggrandizement, and then must persevere in spite of the discouragements and pressures which drive him toward compromise or bitterness; (4) finally he must keep renewing the vision. As Christians, we have an unlimited advantage over the Jews to whom Second Isaiah first came; for them it was a dangerous ideal that had not yet been tried. But we have the cross of Christ. It is still a dangerous ideal, but it has been tried by our Lord and by a few intrepid souls who have dared to follow him. Will the church herself—the New Israel—learn someday how to take up her cross and follow him?

Another sermon on Second Isaiah could be developed along much the same lines, but using the words of the book itself. To read Isaiah

40–55 aloud requires almost exactly one hour; to read chapters 40–66 aloud, an hour and a half. Thus, one-third of the material of chapters 40–55, or a little less than one-third of chapters 40–66, will yield a twenty-minute sermon. The preacher making this approach should observe one caution: Signal each new theme by introducing it with a sentence or two in one's own words. Also, to make sure that this is not merely a literary exercise, set a tension at the beginning between the old order of power and exploitation and the envisioned order of service and justice.

Since so much of Second Isaiah has been set to music by Handel in his *Messiah,* it should be possible to work out a "sermon-anthem," alternating commentary with singing to present the prophetic ideal. Why not propose it to your choirmaster and see what you can work out? To say the least, it will be a sermon out of the ordinary.

A MODERN TITLE

One very attractive way of entitling a sermon on Second Isaiah would be to use one of the many phrases presented by the poetry of the book itself, such as: "In the Desert, a Highway for Our God," or "A Light to the Nations." Various topics suggested by the power of the cross in 1 Corinthians 1:25 are also inviting: "The Nonsense of God," "The Weakness of God, Stronger than Men," and others. Additional possibilities are: "Redemption through Suffering," "Out of the House of Bondage," "The Second Exodus," and "The Gospel before the Gospels."

20

FIRE IN MY BONES
The Book of Jeremiah

JEREMIAH is one of the most arresting personalities of all history. To the persevering reader, the Book of Jeremiah yields up the priceless treasure of knowing the great prophet of Anathoth intimately—as it is given us to know but few men through the channels of literature. The book does not yield up its treasure easily, for that treasure is like ore imbedded in hard rock; but it is there, and it is more precious than gold.

Jeremiah as a prophet rings the changes on four prepositions, as Harold Bosley pointed out a few years ago in a series of lectures to the Kentucky Ministers' Conference: He was at one and the same time all of these: a prophet *from* his people, a prophet *with* his people, a prophet *for* his people, and a prophet *against* his people. He fought his king, his fellow prophets, and his own kinsmen, the priests; he fought the very populace itself; but he was this iron pillar and brazen wall against the whole land because of his compassion for his people and because of a realism rooted in intimate knowledge of God.

I. WORKING YOUR WAY INTO THE BOOK

HISTORICAL SETTING

Jeremiah 1:2–3 is quite exact in dating the work of the prophet—from the thirteenth year of Josiah's reign (626 B.C.) until the fall of Jerusalem in 587 B.C. But Jeremiah 43:6 pictures Baruch and Jeremiah being carried by their fellow Jews against their will into Egypt after the murder of Gedaliah, Babylon-appointed governor of Judah, who is believed to have governed from 587 to 582 B.C. In support of this, Jeremiah 52:28-30 tells of three Babylonian captivities. The third is dated 582 B.C. It must have been the Babylonian reprisal for the murder of Gedaliah. Jeremiah died an exile in Egypt. We do not know how long he had lived, but the facts just summarized give us the span of his prophecy from 626 until at least 582 B.C.

Some scholars believe that these dates cover the whole of Jeremiah's life. J. Philip Hyatt of Vanderbilt University, for example, argues in both *The Interpreter's Bible* and a later book, *Jeremiah: Prophet of Courage and Hope,*[1] that Jeremiah was not born until 626 B.C. and that he began his public ministry about the time of Josiah's death, 609 B.C. The more traditional view, adopted by many scholars, assumes that Jeremiah's ministry began while he was scarcely out of his teens, in 626 B.C. This would necessitate a date nearly twenty years earlier for the prophet's birth—say 645 B.C.

Whether the dates are 645-582 B.C. or 626-582 B.C. they place Jeremiah on the scene during one of the most turbulent and tragic periods of ancient history in the Near East. Two giants—Assyria and Egypt—grappled in what proved to be their death throes, and all but trampled tiny Judah in their struggle. A still younger and more powerful giant—Babylon—arose to fell the others and to batter down the walls of Jerusalem, sack and fire its Temple, topple its Davidic throne for all time, and take thousands of captives into exile. Read the events of these critical years in 2 Kings 17-25 and in Isaiah 36-39. Judah was caught and crushed in the power struggles of three empires.

Egypt, once the master of Canaan, never lost the desire to control it. Assyria all but smashed Palestine in 721 B.C., when the Northern Kingdom was pulverized, and again in 701 B.C., when Judah escaped by the skin of its teeth. The provocation in each case was Israel's attempt to break through the iron curtain of Assyrian domination into the supposedly friendly embrace of Egypt. In the end it appeared that Egypt was too weak to support or to use the political unrest she had stirred up. By 670 B.C., in fact, the Assyrian monarch Esarhaddon had conquered Egypt as well. Under Ashurbanipal (669-633 B.C), Assyria went on from political to cultural triumph in her golden age during an all too ominous peace. Thereafter, with the rise of Babylon, the decay and collapse of Assyria was rapid:

[1] Nashville: Abingdon Press (1957).

Asshur fell in 614 B.C., Nineveh in 612 B.C., and finally the fugitive government at Carchemish in 605 B.C. Accepting the protection of Egypt after this crisis, tiny Judah soon became the victim of mighty Babylon.

Decisions taken by Judah during this clash of the three giants were neither firm nor simple. There were pro-Egyptian and pro-Babylonian parties, first one and then the other gaining the upper hand. Periods of docile submission were followed by explosive revolts. The situation was not greatly unlike that among the Russian satellite countries in the mid-twentieth century before, during, and after the revolts in Berlin, Warsaw, and Budapest.

As pointer-readings for events in Judah, a few dates are here in order:

701 B.C. Hezekiah narrowly escapes Assyrian annihilation
687–642 B.C. Manasseh: the complete collaborationist and Assyrian puppet
621 B.C. The Deuteronomic reform under Josiah: a cultural break with Assyria
639–609 B.C. The reign of Josiah
609 B.C. Josiah killed by Pharaoh Necho at Megiddo
609 B.C. Jehoahaz II (Shallum), three months on Judah's throne
609–598 B.C. Jehoiakim, Egyptian collaborationist and puppet
598 B.C. Jehoiachin, three months on Judah's throne
598–597 B.C. Nebuchadnezzar's first invasion; first Jewish captivity
597–587 B.C. Zedekiah, king of Judah, at first submissive to Assyria, then rebellious
587 B.C. The fall of Jerusalem; second captivity
587–582 B.C. Gedaliah, governor of Judah

RELATED OLD TESTAMENT BOOKS

In addition to the appropriate chapters of 2 Kings and Isaiah already mentioned, Jeremiah has affinities in time with Zephaniah, Deuteronomy, Nahum, and Ezekiel. All of these reflect aspects of the same historical period. And there is also Hosea. Although Hosea performed his ministry more than a century earlier, it seems clear that his written prophecy had a profound influence upon the mind of Jeremiah. The spirit of the two books is similar; both use the analogy of marriage for the relation of God to Israel; both see idolatry as the root of all national evils; both yearn with breaking heart over their people.

READING THE BOOK OF JEREMIAH

The Book of Jeremiah is a mixture of oracles, confessions, and narratives, which appear to have been thrown together without organizational principle. Closer examination will show an arrangement based upon a combination of three principles: chronology, topic, and association by key words; but this multiple basis of arrangement is too complex to untangle without long study. All of this argues against reading Jeremiah continuously from beginning to end, which is the usual manner of coming to understand a book. There is a much more interesting sequence open to us. We shall begin with the mature Jeremiah in conflict with Jehoiakim, king of Judah, in the year 605 B.C.:

Read Jeremiah 36.

This chapter gives us a clue to the writing of the whole book, for we glimpse two editions of it here, and we meet the faithful scribe, Baruch, who recorded both of them and must have been responsible for later additions on the way toward the final version. We see here how some Scripture was written—under peril, a prophet giving witness to his message through writing because he was denied the opportunity of delivering it by word of mouth. This chapter stimulates two questions in the mind of the reader: (1) What was in the scroll to cause so much excitement? (2) Why was Jeremiah debarred from going to the Temple to deliver his own message (36:5)?

Looking at the second question first, we have no difficulty in finding passages which quickly explain Jeremiah's exclusion from the Temple:

Read (in this order) Jeremiah 19:1–2, 10–11, 14–20:6; 18:18, 23.

We cannot date these incidents exactly, but they show Jeremiah offending the priests—the high priest in particular—and being arrested and locked in the stock overnight. There was an even more illuminating incident:

Read (in this order) Jeremiah 26:1–6; 7:1–15; 26:7–24.

Here we see our prophet narrowly escaping death at the beginning of the reign of Jehoiakim.

We have answered the second question; now to look at the first.

What was in the scroll that the king slashed to pieces and burned in his brazier? We notice that it was brief enough to be read aloud no less than three times in one day. Obviously, it would have contained no material later than 605 B.C. It is the "educated guess" of some scholars that this first scroll made up the major portion of the first eight chapters of the present book:

Read Jeremiah 1:4–14, 17; 2:1–37; 3:1–5, 19–25; 4:1–8, 11–22, 27–31; 5:1–17, 20–31; 6:1–30; 8:4–9:1.

FROM CAPTIVITY TO CAPTIVITY

The clearest connected narrative of the book begins with the first Babylonian siege of Jerusalem and the first captivity in 597 B.C. Zedekiah had become king and had reigned four years:

Read Jeremiah 27–28.

Jeremiah thus threw all his weight, by oracle and acted parable, on the side of bowing to Babylon and against armed insurrection. This was not because he had any faith in Babylon but because he did not believe that power politics and military conflict paved the way to national deliverance. It was, he believed, a foolhardy path of suicidal nationalism; Jeremiah threw his body across this path to prevent his nation from taking the fatal road to disaster.

Meantime, Jeremiah wrote to his fellow Jews in exile:

Read Jeremiah 29:1–15, 21–32.

Whereas some prophets and priests were promising the exiles an imminent return to Judah, Jeremiah could see such promises as nothing better than wishful thinking and sheerest fantasy. He took the unpopular but realistic line that the Jews would be in Babylon for a long time and that they would be wise to forsake any other view and to live constructively in the place where fortune had cast them.

Now we leap forward to the second siege of Jerusalem, which lasted two years (589–587 B.C.). From the first, Jeremiah took the most unpopular line imaginable. He advised surrender:

Read Jeremiah 34:1–7; 37:1–10.

During the siege, some Jerusalemites who owned slaves and who had not obeyed the Sabbatical law regarding them developed a belated attack of conscience. They freed their slaves, only to reimpress them when it appeared that their "sacrifice" did not buy God's intervention in their behalf. Jeremiah's scorn was boundless:

Read Jeremiah 34:8-22.

We are not surprised that Jeremiah was soon arrested as a traitor. He chose a time when there was a lull in the siege of Jerusalem to go to his native village of Anathoth (three miles from the city) to purchase a field. His action was interpreted as attempted desertion: *Read Jeremiah* 37:11-15.

The king, however, could sense in Jeremiah an authenticity of insight not evident to his princes and leaders. So we are treated with the startling sight of a king on trial before a prisoner: *Read Jeremiah* 37:16-21.

Returned to his prison, Jeremiah did not languish in utter hopelessness. Amazingly, he took up and completed, through messengers, the land transaction that had been interrupted by his arrest. In just such a dramatic way did he express his hope for the future: *Read Jeremiah* 32:1-15.

As the siege resumed, certain priests and princes determined on the death of Jeremiah. They planned not to kill him outright but to torture him to death through starvation: *Read Jeremiah* 38:1-13.

The Ethiopian eunuch, a palace servant whose name means "Servant of the King," took his own life in his hands in rescuing Jeremiah. And the king himself, after the next interview, apparently took courage from the eunuch's selfless act: *Read Jeremiah* 38:14-28.

The end of Judah and its ruler was catastrophic and bloody: *Read Jeremiah* 39:1-14.

The sequel, leading up to Jeremiah's exile in Egypt, moves quickly: *Read Jeremiah* 40:1—44:30.

AND NOW THE REST

With such an intensive experience of the Jeremiah biography as we have outlined, you are ready to read the rest of the book. Chapters 46–51 are oracles about foreign nations, perhaps later than Jeremiah. Chapter 52 is a historical appendix closely parallel to 2 Kings 24–25. Chapter 45 is a delightful picture of Jeremiah's commission to his self-denying scribe, Baruch, to whom surely we are in debt for most of the narrative we have just read.

Among the things that interest us most in the chapters we have not yet read, there is Jeremiah's clash with his neighbors and kinfolk in his home village of Anathoth:

Read Jeremiah 11:18—12:6.

Though this passage is somewhat cryptic, it leaves no doubt that Jeremiah was a prophet without honor in his own village. He also found himself at odds with other prophets:

Read Jeremiah 23:9–33.

Jeremiah never married, and he held himself aloof from the trivialities and sophistications of polite society:

Read Jeremiah 16:2, 8.

Nothing stirs us so much in the whole book as the intimate glimpses deep into the sorrowing, troubled soul of the prophet, which we have through the sections often called "The Confessions of Jeremiah":

Read Jeremiah 10:23–24; 15:10–21; 16:1–13; 17:9–10, 14–18; 18:18–23; 20:7–12, 14–18.

These show us a man of deep awareness of God and of tender love for Judah, torn between timidity and courage, managing in an apparently hopeless time to keep his integrity and his hope. The story of Jeremiah is the story of a man alone, passing through suffering to the lofty insights of a tested faith.

In no passage does this faith shine more radiantly than in the justly famous new covenant:

Read Jeremiah 31:31–34.

Main Themes

In a chapter on "Permanent Values in Jeremiah's Life and Message," J. Philip Hyatt[2] lists seven points, which we summarize in our own words as follows:

1. The nature of God's servant. A prophet is not perfect, but he is a real man given in strenuous devotion to his God.

2. True prayer is dialogue with God. It involves a sharing of all thoughts and attitudes, including negative ones. It is transparently honest and desperately in earnest. This we learn from Jeremiah's own example.

3. True religion is inward and personal, a spiritual fellowship with God issuing in social justice. It does not depend on Temple and

[2] *Jeremiah: Prophet of Courage and Hope*, pp. 109–115.

sacrifices, nor on rites of circumcision or residence in the land of Judah.

4. God is both power and love—sovereign power and forgiving love. Jeremiah has more to say about repentance than any other prophet, and he is as insistent as Hosea upon the suffering love of God.

5. God works in history, interacting with man in judgment and deliverance.

6. Man by nature is not naturally depraved, though he appears to be so because of his customs and habits; the path of salvation through repentance is open to him.

7. There is hope for the future. The basis of hope is realism in assessing the situation, and loyalty to God who is Sovereign.

Charles E. Jefferson a number of years ago discerned eight *Cardinal Ideas of Jeremiah*, in his book of that title.[3] They are:

1. Religion is an affair of the heart.
2. The individual is the key to the world's problems.
3. The infinite may be temporarily thwarted, but cannot be permanently defeated.
4. The law in the heart is the sole basis of permanent reformation.
5. A sick heart is the source of the world's woe.
6. Prayer is conversation with God.
7. Loyalty to God is above loyalty to government.
8. There is always light ahead.

KEY VERSES

Most students agree that nothing stands so clearly at the center of Jeremiah's thought as Jeremiah 31:31–34.

II. PREPARING YOUR BOOK SERMON

CARDINAL IDEA

God calls to his people out of a suffering love to repent of the idolatries of power and privilege and to make an inward, personal

---

[3] New York: The Macmillan Company (1928). These are chapter headings from the book.

commitment of their whole life to the sovereign power and love of God.

Using the key passage of the book, one could develop several outlines of the main teachings of Jeremiah. Jeremiah 31:31–34, according to Fleming James in *Personalities of the Old Testament,*[4] presents us with five marks of the new covenant. These are: inwardness, fellowship with God, immediacy, universality, pardon. Using these marks, one might develop a negative-positive sermon with two main points: (1) the broken covenant and the old community; here the five marks would be treated through their opposites; (2) the new covenant and the new community; here the five marks would appear positively. In this, as in any sermon on the book, it should be made clear that a covenant community does not exist for its own sake, but as a servant of God among the nations. This will save the preacher from a crude use of piety as the guarantee of national prosperity. God must not be reduced to the status of Chief Friend to state and church; he is Sovereign Lord who works in history to achieve his redemptive purpose for all mankind.

The striking parable-drama of the potter's wheel (Jer. 18:1–6) could serve as the nucleus of a book sermon. An outline developed for my chart, *A Guide to Expository Preaching,*[5] may form the basis of this approach: (1) introduction: the poverty and plight of a nation relying mainly on power politics; (2) it is God who makes history; (3) men sometimes obstruct the will of God for their nation, thus inviting disaster; (4) God is not defeated; he begins to fashion the nation to a new design; (5) conclusion: our duty is to place ourselves at the disposal of the moral will of God, the primacy of moral responsiveness; our confidence is that the clay of nations is all on the wheel of history, in the skillful hands of God.

The central clash of the book is between Jehoiakim and Jeremiah. This might be utilized as the principal framework of the sermon. Jehoiakim represents the strategy of power politics and external social conformity, which has brought Judah to its crisis. Jeremiah represents the unwelcome but redemptive alternative.

[4] New York: Charles Scribner's Sons (1939).
[5] Lexington, Ky.: The College of the Bible (1952).

Several persons in the book may serve as keys to the varying phases of its message: Jehoiakim, prototype of all the princes who moved primarily upon consideration of private interest; Pashur, the high priest of the status quo—religion bent to the purposes of a perishing society; Hananiah (28:10), prophet of salvation without repentance; Zedekiah, a king without the courage of his convictions. Against these, on the side of redemption, stand such persons as: Ahikam, the son of Shaphan (26:24), a man of integrity and courage who stood by a friend in the face of mob violence; Ebed-melech, the Good Samaritan of the Old Testament, who had every reason for caution and no reasons but integrity and love to risk his life to right an injustice; Baruch, the selfless scribe, to whom private ambition was a wasteful luxury in a time of public crisis; and, lastly, Jeremiah himself, an iron pillar and a brazen wall against the whole land; he was himself the complete man for whom he went searching through the streets of Jerusalem.

It remains for us to base a sermon upon Jeremiah alone. This could be done by reconstructing the biography of the prophet, and telling it as a story. Such a poignant story, if well told, will have all the power of authentic drama. If we are moved by Plato's account of the arrest, the trial, and the martyrdom of Socrates, how can we remain unmoved by Baruch's heroic life of Jeremiah?

A Modern Title

Jeremiah 5:1 conjures up the picture of the Greek Diogenes (who lived later than Jeremiah); he went abroad in daylight with a lantern, looking for an honest man. A title for a sermon along this line of thought could be: "Find a Man." "Fire in My Bones" is another phrase from the book itself, which we can hardly resist. "This Nation under God" is appropriate to the figure of the potter's wheel. "One Alone against the Whole Land" would fit the biographical sermon.

21

CRY, THE BELOVED CITY

The Lamentations of Jeremiah

MODERN men know what it is to witness the death of a city and to mourn for her. Hungry civilians poking in the smoldering ruins of Warsaw, Hamburg, and Manila knew what it was to see a city die. The "Hiroshima Maidens" bear the marks of their knowledge in their scarred bodies. This twentieth century has its eyes full of slain cities.

Nevertheless, Americans do not know what it is to see *their* cities in ruins. Suppose atomic fire had rained from the skies upon New York and Washington. Then they would have begun to approach the grief of the Jews at the destruction of Jerusalem in 587 B.C. by Babylon. For Jerusalem was the New York plus the Washington plus the Rome of the Jewish world, and it was more, far more. But after the vengeance of Nebuchadnezzar's armies it lay in rubble, as did their nation and their faith.

I. WORKING YOUR WAY INTO THE BOOK

PLACE IN THE BIBLE

In the Hebrew Bible, Lamentations appears among the five festival rolls. (In the Hebrew Bible the order of these books is: Ruth, Song of Solomon, Ecclesiastes, Lamentations, Esther.) It is read in Jewish synagogues in memory of the destruction of Jerusalem by Babylon (587 B.C.), and again by Rome (A.D. 70); it forms the basis of synagogue services on the 9th of Ab (July-August). The book has the qualities of an elegy or dirge, not only in its content but also in its meter, which suggests constant sobbing.

Our English title for the book is a translation of the title given by the Talmud, which is *Qinoth* (Dirges), and of the title in the Septuagint, which is *Threnoi* (Elegies). The Hebrew text, in keeping with custom, used the first word as title: *Ekah,* *"Ah now!"*

FIVE LITURGICAL POEMS

If you read the Bible in Hebrew or if you have a copy of *The Complete Bible: An American Translation,* you will be able to see at once that the first four chapters of the book are set up in alphabetical form as acrostic poems. This highly stylized form of writing is also found in some of the psalms, an example being Psalm 119. The acrostic, framed upon the twenty-two letters of the Hebrew alphabet, does not translate into English; therefore, much of the stylized, liturgical force of the original Hebrew is lost to readers of English translations of the Bible.

Chapters 1, 2, and 4 have twenty-two numbered verses to each chapter, and each verse begins with a successive letter of the Hebrew alphabet. In chapter 3, the sixty-six verses are grouped by threes, which means that each Hebrew letter is repeated three times in succession before the letter for the next group of verses appears.

Chapter 5 is not an acrostic; neither is it a dirge. It is a penitential prayer.

All of the chapters have the stylized formality which fits them for use in the Jewish liturgy. In other words, they form the basis of a corporate act of mourning and penitence stirred by the memory of the destruction of Jerusalem.

Some scholars feel that chapters 2 and 4 came from eyewitnesses to the tragedy of 587 B.C., who remained in Judah, living among the ruins. Chapter 1 may have come later, from the Babylonian Exile; it has many of the same marks as Psalm 137, which is an exilic poem. The whole book, with the exception of chapter 3, reflects a corporate tragedy to the whole of Israel, and the reaction of a whole people. Chapter 3 shows us one individual as he participated in the tragedy, and how he responded to it.

From this survey, one concludes that the chapters of the book may be read to advantage if rearranged as follows:

Read (in this order) Lamentations 2, 4, 1, 3, 5.

For group reading, the book may be presented in a meaningful manner by using the following assignments:

Two Eyewitnesses: reading chapters 2 and 4 responsively
Two Exiles: reading chapter 1 responsively
One Victim: reading chapter 3 individually
All Together: reading chapter 5 as a unison prayer

OUTLINE OF LAMENTATIONS

   I.   The desolation of conquered Jerusalem, chapter 1
  II.   God's judgment in the desolation, chapter 2
 III.   An individual's lament and prayer, chapter 3
 IV.   The contrast between Jerusalem's past and present, chapter 4
  V.   The nation's prayer for divine compassion, chapter 5

AUTHOR

As we have indicated before, the English titles to the biblical books were not a part of the original text, and the Hebrew and Greek titles differ from the English and from each other. The English title, *The Lamentations of Jeremiah,* is based upon 2 Chronicles 35:25. A reading of that verse will show that Jeremiah's lament was not about the fallen city of Jerusalem in 587 B.C., but about the death of Josiah, king of Judah, who was killed by Pharaoh Necho in 609 B.C. We must conclude that Jeremiah's lamentations over Josiah are among the numerous lost books of antiquity and that our present volume of Lamentations is another writing altogether, probably a liturgical collection from several poets. In any case, the authorship of the book in no way affects its message.

MAIN THEMES

1. The first theme is one of pure and simple mourning over the death of a city. The plight of a dying city under siege is nowhere more shocking than in Lamentations 4:10: "The hands of compassionate women have boiled their own children; . . ." That is the ultimate of hunger.

2. The second theme is the judgment of God. Though Jerusalem

was sacked and burned by the Babylonians, her death was not a murder but a suicide. That is the conviction informing the poems. Arnold J. Toynbee reflects in the same manner upon the death of history's past civilizations: no great civilization is ever murdered, but it dies from internal weaknesses and betrayals; it commits suicide.

3. The third theme is faith in God's compassion and forgiveness (see especially Lam. 3:22–39). Here in the midst of national and personal calamity there is a surprising affirmation of the goodness, compassion, and mercy of God. This is not fair-weather religion. On the contrary, this is hope in the face of great odds. This is hope when faith is at wit's end. Thus, the hope of the poet rests upon nothing temporal. All these things have been torn away. It rests solely upon God. God takes no pleasure in man's suffering; even his punishment is an expression of his compassionate care. He punishes man in order to bring man to his senses, in order to give man the opportunity of changing his ways.

4. The fourth theme is repentance (see especially Lam. 3:40–42).

5. The fifth theme, a minor one, is imprecation. It is not lovely, but it is present in the book, similar to the fiery ending of Psalm 137 (see especially Lam. 3:62–66).

6. Another minor theme bears a glance. It is found in Lamentations 5:7: "Our fathers sinned, and are no more; and we bear their iniquities." This makes difficult theology, but good religion, for it does stir us to grow out of the provincialism and corruption of our forebears. For example, our fathers started Negro slavery, but we bear some of their guilt because we have not yet broken the patterns of discrimination which we inherited from them.

KEY VERSE

How lonely sits the city
    that was full of people!
How like a widow has she become,
    she that was great among the nations!
                    [Lam. 1:1a]

II. PREPARING YOUR BOOK SERMON

CARDINAL IDEA

When a great city dies it is natural and right to mourn her passing and to bring our grief before God as an act of worship; but the full meaning of the tragedy escapes us until, glimpsing God's basic, compassionate goodness, we make of our mourning an act of penitence.

SHAPING A PREACHING OUTLINE

Lamentations is nothing less than a reflection upon the tragedies of history and their religious meaning. Standing at our point in time, we can glance back over the centuries and mark the death of many world cities: Thebes, Nineveh, Babylon, Susa, Carthage. People with passions like our own once inhabited these capitals. Why did they perish? How can we memorialize their passing? What can we learn from them? We hold memorial days for our fallen heroes; why not a memorial day for fallen cities and civilizations?

The major idea of the book as sketched just above offer themselves as one outline for a sermon. Supporting quotations may be taken from Lamentations for each of the five main ideas, and supporting relevant illustrations may be drawn from history. It may be pointed out that the imprecations of the book upon national enemies are a natural response of fallible human nature, but that the nobler response is the call of the book to a national repentance.

A dramatic reading of the book, using a group as suggested on page 154, might serve as a springboard for a topical sermon on the main lessons to be learned from the graveyards of history. There seem to be two of these: (1) Lament! (2) Repent!

A MODERN TITLE

The title of this chapter is, of course, suggested by Alan Paton's compassionate novel, *Cry, the Beloved Country*.[1] More prosaic, "Mourning a City" is suggestive, as is "Dirges over Dead Cities."

---

[1] New York: Charles Scribner's Sons (1948).

22

CAN THESE BONES LIVE?

The Book of Ezekiel

EZEKIEL saw his nation die. He found himself pastor to its displaced persons, searching for a message in the midst of doomsday. He was like Kagawa in his beloved Japan at V-J Day or Martin Niemöller on V-E Day in his native Germany. He saw the catastrophe as the judgment of God, but he yearned over the plight of his people and longed for their recovery. He resolved that Israel should rise from the ruins and live again, but not as it had lived before—rather, with a new kind of national integrity. Envisioning Israel as a valley of dry bones, he articulated the question that must have been nagging at thousands of minds: Can these bones live?

I. WORKING YOUR WAY INTO THE BOOK

OUTLINE OF THE BOOK OF EZEKIEL

In outline, the Book of Ezekiel presents us with a very simple picture. A young priest, deported to Babylon among the first exiles (597 B.C.), received the call of God in the fifth year of that captivity to be a prophet to his own people. Accepting the call, he first preached doom upon the old Israel (Ezek. 1–24). Then he pronounced a series of dirges over neighboring nations (Ezek. 25–32). Finally, he pictured a New Israel, rising to life out of exile, and reuniting in the Holy Land (Ezek. 33–48). There Israel would first repulse the final desperate onslaught of heathen nations, thus ending war and ushering in the reign of universal peace. Thereafter, Israel would rebuild her whole national life, with an ideal Temple and its rituals at the center (Ezek. 40–48). From this center, life would flow out to bless and to renew the whole land.

Such a sober review of the book, however, does scant justice to it, for Ezekiel delivered his message in a spirit of ecstasy: through visions, symbolic acts, and allegories. Seldom do we find in any literature the intensity of motive or the exaltation of mood which throb and thunder through Ezekiel's writings. To move in his world one must leave the prosaic earth and soar high above it into the dazzling realm of fervent imagination. For, as the Negro spiritual puts it, "Ezekiel Saw a Wheel 'Way Up in de Middle of de Air."

HISTORICAL SETTING

A unique feature of the book is the dating of many of its oracles. No less than eleven specific dates by day, month, and year are to be found in the first thirty-two chapters. The year is calculated from the beginning of King Jehoiachin's captivity, i.e., from "the first captivity" in 597 B.C. The earliest of these dates appears in Ezekiel 1:2 and has been calculated as roughly equivalent, on our calendar, to July 21, 592 B.C. The latest date is to be found in Ezekiel 29:17 and is roughly equivalent to April 16, 570 B.C.[1] The reader can figure at least the years of the others as he comes to them by calculating from 597 B.C.

What this means is that Ezekiel began his ministry in the midst of the Babylonian Exile, about five years before the final destruction of Jerusalem and the second captivity, which saw the apparent end of all Jewish national hopes. This means, also, that he extended his ministry through that cataclysm, and beyond it about seventeen years.

In many features of his message, Ezekiel was amazingly like Jeremiah. In the midst of the calamity, he preached not deliverance but further judgment; but he did so from a weeping pastoral heart and in the light of an ultimate hope which originated not in the human situation at all but in his faith in the living God. So as long as Jerusalem was still standing he preached doom, but once it was in ruins he began to formulate his vision of Israel rehabilitated, reunited, and restored.

---

[1] R. A. Parker, and W. H. Dubberstein, *Babylonian Chronology: 626 B.C.-A.D. 45* (Chicago: University of Chicago Press, 1942), pp. 25–26.

READING FOR THE MESSAGE

The Call

The Book of Ezekiel is long to read at one sitting, but a judicious sampling will enable one to get the shape and the sweep of the message in less than an hour. After such a preliminary view, the reader can go back for a more leisurely perusal of the whole book.

Read Ezekiel 1:4–28.

This is a vision of the Glory of the Lord, symbolizing the transcendence, omnipotence, omnipresence, and omniscience of God. Clothed in light as a garment, God dwells in unapproachable splendor and rules the whole world in unrivaled majesty. It was from such a God as this that Ezekiel received his call:

Read Ezekiel 2:1–3:15.

The prophet felt his responsibility with a terrible urgency. If he spoke he might accomplish nothing, but if he did not speak he felt that he himself would become personally guilty for the fall of Jerusalem:

Read Ezekiel 3:16–21; 33:1–20.

Rebellion and Judgment

For a brief glimpse of the ecstatic and dramatic nature of his acted preaching:

Read Ezekiel 4:1–5:17.

If ever a man was wholly consumed by the passion of his message, that man was Ezekiel. Even when his wife died he submerged his personal grief beneath his concern for his nation under siege:

Read Ezekiel 24:15–24.

The offenses of Judah, as Ezekiel saw them, were both ritual and moral, but all sins were against God, and they could be summarized as idolatry. Visiting Jerusalem in an ecstatic vision, Ezekiel surveys the sin of Judah, seeing it as the profanation of the Temple:

Read Ezekiel 8:1–18.

Now we come a second time upon the symbolic vision of the Glory of the Lord which we first saw in chapter 1; through this symbol we meet God in two acts, first destroying Jerusalem and then disowning and deserting his Temple. Judgment, truly, "begins at the house of God":

Read Ezekiel 9:1–10.

Then, after the destruction of Jerusalem, the Lord abandons his Temple:

Read Ezekiel 10:1–22.

Various oracles in chapters 11–24, for the most part, dwell in a somewhat cyclical manner upon the themes of sin (rebellion) and judgment. One unique feature of Ezekiel's view is his insistence upon individual responsibility:

Read Ezekiel 18:1–24.

Such a view leaves room for a righteous remnant which constitutes the hope of a new beginning:

Read Ezekiel 18:30–32.

With the destruction of Jerusalem in 587 B.C., one phase of Ezekiel's message came to a close:

Read Ezekiel 24:1–14, 25–27.

Judgment on the Nations

In a way, the judgment upon neighboring nations is a simple extension of Judah's calamities, but from a Jewish standpoint it is an expression of God's justice, which becomes at least a partial vindication of Judah. Of the many oracles against the nations in chapters 25–32, let us select two for our present purpose. First, there is one against Tyre (Phoenicia):

Read Ezekiel 27:1–36.

As the great sea trader of the ancient world, Phoenicia is symbolized by a ship destined to be sunk.

Second, there are a number of oracles against Egypt. In one of these, Egypt is pictured allegorically as a towering cedar sheltering all the nations, i.e., a world empire. This lordly cedar goes down with a mighty crash, and leaves a lonesome space against the sky:

Read Ezekiel 31:1–18.

The New Israel

The cumulative effect of the destruction of Judah and her neighboring nations is to wipe the international slate clean, and make ready for a new beginning. Israel laid low in captivity and dispersion is apparently dead. Nothing in the whole section on restoration quite equals the allegory of the dry bones:

Read *Ezekiel* 37:1–14.

The meaning is clear. Israel shall rise out of exile and dispersion to make a new beginning.

Chapters 38 and 39 present us with the ultimate apocalyptic war. Gog of Magog, symbolic of all remaining earthly kingdoms, marches against resurgent Israel and is decisively defeated. To find a passage like this elsewhere one must turn to the war in heaven in Revelation. This passage reminds us that evil is often most fanatical and furious when it is about to be defeated.

The New Temple

Chapters 40–48 find the prophet-priest coming to the culmination of his vision. In loving detail he sketches the architect's plans for the rebuilding of the Temple, and then surveys the domain of Jerusalem and of each of the Twelve Tribes. He is so precise in his details, so exact in his measurements, that a reader may get lost in all the "cubits." The essence of his plans is not difficult to see, however; he is providing for a perfect Temple, so isolated and holy that it will be the place of God's throne from which he will rule Israel and the world.

From the final chapters there are some verses of special interest. These depict the visions of God's return to the Temple, and the river of life flowing out of the Temple to irrigate Palestine and to convert the Dead Sea into a fresh-water lake:

Read *Ezekiel* 43:1–5; 47:1–12.

MAIN THEMES

1. *The sovereignty of God.* Ezekiel was a man in earnest, who was conscious of speaking to a nation in its death throes on behalf of the just and living God in whose presence evil could not stand, but by whose power the fallen could rise.

2. *The centrality of the Temple.* Ezekiel had a priest's love for the

Temple, and belief in the crucial and central importance of true worship for the life of a people.

3. *Pastoral concern for people.* Ezekiel's sense of responsibility to individuals was vital; he had a pastor's love for persons.

4. *The restoration of Israel.* Ezekiel had a fervent determination that fallen Israel should experience a resurrection, but not to the old life—a resurrection, instead, to a new life whose center would be God himself, and whose law would be the will of God.

When it comes to assessing Ezekiel's contributions, it is difficult to insist too emphatically upon his uniqueness. His doctrine of individual responsibility is more strongly stated than Jeremiah's, but the doctrines of the remnant and of the true, spiritual Israel found in Jeremiah and in many other prophets surely rest upon some common view of individuality. Ezekiel is new in the emphasis that he places upon it. He is also more intense in his use of prophetic methods, so much so that he is almost considered the father of apocalyptic and allegory. He was apparently the most ecstatic of the writing prophets.

In addition to the contributions just mentioned, two others stand out: He helped to rebuild the morale of a nation at the end of its tether; and he taught the Jews to believe in, and hope for, a future. He even drew a very specific picture of the possible direction of that future. To put it simply, he dismissed the dream of resurrecting the monarchy and concentrated upon the shaping of a theocracy. Israel was to be ruled from the Temple by priests. Since this became the actual pattern of Jewish life after the Exile, Ezekiel is to be credited, at the very least, with accurately predicting its general character and, at the most, with a major share in shaping it. For this reason he has often been called the Father of Judaism.

One cannot help but contrast Ezekiel with Second Isaiah. Ezekiel may have longed as much as the other for God's universal kingdom, but he saw no place for vicarious sacrifice or for an Israel losing her life in a superb missionary effort. Instead, he foresaw Israel devoting her first energies to guaranteeing her own purity and strength. In practice this meant isolationism and provincialism, and it led rather naturally to the position which came to be held by the Pharisees. Nevertheless, though lacking Second Isaiah's universalism, Ezekiel did call the turn on the flowering of Hebrew religion into postexilic Judaism. Without that achievement, it is doubtful if Christianity could ever have come into being, for it is sober fact that Christianity arose not merely out of the prophet's dream but also out of the concrete life and institutions of Judaism.

KEY VERSES

No passage is more appropriate than the vision of dry bones (Ezek. 37:1-14).

II. PREPARING YOUR BOOK SERMON

CARDINAL IDEA

Israel, fallen because of her rebellion against God, may rise again in repentance to a new life as a theocracy. To do this she will need to center her life in the Temple, and shield herself carefully against alien influences.

SHAPING A PREACHING OUTLINE

In trying to universalize Ezekiel's message so as to apply it in a modern setting, we find ourselves frustrated at the outset by our unhappy experiences with priestly rule. Priests in the seat of government can be just as corrupt or tyrannical as secular politicians. We can document this observation from many periods of history: from postexilic Judaism, from medieval Roman Catholicism, from Savonarola's Florence and Calvin's Geneva, and from our own early American attempts at theocracy in Puritan New England. And if these are not enough, we are further warned by the power of the Eastern Orthodox church allied to the throne of the Czar in prerevolutionary Russia, and a like power of the Roman church in Spain and certain Latin-American countries. We can have no sympathy with Ezekiel's vision of a nation or nations ruled by priests from a Temple, however glorious.

Does this mean that Ezekiel has no message for us? Far from it. The worship of God need not be united with political power to exert its saving influence. Ezekiel insists upon the sovereignty of God, upon the centrality of worshiping the one God, upon the suicidal nature of profaning this one, central loyalty, and upon the grace of God available to any people who will return to the true source of its life. He makes sin and repentance more crucial than natural resources and military might; he makes loyalty to God paramount to pleasure or security. These are valid truths needed now as much as six centuries before Christ or at any other time.

A good sermon lies in the most vivid of Ezekiel's visions: the chariot-enthroned Glory of the Lord, which appears in three different roles in the book. First, there is the sovereign glory of the one transcendent God (1:4–28). As the real Sovereign of the world, God broods over the power of nations as well as the lives of individuals, calling them to honor and serve him. Second, the Glory of God departs from a sinful people (10:1–22). This is the ultimate symbol of judgment upon a people who have forsaken their integrity, their central spiritual loyalty. Third, the Glory of God returns to a new people who have a new heart (11:19–20; 43:1–5).

If one is looking for another single vision epitomizing the whole message of Ezekiel he may well use the Valley of Dry Bones (37:1–14). Why are the bones there in the first place? The answer to this question will involve the sins named in chapters 1 through 24, together with the note of divine judgment. Can these bones live? By the power of God's grace, yes. But this calls for repentance, for a genuine turning toward God.

A sermon centered on the personality of Ezekiel could begin in the sense of urgency so well represented by Ezekiel 3:16–21 and Ezekiel 33:1–16. It could then go on to include the prophet's call, some of his symbolic acts and oracles, and end with the vision of restoration and renewal.

Passages indicated earlier as we worked our way into the book could be the basis of a book condensation presented in its own words. Properly prepared and fully rehearsed, such a message may well have an electric effect.

A Modern Title

"God Will Strengthen" (the literal meaning of *Ezekiel*), "Watchman for the World," "The Church at the Center," "Can These Bones Live?" "Dry Bones," and "A Nation after God's Heart" are appropriate titles.

23

FAITH UNDER FIRE

The Book of Daniel

WHAT do you think of when the Book of Daniel is mentioned? The fiery furnace? The lions' den? These are good symbols for the central message of Daniel: Men of faith are imperiled because of their faith, but saved by it.

I. WORKING YOUR WAY INTO THE BOOK

Daniel is one of the least understood and most abused books of the Bible. There are two reasons for this: (1) It belongs to a special type of literature which few modern readers understand. (2) Understanding it requires a far more exact and detailed knowledge of history of the Near East prior to 165 B.C. than most of us possess.

TYPE OF LITERATURE[1]

The type of literature is *apocalyptic*, a kind of writing which flourished in late Palestinian and early Christian times. Two biblical books belong *in toto* to this peculiar kind of writing; these are Daniel and Revelation. But there were apocalyptic elements in the prophets, such as Isaiah 6:1–6; Ezekiel 1:1–3:27; Joel 2:28–3:17. It is in the Pseudepigrapha of the Old Testament, however, that we find most of the Jewish apocalyptic writings, such as the Book of Enoch, the Assumption of Moses, the Secrets of Enoch, the

[1] This section is based upon my book, *Preaching on the Books of the New Testament* (New York: Harper & Brothers, 1956), pp. 244–245.

165

Apocalypse of Baruch, 4 Ezra, and the Sibylline Oracles. There is the little Christian apocalypse of Mark 13; and outside the New Testament there are the Christian books, the Apocalypse of Peter and the Shepherd of Hermas.

When these writings are taken together and read as a group, they will be seen to shed light upon one another. All are characterized by ecstatic feeling, by allegory of an extremely bizarre variety, so extreme in many instances as to lead into an obscurity which serves to heighten the sense of mystery. There is also a peculiar fondness for numbers. All of the writings deal with a cosmic drama showing two worlds in conflict; they abound in prayers and hymns; they are visions; and they are tracts for times of crisis. They have a pastoral aim, to encourage the faithful in a period of persecution and danger. Much of the imagery of these books is standard; for example, beasts quite generally represent nations or empires. This last symbol should not be difficult to understand; we do the same thing today. Witness the British lion and the Russian bear.

HISTORICAL SETTING

The writer of Daniel moves with ease back and forth over the history of the Near East from Nebuchadnezzar to the fall of Alexander the Great and the rise of his successors. He presupposes a good working knowledge of the history of the Jews and their contacts with the empires of Babylon, Medo-Persia, Greece, Syria (the Seleucidae), and Egypt (the Ptolemies). Rome stands just offstage. It is quite obvious to anyone having this background that the focus of interest is upon the successors to Alexander the Great, and more especially upon one Seleucid king, Antiochus IV, who was called Epiphanes. The dates of Antiochus Epiphanes were 175–164 B.C. The backdrop of the book is a stretch of time covering almost four and a half centuries, but the spotlight is upon a cataclysm in Judah during the last four or five years of Antiochus Epiphanes.

For the easiest available account of this immediate background, secure a copy of the Apocrypha and:

Read 1 *Maccabees* 1:1–4:60.

Antiochus IV seems to have had two ruling ambitions, to dominate Egypt and to Hellenize the culture and religion of the whole Near East. One ambition was political and the other was cultural. The

Jews stood astride his path to both goals. The road to Egypt led through Judah, and though the Jews offered no opposition to his Egyptian campaigns, they were there to be the scapegoats after his defeats and setbacks. Many Jews offered no resistance to his Hellenizing program; he found high priests who were willing to collaborate with him. They even paid for the office. But there was a hard core of loyal Jews who resisted. This soon led to bitter feuds among the Jews themselves between the two factions, Hellenistic and Judaistic. Antiochus used the feuds as an excuse to intervene and ruthlessly to dislodge the Jewish cultus and impose the Greek cultus in 168 B.C. He made it a capital offense to circumcise a baby, to own a copy of the Jewish Law, to keep the Sabbath, to make an offering to Yahweh. He consecrated the Jerusalem Temple to Zeus and offered swine upon its altars. He set up Greek altars throughout Judah, commissioned priests to officiate at them, and compelled Jews to worship Zeus, on pain of death. The desecration of the Temple took place on December 25, 168 B.C. The next year the Jews, under the leadership of the Maccabees, rebelled. Through a series of military campaigns brilliantly led by Judas Maccabeus (who reminds us of David), the forces of Antiochus Epiphanes were defeated, and the Temple was rededicated exactly three years after its desecration, on December 25, 165 B.C.

Other details of Seleucid and Ptolemaic history are needed, especially to understand Daniel 11, but we shall leave those for the section of symbolism, below.

THE DATES OF DANIEL

In the light of all this, why is Daniel represented as living in the sixth century? He did his work, according to the book, as the Babylonian empire was breaking up and the new empire of Persia was emerging. There may have been several reasons. First, there is always value in going into the storied past to find inspiration for present crises. Witness the current vogue of historical fiction in contemporary America. The Bible does this with other books as well: Ruth, Jonah, and Esther, for example. Second, a book which appeared to be about ancient Persia would not arouse the suspicions of the Greek persecutors of the Jews. (Clear allusions to the Seleucidae were safely buried in the last six chapters of the book; a Greek censor would probably toss the book aside after reading the story of Daniel in the first six chapters. The elaborate imagery of chapter 7 would bring his reading to a halt.) Third, apocalyptic literature had taken the place of the prophets (see Zech. 13:3–6). And apocalyptic writing often makes use of past history for present purposes. (Notice, for instance, that Babylon stands for Rome in Revelation.)

A few simple arguments support a date during the Antiochian persecution and the Maccabean Revolt. The symbolic details of the visions in Daniel 7–12 are preoccupied with the years 168–165 B.C. The foregoing years, even whole centuries, are passed over quickly and lightly. Moreover, they are treated in a very cursory manner. For example, Darius is represented as the first of the Persian kings, with Cyrus coming later, the reverse of actual fact. And three Babylonian kings who ruled between Nebuchadnezzar and Belshazzar are omitted entirely. We can understand this. An American living in A.D. 1960 will be much clearer about the major events of the Truman and Eisenhower administrations than he will be about those of Madison and Monroe. (By the way, in what order did those two serve—Madison-Monroe or Monroe-Madison?) When we look closely at the main point of the Book of Daniel we see that it fits the Maccabean period far better than it does the Babylonian or Persian: For while the Babylonian Jews were deprived of their political freedom, they were not subjected to religious tyranny. And one last argument: The language of Daniel 2:4–7:28 is Aramaic, the spoken language of the Jews in the latest period of the Old Testament and in the early Christian era. Most scholars feel that the whole book first appeared in Aramaic and that parts of it were later translated into Hebrew.

OUTLINE OF THE BOOK OF DANIEL

I. The story of Daniel and his friends, chapters 1–6
II. The visions of Daniel, chapters 7–12

The story of Daniel and his friends is as clear and easy to understand as the Book of Jonah, although it is a bit more flamboyant and stylized. It shows us Daniel, wise and good, remaining strong and victorious in the face of temptations and pressures to forsake his God and worship idols. The message and main point of the whole book is found in its first division; Daniel 1–6 is really complete without the remaining chapters.

When we come to the visions, we are in a bizarre and confusing realm, and we need an experienced guide who knows the history of the Near East from 600–165 B.C. He also needs to know the peculiarities of apocalyptic literature. We find such a guide in Arthur Jeffery, from whose Introduction to the Book of Daniel[2] the following material is adapted.

Read Daniel 7:

The four beasts are four empires: Babylonia, Media, Persia, and Syria (the Seleucid kingdom). The ten horns represent ten Seleucid kings and pretenders, the little horn being Antiochus Epiphanes. "A time, two times, and half a time" equals three and one-half years, the predicted period before the defeat of Antiochus.

Read Daniel 8:

The two-horned ram is Medo-Persia. The he-goat is Greece; the first, big horn is Alexander the Great. The four horns which displace him are four generals contending for his empire. The little horn is the one that concerns us most—the Seleucid king, Antiochus IV. It was he who desecrated the Jerusalem Temple and stopped the sacrifices for the three years, 168–165 B.C. (Dan. 8:11–14).

Read Daniel 9:

The writer reflects upon Jeremiah's prediction that the captivity would last seventy years (Jer. 25:11–12; 29:10). He interprets this to mean seventy weeks of years—that is, from the beginning of the Babylonian captivity in 587 B.C. to the final overthrow of Antiochus. (He died in 163 B.C.)

Read Daniel 10:

Angels come to Daniel to tell him of the futures of Persia and Greece.

Read Daniel 11:1–6:

As you read this chapter from the Bible, the following identifications will help to clarify the historical references: Darius I, Xerxes, and Artaxerxes (11:2); Alexander the Great and the generals among

[2] *The Interpreter's Bible*, Vol. VI, pp. 346–348.

whom his kingdom was divided at his death in 323 B.C. (11:3–4); Ptolemy in Egypt, Seleucus in Syria (11:5); Berenice, daughter of Ptolemy II, who married Antiochus in 246 B.C. and who, with her son, was later assassinated (11:6).

Read Daniel 11:7–12:

The "branch" is Ptolemy III. To avenge his sister, Berenice, he plundered Syria, defeated Seleucus II (vss. 7–9). Seleucus III and Antiochus III made war against Egypt (vs. 10). Ptolemy IV defeated Antiochus III in 217 B.C. at Raphia, but did not break him (vss. 11–12).

Read Daniel 11:13–16:

Antiochus III took Palestine from Ptolemy V.

Read Daniel 11:17:

Cleopatra (not *the* Cleopatra, but daughter of Antiochus III) was married to Ptolemy V in 194 B.C. for political reasons, which did not work out.

Read Daniel 11:18–20:

Antiochus III attempted to take Asia Minor and Greece, but he was defeated by a Roman commander at Magnesia in 190 B.C. He was killed in 187 B.C. while plundering a temple at Elymais. Seleucus IV was assassinated in 175 B.C.

Read Daniel 11:21:

Antiochus IV (Epiphanes), brother of Seleucus IV, obtained the throne that should have gone to Demetrius, son of Seleucus IV.

Read Daniel 11:22–24:

The "prince of the covenant" was the Jewish high priest, Onias III, assassinated in 171 B.C.

Read Daniel 11:25–30:

Antiochus IV returned from a campaign against Egypt in 170 B.C. with much booty (vss. 25–27). He began his attack against the Jewish religion (vs. 28). The Kittim are the Romans who halted the Egyptian campaign of Antiochus Epiphanes in 168 B.C.

Read Daniel 11:31:

Antiochus Epiphanes captured Jerusalem, installed a Syrian garrison in the Temple, offered swine on its altar, decreed an end to Jewish religion, and dedicated the Temple to Zeus. That happened on December 25, 168 B.C.

Read Daniel 11:32–35:

The Jews themselves were divided into two parties, Hellenizers and Hasadim. The Maccabean Revolt began.

Read Daniel 11:36–39:

Antiochus Epiphanes plundered temples and even took to himself titles of divinity. He worshiped the non-Syrian deity, Olympian Zeus.

Read Daniel 11:40–43:

Ptolemy VI attempted to conquer Syria but suffered crushing defeat—both he and his allies.

Read Daniel 11:44–45:

This is a prediction that Antiochus Epiphanes on his return from Egypt will die in camp between Jerusalem and the Mediterranean. Actually, he died in Persia in 163 B.C. trying to raise revenues for his depleted treasury.

Read Daniel 12:1–4:

This is an anticipation of the end of the persecution, to be followed by a general resurrection and by the beginning of the kingdom of God.

Read Daniel 12:5–13:

Daniel sees a vision assuring him that the persecution, now fairly advanced, is about to end. Calculations about the length of the persecution (see vss. 7, 11, 12) present difficulties. But verse 7 is clear; the time is three and one half years.

Main Themes

1. *God in history.* Human history is a whole; successive contemporary empires must be viewed together from the standpoint of God and his moral requirements, for he is the ruler of all nations. He punishes the wicked and vindicates the righteous—but not without struggle.

2. *Belief in angels.* Great prominence is given to angels (8:16; 9:21; 10:13, 20). This belief was taken up by the Pharisees. The Sadducees, being more traditional, resisted innovations from the Persian period, including this one.

3. *A supernatural Messiah.* The son of man (7:13–14) is Daniel's picture of a supernatural Messiah. This picture may have influenced Jewish thought in New Testament times; this idea represents a revision of the older view of a political Messiah.

4. *The general resurrection.* The kingdom of God is to be ushered in by a general resurrection (12:2). The Old Testament has little to

say about life after death; this is one of the few passages to present the belief.

KEY VERSES

". . . our God whom we serve is able to deliver us from the burning fiery furnace; and he will deliver us out of your hand, O king. But if not, be it known to you, O king, that we will not serve your gods or worship the golden image which you have set up" (Dan. 3:17–18).

II. PREPARING YOUR BOOK SERMON

CARDINAL IDEA

Remain faithful to God at all costs and you will be vindicated, if not now, then in the resurrection.

SHAPING A PREACHING OUTLINE

Daniel was written for a time of martyrdom and persecution. There are situations in the world today which duplicate this basic condition; within such situations the message of Daniel will be timely and relevant. Aside from that, the relentless pressure of a secular culture to suppress all that is unique in our religious faith is a very present trouble. Hellenization finds its modern counterparts in secularization. There is always the danger that the temple of true faith will go on standing but that the alien fires of substitute religions and antireligion will burn upon its altars. This is not always imposed upon us from without by military dictators—though our age has seen plenty of that; it is often self-imposed by the worshipers. Unwittingly they come to worship civilization rather than God. Such is the modern abomination of desolation—the desecration of the Temple.

The simplest kind of sermon would be a double narrative: (1) the story of the Maccabean Revolt, drawn from 1 Maccabees in the Apocrypha or from any good Jewish history; (2) the story of Daniel from the first six chapters of the book. When these two narratives come together, the book will register its point without the laboring of a moral. Care must be taken to streamline both narratives so they may be fitted into the limited time allotted to a sermon.

A former student, Coleman Games, submitted the following outline for a book sermon to a seminary class in preaching: Text: Daniel 3:17-18: (1) the hostile opposition of the world; (2) the consuming loyalty of the faithful; (3) the final vindication of the righteous.

There is a sermon to be found in the binding together of the exploits of Daniel and the visions of Daniel, with the following key: Those who see into history with religious and moral insight are those who become wise and who will make history by remaining loyal under persecution. This idea is suggested by my colleague, William L. Reed. It would seem desirable to reverse the order of the two sections: (1) insight into history, in particular the history of the Maccabean Revolt (Dan. 7-12); (2) the wisdom of those who remain faithful (Dan. 1-6).

A MODERN TITLE

Possible titles are: "The World against the Church," "Unconditional Loyalty," "But if Not" (Luther A. Weigle's title), and "Faith under Fire."

24

NEWS OF GOD FROM A BROKEN HOME
The Book of Hosea

I N THE play *The Green Pastures,* by Marc Connelly, it was Hosea who taught God the meaning of mercy. Alienated from mankind by its sin, God had withdrawn from the earth for a long time, when belatedly he appeared in a lull of battle during a siege of Jerusalem, to see how man had been faring. He spoke to a soldier, who mistook him for a country preacher. We pick up the story in the midst of the scene:

HEZDREL (*A soldier,* alter ego *for Adam*): How come you so puzzled 'bout de God of Hosea?

GOD: I don' know. Maybe I jest don' hear things. You see, I live 'way back in de hills.

HEZDREL: What you wanter find out?

GOD: Ain't de God of Hosea de same Jehovah dat was de God of Moses?

HEZDREL (*contemptuously*): No. Dat ol' God of wrath and vengeance? We have de God dat Hosea preached to us. He's de one God.

GOD: Who's he?

HEZDREL (*reverently*): De God of mercy.

GOD: Hezdrel, don' you think dey must be de same God?

HEZDREL: I don' know. I ain't bothered to think much about it. Maybe they is. Maybe our God is de same ol' God. I guess we jest got tired of his appearance dat ol' way.

GOD: What you mean, Hezdrel?

HEZDREL: Oh, dat ol' God dat walked de earth in de shape of a man. I guess he lived wid man so much dat all he seen was de sins in man. Dat's what made him de God of wrath and vengeance. Co'se he made Hosea.

An' Hosea never would a found what mercy was unless dere was a little of it in God, too. Anyway, he ain't a fearsome God no mo'. Hosea showed us dat.

GOD: How you s'pose Hosea found dat mercy?

HEZDREL: De only way he could find it. De only way I found it. De only way anyone kin find it.

GOD: How's dat?

HEZDREL: Through sufferin'.[1]

I. WORKING YOUR WAY INTO THE BOOK

THE TIMES OF HOSEA

According to the preface—written long after the book itself— Hosea was contemporary with the Judaean kings Uzziah, Jotham, Ahaz, and Hezekiah. Uzziah died *ca.* 742 B.C. and Hezekiah became king *ca.* 715 B.C. Also, according to the preface, he began to preach under Jeroboam II, who died in 746 B.C. Thus the title of the book would place Hosea's work within the last quarter-century of Israel's national existence, when crisis after crisis was leading on to the final calamity.

Evidence from the text of the book itself indicates that Hosea preached during the period of anarchy and bloodshed following the death of Jeroboam II, who was the fourth king of the house of Jehu. The fifth in the line, Zechariah, lasted only six months before he was assassinated by Shallum, who then seized the throne:

Read Hosea 1:4; 2 *Kings* 10:11.

The name Jezreel in Israelite history was a name with definite historical associations, as the Alamo, Gettysburg, and Pearl Harbor are for Americans. It recalled the slaughter by which Jehu had obliterated the house of Omri and usurped the throne of Israel a century before. For the biblical record of these final, tumultuous years in Israel:

Read 2 Kings 14:23–17:6.

After Jeroboam, until the fall of Samaria a scant twenty-five years later, the dynasty in Israel changed no less than four times.

---

[1] Marc Connelly, *The Green Pastures* (New York: Farrar and Rinehart, 1930), Part II, scene 7.

Four of the six kings of this period were assassinated, and a fifth was carried into Assyrian captivity. The political life of Israel had become as unstable as that of certain Latin-American republics in the twentieth century.

The balance of power in Israel lay between pro-Assyrian and pro-Egyptian parties. This accounted for most of the intrigue and bloodshed. Students of Hosea's text think that we have no prophecy later than 732 B.C., the date of the Syro-Ephraimitic War:

Read Isaiah 7:1; 2 *Kings* 15:29.

In a massive rebellion against Assyria in 734–732 B.C., the kings of Syria and Israel sought first by persuasion and then by force to bring Judah into their coalition. The result at this time was disastrous for Syria, Galilee, Gilead, and the plain of Sharon (732 B.C. marks the beginning of the Assyrian captivity for those regions), as it was disastrous for Israel ten years later.

Thus we arrive at the probable dates of Hosea's activity: 746–734 B.C. This was contemporary with Amos. Both prophets preached in a time of social injustice and religious corruption. Amos was engrossed largely with the social injustices of the period; Hosea was more concerned with its religious corruption.

The Book of Hosea

The Book of Hosea falls into two divisions, chapters 1–3 dealing with Hosea's marriage and home life, and the lessons learned from it; and chapters 4–14, the record of his preaching. The arrangement of the book seems haphazard; there is no carefully wrought, analytical outline.

The details of Hosea's home life are by no means clear. The Hebrew text is corrupt in many places, and the translation of certain passages is conjectural. And yet, in spite of all this, we are not in doubt about the kind of person Hosea was, the nature of his personal life, or the main themes of his preaching. Detail for detail, we cannot tell exactly what happened in his home life; but we do know that his wife broke his heart, but not his love. We do know that the lessons he learned in his broken home showed him a new face of God's love for Israel. His suffering and his consequent insight brought him into the shadow of the cross. As to his preaching, Hosea, like Amos, foresaw destruction and captivity for Israel; but unlike Amos he spoke from the inside of Israel as a citizen who loved his fatherland. His voice of doom is choked by sobs of love and compassion, his indignation by sorrow and yearning.

Main Themes

1. *Israel's sins:* religious apostasy, social injustice and crime, foreign intrigue.
2. *Israel's punishment:* destruction, dispersion, captivity.
3. *God's long-suffering love* for wayward Israel.
4. *The call to repentance.*

These themes are like the spokes of a wheel, turning over and over throughout the book. The main emphases upon God's long-suffering love occur in chapters 1, 2, 3, and 11. The main call to repentance is in chapter 14.

Reading the Book

Because the arrangement of the book is not analytical but episodic and oracular, there is little point in outlining it. A categorical analysis will serve our purposes much better. What we propose, therefore, is a fourfold reading of the book, as follows:

1. Read the last eleven chapters for Israel's sins. List the passages under three headings: (*a*) Social injustices and crimes; (*b*) foreign intrigue; (*c*) religious apostasy. You will see that they are often interwoven with each other, and that the theme of Israel's sins in turn is interwoven with the other themes of the book. It becomes clear, however, that Hosea regarded religious apostasy as the fountainhead of the other sins. Like a faithless wife to God, Israel was playing the harlot to other gods. From this unfaithfulness grew injustice, crime, and political weakness. Specifically, the apostasy was to the fertility cults of Canaan—cult prostitution, idolatry, and festival drunkenness. Apostasy is perhaps too strong a term, for the cultic practices of Canaan's Baal may have been joined with the cultic practices of Israel's Yahweh, producing a mongrel religion in which the ethical emphasis was smothered under ritual and magic. Religion was booming, but it was orgiastic, demoralizing.

2. This time reread the last eleven chapters and list the passages dealing with the results of Israel's sins. These will be found to be a

general decline in spiritual sensitivity (4:1b; 5:3–4) relieved by occasional remorse and shallow repentance (6:8–11; 7:1–7). Social breakdown and loss of political prestige will follow, and all the troubles will lead in the end to the scattering of the Israelites, and to their captivity, some in Egypt, others in Assyria. A key passage to this theme is 5:5–6; Israel has so consistently violated the covenant that God is compelled at last to withdraw from Israel and turn his back upon her.

3. For the third reading, focus upon passages indicating God's yearning for Israel and his long-suffering love. Most of your findings will be in chapters 2 and 11. Hosea 2:14–23 and 11:1–9, in particular, stress God's brokenheartedness at Israel's sin and his unbroken love for her; God cannot give Israel up to reap the whirlwind she has sown; he suffers with her and for her. This is Hosea's unique emphasis. We suspect that this insight into God's long-suffering love for Israel has come to him through his own long-suffering love for Gomer, his faithless wife.

4. The final reading of the book will center upon passages calling for repentance. Here the principal material will be found in chapter 14, but there are other passages, such as 10:12 and 12:6, as well as many passages in which a call to repentance may be inferred.

HOSEA'S HOME LIFE

We are now led to the knotty problems of the first three chapters. These have been subjected to a variety of interpretations; scholars disagree about them. Some of the views follow: (1) Hosea deliberately married Gomer, a cult prostitute, and by calculation used his marriage and even his children as a symbol to preach against Israel's faithfulness to Yahweh. (2) Hosea did no such thing; instead he merely spun out a tale of marriage as an allegory; the husband is God, the faithless wife is Israel. (3) Hosea married two women, Gomer a respectable woman (in chapter 1), and a second woman, an unnamed prostitute whom he bought out of slavery (in chapter 3). (4) Hosea married Gomer, a respectable woman who had tendencies toward promiscuity which were latent at the time of the wedding but which later became overt. Hosea had a son by this marriage, and then Gomer bore a daughter and a son who were of dubious paternity. Finally Gomer's loves grew so numerous and so flagrant that Hosea turned her out of the house. She then went from bad to worse and ended up in slavery. Meantime, Hosea tried without success to put her out of his heart, but he found that he still loved her in spite of all her unworthiness. So in the end, when she had reached the very bottom, he bought her out of slavery, forgave her, and tenderly restored her to his home as his wife.

The fourth interpretation appeals to the present writer. Hosea's home experience was one that broke his heart, and from his broken-hearted efforts to save his home and his love, he learned lessons of mercy which tempered his justice in his preaching to Israel. He did not come to his marriage with his complete message, but through the inexpressible suffering which that marriage brought him he penetrated to religious truths which he could not have learned at lesser cost.

As you read the first three chapters of the book you will find details of Hosea's home life woven allegorically into the second chapter, which deals bifocally with Gomer and with Israel. This chapter may be read on one plane as a part of Hosea's biography, on another plane as a part of his preaching. There are two movements in it: (1) the husband puts his faithless wife away because of her persistent sin; (2) the husband forgives her, tenderly wins her back, and reinstates her. The only clear departure from the biographical interest of these chapters is 1:10–11, where the theme of restoration of Israel interrupts the story. For the rest, though the details are seen through a mist, the story unfolds logically: (1) the wedding of Hosea to Gomer, a woman with harlot tendencies; (2) the birth and naming of the children; (3) the emergence of Gomer's tendencies into overt faithlessness; (4) the putting away of Gomer; (5) the unbroken love of Hosea; (6) Gomer's redemption and restoration through the tender, long-suffering love of Hosea.

OUTLINE OF THE BOOK OF HOSEA[2]

I. The story of an unfaithful wife, and its application, 1:2—3:5
II. Prophecies against a guilty nation, 4:1—13:16
III. Words of encouragement and promise, 14:1-9

[2] Sydney Lawrence Brown, *The Book of Hosea with Introduction and Notes* (London: Methuen & Company, 1932), p. xxxvi.

As we have seen, the basic sin in Israel as Hosea understood it was religious faithlessness. The Hebrew concepts of *knowledge* and *faithfulness* are closely woven together, in the following manner: The Hebrew verb *to know* (*yadhah*) stands equally for knowledge and for sexual intercourse. Knowledge, in the Hebrew sense, is never a detached kind of knowing; it is a commitment, an involvement of the whole person in personal relationship. And the knowledge of God means being bound to God, as in a marriage. Thus, passages in Hosea dealing with the knowledge of God, or the lack of it, come close to the center of his message. We nominate two passages, which, when taken together, form a good summary of Hosea's preaching: Hosea 4:1b; 6:6. These contain the negative and the positive sides of the message: the faithlessness of Israel and her repentance and returning.

A longer passage, at the heart of Hosea's message, is Hosea 11:1–9.

II. PREPARING YOUR BOOK SERMON

CARDINAL IDEA

When man sins he brings degradation and ruin upon himself, and suffering to God; but God goes on loving him and suffering for him, pleading for his repentance in order to restore him to full companionship.

SHAPING A PREACHING OUTLINE

If we could be more certain of the biographical details in the marriage of Hosea and Gomer, we could make that story the basis of the sermon. Certainly the main features of the story have been repeated in enough homes since then to make the theme familiar. In the love of a husband for a faithless wife, or of a wife for a faithless husband, and in the seeking, the suffering, the forgiving, and the restoring, we find a parable of God's relations to man. Israel or America, Hosea or us, the lesson is the same. Without being dogmatic about the biblical story of Hosea and Gomer, we can say that it may have happened so, and if it did, we can learn much about

God's love for man from this picture of a broken home where forgiving love prevails and conquers. Religion and marriage will be treated analogously.

The main themes of Hosea, developed in a previous section, may be used as the main divisions of a sermon. The story of Hosea and Gomer may be introduced into the development as a transition between the punishment of Israel for her sins and the strange, new accent upon God's long-suffering love. Hosea saw Israel's sin and he pronounced doom upon her, as Amos had done. But then his harsh judgment softened; mercy crept in to season justice. Whence did it come? From his broken home and his efforts to redeem his wayward wife. The sermon will then have five main points: (1) the sins of Israel; (2) the devastating results; (3) Hosea's personal experiences; (4) the long-suffering love of God; (5) the call to repentance.

Another outline, developed somewhat chronologically in terms of Israel's history, might develop along the following lines: (1) God's love for Israel and his initial act of redemption (Hos. 11:1); (2) God's love revealed in education and nurture of man (Hos. 11:3–4); (3) Israel's spurning of God's love (Hos. 11:2), with its apostasy (13:1–2; 7:11) and penalty (13:3–6); (4) God's unyielding love (11:8–9); (5) God's invitation to return home (14:1–4).

A Modern Title

A topic suggested by H. Wheeler Robinson's fine title will appeal to many: "The Cross of Hosea." "News of God from a Broken Home" is quoted from memory, I think from a book by Struthers Burt. Using the words of the marriage contract, we may arrive at a title like: "God Takes Us for Better or for Worse."

25

WHEN NATURE FROWNS

The Book of Joel

MOST of the time Nature smiles upon us. The Earth is a tender Mother to her children. But now and then Nature frowns and Mother Earth turns shrew for a season. It was from such a season of natural calamity that the Book of Joel was born.

I. WORKING YOUR WAY INTO THE BOOK

THE LOCUSTS

The Book of Joel is based upon an unprecedented plague of locusts which at some time in the postexilic period overran the land of Palestine, stripping it of all plant life and plunging the people and the domestic animals into famine. Those who have witnessed such an army of locusts in action tell us that the book is matchless in its description. Since the second chapter is somewhat more vivid than the first, we shall begin our reading with chapter 2:

Read Joel 2:3-10; 1:2-12, 16-20.

Perhaps we do not live sufficiently close to Nature in the twentieth century to realize how very dependent we are upon its rains, its sunshine, its balanced seasons, its seedtime and harvest. In our urban culture, where thousands of children have never seen a cow being milked, nor put a hoe into the earth to tend growing beans, it is possible to suppose that milk comes from pasteboard cartons and beans from the deep freeze. In a word, we lose our sense of living dependence upon the living earth.

If a plague like that pictured in Joel should assail America, the people of our cities would be starving in a few weeks. Pastures, denuded of grain, would support no cows; milk would fail; beef and veal would vanish from the meat counters. Cornfields would disappear, and the hogs and chickens dependent upon their grain would starve in the fields by empty granaries. There would be no bacon and eggs for our tables. Fruit and vegetables would be at an end. All that would be left after a few days would be the things that the ancients did not have—frozen foods from storage, canned goods, and dried foods. But these stores would quickly give out. Rationing would soon put everyone on a single meal a day, and that a small one. How quickly we would learn that we are dependent on the bounties of Nature.

A Call to Repentance

Such a calamity might have upon us the same effect it had upon the Jews: It might start us thinking about ultimate things, about our relation to God and about the final judgment. Repentance is the second movement of the book. It follows the call of the priests and the prophets in the face of the disaster we have just seen:
Read Joel 1:13–14; 2:12–17.
In the original order of Joel, verses calling for repentance are intermingled with verses describing the plague. This is as we would expect it to be, for the repentance is induced by the trouble. For purposes of analysis we have separated the two.
A penitent mood is a natural response to disaster. Such a response does not necessarily prove that the people who make it believe that natural calamities are the fruit of human sin. Drought and dust bowls, to translate the disaster into recent American difficulties, do not mean that the people have been guilty of moral failures. They may have been agriculturally unwise, and the plundering of the soil is a sin; but God continues to send his rain on the just and the unjust, and Nature responds on naturalistic bases, not on moral ones.
What disaster did, and still does, is to impress upon those involved in it the fact of their dependence. And this in turn evokes a mood of repentance. Nothing produces moral laxness quite as surely as the independence of arrogant human pride. When all is going well, even though we are all dependent upon Nature and upon each other in a thousand ways, we can easily develop the illusion that we are all

self-made and self-sustained. And in our pride we can take our life to be our own, for us to use as we wish. This is sin.

It is the sin of independence, of isolation and pride, that needs repentance. The calamity of the locusts underscored that in Israel. Other natural calamities—tornadoes, earthquakes, floods, and droughts—underscore the same truth. Trouble may deepen the religious mood of a people.

THE LAST JUDGMENT

Repentance brings us to the threshold of another mood which is also reflected in this book. It is the conviction that we are morally accountable. There is a final judgment, and it is final not only in the sense of coming at the end of mortal time, but in a more immediate sense: it is ultimate. It is the judgment of God that takes the measure of all human deeds and attitudes in every moment and every hour of every day. And it is the accounting that must take place between man and God in the final reckoning. In this reckoning God shows himself to be the Creator and Master of both Nature and nations.

Read Joel 1:15; 2:1–2, 11, 30–32.

These verses on the Day of the Lord follow the best prophetic tradition. When man has had his say and done his deed, then God acts. He shatters complacency and pride. He judges evil. The judgment of God means human crisis. As pictured by Joel, the coming of the Day of the Lord will result in three deep changes in the world: (1) a renewal of Nature; (2) a renewal of man's spirit; (3) the coming of international justice.

1. *A renewal of Nature.* Joel pictures a revival of Eden:

Read Joel 2:18–27; 3:18.

The "northerner" in 2:20 refers to the invading locusts, which are to be banished so that Palestine may again become verdant and productive. We have here a dream of an economy of abundance. It is the dream of hungering, undernourished humanity wherever Nature's scarcity is matched with teeming humanity's millions.

2. *A renewal of man's spirit.* This is the inner, religious renewal of man; it is nothing less than a spiritual rebirth, and it depends upon God's creative touch:

Read Joel 2:28–29.

These verses are very familiar to readers of Acts, for Peter quoted them at length in his sermon on the Day of Pentecost (Acts 2:17–21). The things that happened in the minds of the early Christians were so cataclysmic and so transforming that they were seen to be a fulfillment of Joel's prophecy. Men must be renewed from within— they must be born again; then they will develop the insight from which good lives alone can spring.

3. *The coming of international justice.* Joel's picture of international justice does seem to be rather biased in favor of the Jews. In this respect, his book is closer to Nahum and Obadiah than to Jonah and Ruth. It is both militaristic and nationalistic. Notice, for example, the amazing reversal of Micah's and Isaiah's dreams of peace:

Read Joel 3:9–19; *Micah* 4:1–3; *Isaiah* 2:2–4.

On the surface, at least, Joel issues a battle cry for the Final World War. He appears to gather the righteous from all over the world into one army, and the wicked into the opposing army. He further appears to equate the Jews with the righteous, and the Gentiles with the wicked.

But there is a dimension of meaning which transmutes all these nationalistic and moralistic values into something higher. It is God who gathers the nations and peoples. He assembles them to face him in judgment. All people stand on trial before the Most High:

Read Joel 3:1–17, 19, 21.

The valley of the Jehoshaphat was not a geographic location. Long, long afterward the Kedron valley was sometimes called by that name, but in the thought of Joel it is an allegory of God's judgment. Jehoshaphat means *Yahweh has judged.* The ultimate moral issues of the world are not in human hands; they are in the hands of God.

Though Joel seems unable to rise entirely above his own nationalistic prejudice, his vision places even that under the final judgment of God, who alone is worthy to test the self-righteousness of the world's peoples, and of his own prophets.

II. PREPARING YOUR BOOK SERMON

CARDINAL IDEA

A natural calamity starkly reveals our living dependence upon Nature; moreover, it tends to call us to repentance and to consider how God measures our whole way of life.

The three movements in the Book of Joel have been clearly sketched above. They seem to offer themselves as the most natural structure for your book sermon. Such a sermon will come most suitably after some contemporary catastrophe in Nature's realm— tornado, flood, drought, earthquake—affecting your hearers. The sermon will have three main divisions:

1. The catastrophe
2. Our dependence on Nature, and repentance for our arrogant self-sufficiency
3. A new insight into what God wants
   a) Economic abundance, with the world a well-cultivated garden
   b) A new humanity, reborn from within
   c) International justice

Thus the eyes of the congregation will be lifted beyond their temporary plight to the usual fertility of the earth and the bounties of Nature, which will be renewed shortly; and their eyes will also be lifted to the ultimate measure and meaning of our human lot.

Using the same outline, you may fashion a sermon on the "disasters of Nature" caused by man. That predatory, two-legged animal has wrought havoc with the earth and is storing up trouble for his children's children by his waste of Nature's resources. He has slaughtered the wildlife of continent after continent. He has denuded the hills of their forests. He has broken the prairies with his plow, exposing precious topsoil to the slow erosion of water and the dramatic disaster of dust storms. He has been prodigal of coal and petroleum, and has looted the deep earth's treasures of iron and copper. When some future generation, as yet unborn, inherits from us a plundered planet, its members may well ask what madness possessed us.

A Modern Title

Besides the title of this chapter, which we recommend as a good sermon topic, the following may be used: "The Valley of Decision" (suggested by Joel 3:12), "Prelude to Pentecost" (based upon Peter's use of Joel in his Pentecostal sermon), "The Outpouring of God's Spirit," and "Calamity Calls us Back to God."

26

JUSTICE OR DEATH

The Book of Amos

Amos is known as the first of the writing prophets. Before him the word of prophets was spoken but not committed to writing. And though strands of our scriptural record were composed before this time, probably no entire biblical book existed in final form at an earlier date.

This first of the writing prophets does not steal upon us quietly, in genteel grace like an author at a literary tea. He bursts upon us like an earthquake.

I. WORKING YOUR WAY INTO THE BOOK

HISTORICAL SETTING

For the original readers of the book, the date of Amos' oral prophecy was rather precisely fixed—within the reigns of King Uzziah of Judah (783–742 B.C.) and King Jeroboam II of Israel (786–746 B.C.), "two years before the earthquake." The earthquake, which would have been such a vivid memory to the original readers (just as the 1906 'quake of San Francisco is still *the* earthquake for Americans) has left no record in history. Therefore we have to rely on other indications to date the prophecy:

Read 2 *Kings* 14:23–28.

Assyria was quiescent in the eighth century until the rise of Tiglath-pileser III in 745 B.C. This peace provided Israel and Judah with the opportunity to regain lost territory, to collect tribute from the caravans passing through these lands astride the trade routes, and to enjoy a period of prosperity. By the time in which Amos spoke, this condition had lasted long enough for Israel's prosperity to have caused a general corruption—landlords foreclosing mortgages, large estates swallowing up small farms, judges taking bribes, the rise of a leisure class with elaborate forms of amusement to keep it entertained, and the emergence of a whole scheme of luxury living for a few exploiters:

Read Amos 3:15; 6:4–6; 4:1; 5:11, 12.

It seems safe to assume that these conditions would not have prevailed earlier than the middle of Jeroboam's reign. Probably they would come even later. A scholar who has carefully sifted the evidence, J. Jorgenstern, gives the dates *ca.* 752–738 B.C.

The book itself, as the first verse indicates, was written as a record of the prophecy, some years later. Probably the writing took place not too long after the prophecy. (We shall have to except Amos 9:11–15, which bears the marks of an appendix added sometime after the fall of Jerusalem in 587 B.C.)

The Man Amos

What we can know about the prophet must be learned from the book itself. There are some autobiographical details:

Read Amos 1:1; 7:14, 15.

Tekoa may have been situated two hours by donkey southeast of Bethlehem in a rocky, barren waste, affording a grudging existence to even the most industrious. Residents of this region would be poor. Here Amos eked out a living by herding sheep and goats, and by pricking and harvesting sycamore figs, the food of the poor. But this poor village was a kind of balcony seat from which one could look out upon the world. The Dead Sea and the plains of Moab were in full view to the east, as was Jerusalem to the north.[1]

Receiving a prophet's call, though a layman himself, Amos made his way north, perhaps to Samaria, certainly to Bethel, and there he preached against Israel at the royal shrine. This brought him into

---

[1] "Since Thekua has not been excavated, its identification with Tekoa is uncertain. Some scholars have thought that it was southwest of Jerusalem where there are sycamore trees. In this case, it would have been possible for Amos to see the coastal plain, possibly even the marching armies of Assyria and Egypt."—William L. Reed, in a note to the author.

direct conflict with Amaziah, the priest of Bethel, who drove him out in the name of the king.

In addition to direct information about Amos, there is much that we may infer from the nature of his words. Here was a man at home in Nature and in history. He knew and loved the out-of-doors with its dangers and its beauties. He was alert to what was happening in neighboring nations, and in Judah and Israel. He was possessed of a fiery social conscience—great sympathy for the poor, holy indignation against the rich and exploiting. He was passionately devoted to social justice; but his justice was little seasoned by mercy. His keen ethical sense intuited disaster for Israel in the near future; he felt sure that Israel could not go on as she was without meeting calamity. He felt himself under constraint to speak this unhappy truth. And thus he left his flocks and his trees, and invaded the happy and heedless land of Israel. There he tossed his words like firebrands into the festival crowds.

Amos was himself something of a human earthquake. And he was not mistaken about the social earthquake which was then gathering to destroy Israel; for it was only a few years later (722 B.C.) that Samaria was destroyed, and the Ten Tribes disappeared from history.

OUTLINE OF THE BOOK OF AMOS

   I. Indictments against the nations, chapters 1–2
  II. Oracles against Israel, chapters 3–6
 III. Visions and narratives, chapters 7–9

The oracles against Israel in chapters 3–6 are brief and numerous. Are they fragments of Amos' preaching, or did Amos emerge from the crowd to speak a quick dramatic word, and disappear as quickly? The text of the Revised Standard Version of the Bible is printed with double spacing between oracles so that a reader can separate them at a glance.

In the third main division of the book there are five visions. They seem, in part at least, to have constituted the call of Amos to his prophetic work. In these final chapters we also learn where Amos preached and how he was received. We have, as well, a kind of summary of the main features of his preaching (8:4–14). And we also have the appendix (9:11–15) with its vision of a restored Israel following the Exile.

READING THE BOOK OF AMOS

One way of reading the Book of Amos would be to begin with the visions:

Read Amos 7:1-9; 8:1-3; 9:1-4.

Though Amos may have shared these visions with his hearers later, they seem to lie at the beginning of his prophetic call. All of them are visions of doom: locusts devouring every blade of grass and every green leaf so that life will perish, fire licking up the water of life, a plumb line condemning a crooked wall, summer fruit whose very name (*qāyiç*) suggests the end (*qēç*), the Lord by his altar executing judgment.

Next we may read the dramatic beginning of Amos' preaching:

Read Amos 1:1—2:16.

With irresistible psychological force, Amos "zeros in on his target." His hearers would have given enthusiastic assent to everything he said up to 2:6, and they would then have found themselves captives of their own prejudices. Before they could have closed their ears, the message would have found its mark.

Next, read the oracles of chapters 3-6. Finally, read of the clash between priest and prophet in 7:10-17. This completes a reading of the greater part of the book within a narrative sequence beginning with the prophet's call and ending with his banishment.

MAIN THEMES

1. *Social wrong.* In analyzing the message of Amos, let us begin with the injustices and evils which aroused him:

Read Amos 2:6, 7, 12; 3:9, 10, 15; 4:1, 4-5; 5:7, 10-12, 21-26; 6:4-6; 8:4-6.

From these verses, like the pieces of a puzzle, we put together a picture of the economic exploitation of the poor. They were ground down through dishonest business practices, driven into debt, their farms foreclosed and added to large estates. In many cases they themselves were sold for debt. From the courts there was no recourse, for the judges were corrupted by bribes. From prophets and holy men there was no voice of social protest, for these men also had been seduced by prosperity. Luxury and idleness made women greedy, and they in turn drove their men to new deeds of callous injustice.

Sexual indulgence quite naturally flourished. But surprisingly, the public services of religion also flourished. This religion was almost exclusively ritualistic, however; corrupted by idolatry, it existed as a cult of assurance to bless and perpetuate the status quo.

2. *Election and calling.* In the face of this, Amos found himself confronted by a nation which had been elected by God himself to be his Servant for righteousness:

Read Amos 3:1–2.

In the light of such election, Israel's present behavior could lead only to divine judgment; for Israel was elected not to privilege but to service.

The prophet, too, found himself elected:

Read Amos 3:3–8.

It did not matter what his private feelings were, how much he longed to be liked; he was under divine constraint. He had no choice but to prophesy.

3. *Unheeded past warnings.* God's word of judgment did not fall upon Israel without prelude or pretext. There had been past warnings, past attempts at discipline:

Read Amos 4:6–12.

But none of these disciplines and warnings had driven Israel to repentance.

4. *Inevitable doom.* Therefore, the harvest of error could not be avoided. Judgment would come; doom would fall:

Read Amos 2:6, 13–16; 3:2, 11, 14–15; 4:2–3, 12; 5:1–2, 16–20; 6:7–11, 14; 7:17; 8:3, 7–14; 9:1–4, 8–10.

Amos thought of punishment as falling not upon individuals but upon the corporate body of the whole people. And he thought of it in historical terms; it would happen through political and military channels. This would mean the end of Israel at the hands of a conqueror. The causes, however, were not political or military; they were ethical and religious.

5. *A call to repentance.* There is no glee in the prediction. Amos pleads, without hope, for repentance:

Read Amos 5:4–6, 14–15.

But, of course, he is speaking to a people who are blinded by prosperity. They imagine that their happy state will continue forever. They cannot see that their boom is about to burst.

6. *Hope for a remnant.* In the book as we now have it there is a

faint glimmer of hope that a remnant will return from the anticipated disaster:

Read *Amos* 5:15.

It is by no means impossible that this ray of light is from a later editor. In any case the Book of Amos touches upon it very lightly. It is not a major theme.

7. *Doxologies.* There is one other bit of bright relief from the somber doom of the book. This is found in the doxologies:

Read *Amos* 3:13; 5:8–9; 9:5–6.

These beautiful words dwell upon the sovereign majesty of God, ruler of Nature and history. From these, and also from the indictment of foreign nations in the first two chapters, we meet in Amos a mind of cosmopolitan and cosmic breadth. He sees Israel among the nations; he sees God over the nations; he sees the power of God more vividly than he sees the power of nations. The first word and the last word is with God.

KEY VERSE

The golden text of the book, so frequently quoted, is 5:24. But we must be careful to couple this with the idea in 3:2. God's requirement of justice springs from the covenant. Israel had experienced God's grace in deliverance and had entered into an agreement to be his people. It was from this that the acute sense of justice derived. The question is not what justice requires of us, but what justice God requires.

II. PREPARING YOUR BOOK SERMON

CARDINAL IDEA

Prosperity—even prosperity in the institutions of religion—if it cloaks social injustice, may be a prelude to national disaster, for God's call to justice may not be flaunted.

SHAPING A PREACHING OUTLINE

One of the most popular ways of presenting Amos is to do so in terms of a biographical narrative. This requires some creative imagination, but if Amos can be made to live as a person, his timeless message will grip modern hearers. We have suggested earlier that this could be done by beginning with Amos 7:1. To this suggestion may now be added a description of Tekoa and the life of a shepherd and dresser of sycamore trees in such a surrounding. Such a narrative sermon requires a great deal of skill. Help may be gained from a good historical novel like *The Herdsman* by Dorothy Clarke Wilson.[2]

Still following biography as the key to the sermon, one may use the clash between Amos and Amaziah as the focal point. On the one hand, there is all that Amos was and represented: the common people, the simple ethical faith, the keen sense of history. On the other hand, there is all that Amaziah was and represented: vested power, the rights of privileges, shallow assurance of surface prosperity. Then cast up the balance between these two, and state the final judgment of God as shown in the preaching of Amos and in the verdict of history at the destruction of Samaria.

A topical approach to the message of Amos may follow the lines laid down under "Main Themes" in the pages just preceding. They may be rephrased slightly, in these terms: (1) social wrongs; (2) divine imperatives; (3) past warnings; (4) a harvest of disaster; (5) a call to repentance; (6) hope for the future: (*a*) a righteous remnant, and (*b*) the sovereign and everlasting God, ruler of Nature and nations. Care must be taken under the last point not to lapse into easy optimism, for in the Book of Amos the note that dominates and prevails is one of judgment.

A MODERN TITLE

A triple use of the earthquake which appears in Amos 1:1 (the literal earthquake, Amos as a very disturbing man, and the national cataclysm which befell Israel) suggests: "Just before an Earthquake." A variant would be "Prescription for an Earthquake." Melodramatic but accurate is "The Death of a Nation." Since justice is the one word most naturally associated with Amos, a title bearing that word seems almost automatic: "We Are Meant for Justice," "Justice among the Great Powers," and "Give Me Justice or Give Me Death."

[2] Philadelphia: Westminster Press (1946).

27

THE RED HARVEST

The Book of Obadiah

THOSE who live by the sword will perish by it. This is the red harvest reaped by nations who are "bad neighbors." This is the cup of God's fury for peoples who live by prey and plunder. "As you have done, it shall be done to you, your deeds shall return on your own head" (Obad., vs. 15).

Of all the enemies ringing Israel and harassing her, Edom came to be the most hated. The Old Testament bears witness to this fact through many oracles against Edom (Ezek. 25:12–14; 35:1–15; Mal. 1:2–5; Isa. 34:5–15; 63:1–6; Jer. 49:7–22; Amos. 1:11). This bitter enmity is all the more tragic because of the kinship of the two peoples; the patriarchal stories in Genesis show that Jacob and Esau were twin brothers—Jacob the father of the Israelites, Esau the father of the Edomites. Both peoples were from the stock of Abraham and Isaac; but they were enemies, caught in the endless cycle of hate and retaliation. Obadiah shows us nationalism in its most vehement mood; that is clear. But is it religion? The biblical student is hard pressed to read Obadiah's oracle against Edom for a positive religious message. Is there any word of God that comes to us through such a book?

I. WORKING YOUR WAY INTO THE BOOK

HISTORICAL SETTING

The grievance against Edom was an ancient one, but Obadiah was chafing under the recent memory of Edom's behavior at the destruction of Jerusalem by the Babylonians in 587 B.C. Edom, acting as an ally of Babylon, was guilty of at least three kinds of unbrotherly behavior: (1) they gloated over the misfortune of the Jews, enjoyed their downfall, openly added their insult to the Jewish national calamity; (2) they "looted his goods in the days of his calamity," actually making profit out of the Jews' adversity; (3) they aided Babylon by capturing Jewish refugees who sought sanctuary in Edom. For the record of these three unneighborly actions:

Read Obadiah, verses 10–14; Psalm 137:7; Ezekiel 35:5.

It is a matter of historical record that the Edomites were pushed from their homeland by the invading Arabs sometime near the end of the sixth century or at the beginning of the fifth century B.C. Arabian tribes eventually established the Nabataean kingdom. Thus disfranchised, the Edomites invaded the Jewish Negeb, or southland, and occupied it from that time forward. Their new territory was known as Idumaea. Finally an Idumaean, Antipater, made himself master of Judah, and his son, Herod the Great, became king of the Jews. Thus, ramifications of the Edom-Judah interrelationship continued as long as the nations themselves continued.

The dispossessing of Edom by the Nabataeans seems to be mirrored in Obadiah's record:

Read Obadiah, verse 7.

MAIN THEMES

The theme of the first section of the book is Edom's punishment by her national enemies—her dispossession and her consequent plight. All of this is seen as the just reward of her misuse of the Jews:

Read Obadiah, verses 5–9.

Edom's pride is humbled:

Read Obadiah, verses 1–4.

Thus we see the working out of the central moral principle with which we opened the present chapter; it is a Golden Rule in reverse. One might call it the pagan world's Iron Rule: "As you have done, it shall be done to you, your deeds shall return on your own head" (Obad., vs. 15).

In the remaining third of this slight book the scope of the treatment is expanded to include God's judgment and rule over all nations. The Jews are pictured here as a remnant of those who have passed through their own national punishment; they are the returning exiles who are again taking up their habitation in Palestine:

Read Obadiah, verses 17, 20.

All nations among the pagans will come under God's wrath and judgment:

Read Obadiah, verse 16.

Israel will be restored, both in its Southern and Northern parts, and it will occupy its full territory, the kingdom as it had been in the golden age of David and Solomon. And, in the possessing of "their own possessions," the Jews will act as God's agents; in particular, they will punish Edom:

Read Obadiah, verses 17–19.

Though the note of national revenge seems to predominate in this book, the Jew does not picture himself as acting merely on his own behalf. He thinks of himself as God's agent. And when the Jews triumph over Edom, the kingdom will be the Lord's:

Read Obadiah, verse 21.

From this sketch of the book and its background, we can see that it was written after the fall of Jerusalem in 587 B.C. As for the date of writing, we can only say that since it is quoted in Joel 2:32 (cf. Obad., vs. 17), it was in existence by 400 B.C., the probable date of Joel. A date sometime near the middle of the fifth century (450 B.C.) does not seem too far afield.

OUTLINE OF THE BOOK OF OBADIAH

I. The downfall of Edom, verses 1–14, 15b
   A. The title and author of the book, verse 1a
   B. Edom's dispossession, verses 1b–9
   C. The reason: Edom's past mistreatment of Judah, verses 10–14, 15b
II. The coming judgment and kingdom of God, verses 15a, 16–21

KEY VERSE

For the day of the Lord is near upon all the nations.
As you have done, it shall be done to you,
   your deeds shall return on your own head.
                              [Obad. vs. 15]

II. PREPARING YOUR BOOK SERMON

CARDINAL IDEA

Nations which live at the expense of their neighbors will fall into their own time of troubles, for all history is under the sovereign rule of God.

SHAPING A PREACHING OUTLINE

The modern Christian reader may well feel that Obadiah was half right and half wrong. He was right to condemn predatory nationalism in Edom; he was wrong to exalt vindictive nationalism in Israel. "Beloved, never avenge yourselves, but leave it to the wrath of God; for it is written, 'Vengeance is mine, I will repay, says the Lord' " (Rom. 12:19). For this reason, the Word of the Lord which comes to us through a writing such as this will be deeper and more searching than the word which the prophet intended. Not only does it probe the life of our enemies; it probes us. And, if it is God's Word, it probes us first.

Alfred North Whitehead once wrote: "The fact of the instability of evil is the moral order of the world."[1] A book like Obadiah, which appears to be almost entirely negative, does have a positive religious message. History is not on the side of ruthless force and social injustice; its final edict is for neighborliness and honor. When a people have little reason for being except to be against another nation, that people is nourishing itself on poison. We can see this in other nations, but we are not equally astute at seeing the same traits when they appear in our own national behavior.

We may well remind ourselves that the Book of Obadiah contains no nations which did not come under God's judgment. The Jews themselves had been chastised by national defeat and by captivity and exile; only a remnant returned. The other nations, with Edom at their head, also fell under God's judgment.

The Book of Obadiah can be approached as the final chapter in the story of Jacob and Esau. That story will be seen as the natural biography of two contrasting types of men: one religious, the other

[1] *Religion in the Making* (New York: The Macmillan Company, 1926), p. 95.

materialistic. The religious man was not a markedly "good" man, but he did come to his time of repentance and surrender; he underwent discipline and correction. The materialistic man was not a markedly "evil" man; he merely measured his life in terms of money, possessions, and immediate advantage; he was the perfect representative of a secular culture. Edom represents the ultimate development of secularism. Its nationalistic expression is Stephen Decatur's motto: "Our country! . . . may she always be in the right; but our country, right or wrong." Moral questions recede into the background, and self-interest rules. But there is a Lord of history; there will be a moral accounting.

A good text of the book is verse 15. This could be taken as the Iron Rule, contrasting with the Golden Rule. Has any nation ever sought really to live by the Golden Rule? Certainly many have lived—and died—by the Iron Rule. One of the chief values of looking at other nations and making moral judgments upon them is that these nations become the mirrors in which we may see ourselves.

Still another approach to outline may be made from one of the Beatitudes: "Blessed are the merciful, for they shall obtain mercy" (Matt. 5:7). Edom's actions, as shown in Obadiah, are a reversal of this Beatitude; and so they become a woe: Woe to the unmerciful, for they shall suffer judgment.

No matter which of the approaches to outline may be chosen, the thought of Obadiah must be presented in three phases: (1) the sowing of injury; (2) the reaping of disaster; (3) the ultimate sovereignty of God.

A MODERN TITLE

In the foregoing discussion we have already used a number of phrases which may serve as possible titles to the book. It is sufficient here merely to list them: "The Red Harvest," "The Iron Rule," "The Cup of God's Fury," "Secularism—Final Chapter," and "The Moral Order of the Universe."

28

THE WIDENESS OF GOD'S MERCY

The Book of Jonah

FATHER MAPPLE in *Moby Dick* by Herman Melville preaches an exciting sermon on Jonah. No one can improve on his beginning: "Shipmates, this book containing only four chapters—four yarns—is one of the smallest strands in the mighty cable of the Scripture. Yet what depths of soul does Jonah's deep sealine sound!"[1] It *is* a noble book, with a message of God's unbounded love for all kinds of men. The commentaries praise it in this manner: "The clearest note of universalism to be found anywhere in the Old Testament." "The noblest missionary tract in the Bible."

And yet, so great has been the controversy over the big fish that few, even among churchgoing people, have really heard what this book has to say. Early in the 1930's Clarence Darrow, the doughty foe of Fundamentalism, and Gilbert Keith Chesterton, the British author, debated in New Haven, Connecticut. The subject was "Can Religion Continue?" Darrow had his doubts, and one of them had to do with Jonah in the belly of the whale. After Darrow had poured scorn upon the story, with all his arts of sarcasm and ridicule, Chesterton arose in his mountainous bulk and with his squeaking little voice to ask this question: "Well, now, are we going to let a whale block up the whole path of human progress?" The question was a good one. It is not the big fish but Jonah who is the central character in this book, and if we are going to learn what this book has to say we must keep our eye on Jonah.

---

[1] Chapter IX, "The Sermon" (New York: Modern Library, 1926), p. 40.

199

I. WORKING YOUR WAY INTO THE BOOK

THE MAN JONAH

The "hero" of our tale finds his historical counterpart in a prophet contemporary with Amos and Hosea, living in Israel during the reign of Jeroboam II (786–746 B.C.). In the only Old Testament reference to Jonah outside the book bearing his name, we find him acting as a nationalistic voice of Israel's expansion and prosperity: "He [Jeroboam II] restored the border of Israel from the entrance of Hamath as far as the Sea of the Arabah, according to the word of the Lord, the God of Israel, which he spoke by his servant Jonah the son of Amittai, the prophet, who was from Gath-hepher" (2 Kings 14:25). This is the man on whom the Book of Jonah is based.

In our story he emerges as a narrow nationalist who hates Assyrians. When God commands him to go to Nineveh and call the Assyrians to repentance, Jonah flees—to escape doing what is hateful to him:

Read Jonah 1:1–3.

Later, when God has overtaken him and all but compelled him to go to Nineveh; and when, as a result of Jonah's reluctant call to repentance, all Nineveh turns to God, Jonah becomes angry and petulant. He wants nothing to do with a world where both Assyrian and Jew stand side by side in God's mercy and favor:

Read Jonah 4:1–4.

Jonah, in fact, is so narrow in his sympathies that he is more concerned about a vine that grows up to shelter him from the sun than he is about the fate of thousands of people:

Read Jonah 4:6–11.

THE "HEATHEN"

Throughout the book, Jonah is the foil for points of view contrasting with his own narrow provincialism. There is, to begin with, the attitude of the "heathen." These are represented by the sailors on the ship and by the inhabitants of Nineveh.

Untutored and misguided as they were, the heathen sailors had broader human sympathies than Jonah, a prophet of God! They were reluctant to do him harm, even as the price of their own safety, and they tried every device to save Jonah's life, at great peril to their own:

Read Jonah 1:11-15.

In the same way, in sharp contrast to Jonah's rebelliousness and unrepentant vindictiveness, the heathen residents of Nineveh repented, from king to lowly beast:

Read Jonah 3:6-9; 4:6-10.

Jonah did not come off well in the comparison. The polyglot crew of heathen sailors had broader human sympathies than he; and the arch enemies of Israel for all time, the hated Assyrians, were more responsive to the call of God than he had been.

The word that is being spoken to narrow-minded Judaism through Jonah is not unlike what Paul said centuries later to the Jews of Pisidian Antioch: "It was necessary that the word of God should be spoken first to you. Since you thrust it from you, and judge yourselves unworthy of eternal life, behold, we turn to the Gentiles" (Acts 13:46).

While we are quoting from Acts, we may well continue in the same passage. Paul recalls the ancient words of Second Isaiah (Isa. 49:6) to charge the Jews with a missionary responsibility to foreigners—the very kind of mission that Jonah fled from: "For so the Lord has commanded us, saying, 'I have set you to be a light for the Gentiles, that you may bring salvation to the uttermost parts of the earth' " (Acts 13:47).

Jonah, the special servant of God, is very unlike his God. For, whereas God is merciful toward all people and yearns for the heart of "aliens" and "foreigners," Jonah feels nothing but hatred toward them. In the face of this, how can Jonah call himself God's spokesman? For God's spokesman is not the man who takes the title but the man who does the will of God. In this book, Jonah, God's special spokesman, finds himself being spoken to by God himself; he finds himself under God's judgment. To little-minded Jonah, pining over his dead vine and his own solitary comfort, God tries to present the claims of a city full of *people*, including *babies:*

Read Jonah 4:11.

OUTLINE OF THE BOOK OF JONAH[2]

I. A prophet flees from his missionary commission, 1:1–17
II. A song of thanksgiving for deliverance from drowning, 2:1–10
III. A reluctant missionary at his task, 3:1–10
IV. The absurdity of trying to limit God's mercy, 4:1–11

WAYS OF INTERPRETING THE BOOK

1. *As literal history.* The barbs of Clarence Darrow in his debate with Gilbert Keith Chesterton, mentioned earlier, took their sharpness from the assumption of many Bible readers that the book of Jonah is meant to be read as literal history. Millions of sincere people through many centuries have understood it in that light. Science and literary criticism have made such a belief impossible to other millions of modern readers. Unfortunately, a debate has raged between these two camps—between those who do and those who do not believe that all events in the book were literal happenings. This debate has tended to obscure the real Word of God which is there for any person, literalist or not, who keeps his attention on the central question. For the central question is not in the details of the book nor in matters of literary form but in the way in which the mirror of God is held up to a narrow, prejudiced man, who sees himself exposed and judged by universal love. No person who reads the Book of Jonah with complacency and self-congratulation has read the Word which God seeks to convey through it, for no man, however merciful or humanitarian he may be, has fully attained to the wideness of God's mercy. It is possible, for those who find no intellectual obstacles to such an interpretation, to read the book as literal history and to be conducted directly to a personal encounter with the God of all mercies, an encounter which exposes our human prejudices in all their ugliness and absurdity. It is this meeting with God, and with ourselves in the light of God, that really matters.

"Enlightened" Bible readers who find it impossible to accept Jonah as literal history need to be on guard against the limitations and dangers of their emancipation; for believing the Book of Jonah is not merely the entertaining of a correct opinion about the nature of

---

[2] Adapted from James D. Smart in *The Interpreter's Bible*, Vol. VI, p. 874.

the book as a literary composition. Believing the book means reading it in such a way as to believe, and to be personally convicted by, the central thrust of its message, i.e., that we, as God's people, must learn how to share and express God's love for our enemies and other human beings "not of our kind."

2. *As allegory.* Another venerable method of interpreting the book is through allegorization, somewhat after this manner: Jonah represents the people of Israel; Nineveh, paganism, at its worst; the sea, world politics; the ship, diplomacy; its polyglot crew, the nations who were Israel's neighbors; the storm, Babylon overthrowing Assyria with the consequent troubling of the world; the great fish, the Babylonian empire; Jonah's sojourn in its belly, the Babylonian Exile; his deliverance, the return from the Exile. Though such allegorization seems overdrawn, it is possible to read the Book of Jonah in that light and to be conducted by it to a genuine meeting with God. But here again we should be warned against undue attention to details: The purpose of the book is not to give us a disguised history of Israel before, during, and immediately after the Babylonian Exile; it is to judge the Jonahlike attitude and to enlarge the sympathies and services of the "people of God."

3. *As parable.* The book can be read as parable, or as a short story with a point. When seen in this light, it stands beside the parables of Jesus as one of the truly moving revelations of God's truth. Modern scholars like S. R. Driver understand it as a Midrash, that is, as "an imaginative development of a thought or theme suggested by Scripture, especially a didactic or homiletic exposition or an edifying religious story."[3] The Book of Tobit and the Story of Susanna in the Apocrypha belong to the same type of literature. And, as we have said, the parables of Jesus are of this nature.

As a parable, the Book of Jonah confronted the difficult task of pricking the narrow nationalism which grew up in postexilic Judaism from the time of Ezra-Nehemiah until about the beginning of the third century B.C. Crowded in and harassed by enemies under conditions of poverty and duress, the postexilic Jews tried to get a toehold and enlarge their living space in the land they had lost to encroaching peoples while they were far away in captivity. They responded to this challenge by becoming exclusive, nationalistic, and vindictive

[3] R. F. Horton in *The New Century Bible: The Minor Prophets* (New York: Oxford University Press, n. d.), Vol. I, p. 198.

toward outsiders. Other peoples in other times have known the same vindictiveness, the same isolationism, the same exclusiveness. It is one of the natural fruits of international strife, as can be seen in the Near East in our twentieth century. But not every Jew was overwhelmed by this retaliatory spirit. There were some who saw Israel in a very different light—as God's special, suffering messengers to the whole of humanity. They lifted their minority voices to give song to their differing vision; and the result is writings like Isaiah 40–55, the Book of Ruth, and our present Book of Jonah.

Once again, however, we should be alert to notice that the purpose of the book is not to create in us the opinion—perhaps correct—that it is a parable written to convey an unpopular truth in a fear- and hate-ridden time; its purpose is to prick the bubble of our pride and prejudice, and to show us that we are not to be obsessed with our own rights, but with God's love to all men. This truth must come home to us, convict us of sin, and call us to a new commitment.

MAIN THEMES

1. God's love and concern for all peoples: his desire to bring all to repentance and to forgive all.

2. The nature of God's election: not to special privilege but to sacrificial service.

3. The judgment that falls upon those who interpret God's purposes narrowly and selfishly.

4. The absurdity of many of the petty concerns of supposedly religious people.

KEY VERSE

As to the key verse of this humanitarian, missionary document, we cannot be in doubt for an instant: "That is why I made haste to flee to Tarshish; for I knew that thou art a gracious God and merciful, slow to anger, and abounding in steadfast love, and repentest of evil" (Jonah 4:2b). Notice that this verse contains not only the wideness of God's mercy but Jonah's attempt to flee from the claim of that mercy upon him.

II. PREPARING YOUR BOOK SERMON

CARDINAL IDEA

When God, in his love for all men, confronts us with his call to serve the people we tend to exclude, we, because of our human prejudice, try to flee from his demand; but God overtakes us, exposes our pettiness, and calls us to a wider sympathy. Righteous people who profess to serve God will find their prejudices against their fellows coming under God's judgment.

SHAPING A PREACHING OUTLINE

To begin with, make sure that your subject is correctly limited. The subject is not "The Fatherhood of God" or "The Brotherhood of Man." It is more restricted and more specific than that. It is "The Judgment of a Universal God upon a Narrow and Prejudiced Servant." The "servant" may be a church or an individual, any group or person acknowledging God's sovereignty and claiming to serve him as human agent. And the purpose of the sermon is to bring conviction of sin to us for our prejudice against our particular brand of "Assyrians"—Negroes, Mexicans, Japanese, Poles, Russians—whoever they may be. Further, the purpose should be to lead us out of our prejudice toward the wideness of God's concern for our enemies. God loves and yearns for the very people we despise the most! And he wants us to serve them!

One good approach may be a story-sermon. Begin by mastering the book for a public reading or retelling. If the situation is sufficiently informal, and if the practice of your church will allow it, much can be gained from a group reading. The cast includes: Narrator, Captain, Sailor (a spokesman for the crew), Jonah, Royal Herald, and God. Thus, the book may be presented in three ways: by yourself, read from the Bible; as a story told from memory; or as a group reading. Follow the reading with a brief sermonette, eight to twelve minutes long, driving home the main point of the story and applying it to our contemporary situation.

The structure of the book is itself a good basis for a sermon outline: (1) when God calls us to cross lines of prejudice, we rebel and flee from him; (2) he pursues and overtakes us, to save us from destroying ourselves and also to confront us with our hated responsibility; (3) people turn to God almost in spite of us, and God accepts as his own those whom we have rejected as brothers; (4) meantime, while we wallow in our misery of hate and self-pity, God shows us our pettiness and lets us glimpse his own magnanimity. Thus we have a sermon with four major points, each stated by seeing Jonah as a symbol of any man in any time who claims to be God's servant.

Here, under the title of "My Brother Faraway" is a sermon outline by a student. The word "faraway" expresses social distance, not miles: (1) we see the man "faraway" as a foreigner; God sees him as our brother; (2) we, refusing God's view, flee from our brother; God overtakes us and confronts us with our diminishing selves; (3) we, giving in to God, return to discover our brother; God, binding our brother to us, increases us.

A two-point outline might well stress: (1) the narrowness of man's sympathies (the Jonah spirit did not die in the Old Testament); (2) the wideness of God's mercy (which includes us, even though we are in rebellion against God, and the brother whom we try to exclude and make into an enemy).

Do not seek a too-easy resolution of the conflict that is going on between Jonah and God, and the conflict that is going on within the half-repentant soul of Jonah. The book closes on that note. Perhaps the sermon should also close there: Will we, imprisoned within our prejudices, ever outgrow them, or will we end our days in selfishness and self-pity? This is a sermon that will have to be finished out of the church, each member writing his own conclusion in his own life's blood.

A MODERN TITLE

To "The Wideness of God's Mercy" and "My Brother Faraway" add these: "Your God is Too Small," "Running Away from God," and "A Man of Prejudice."

29

THE SHAME OF THE CITIES

The Book of Micah

IN THE cities, civilizations flower—and fade. In the cities, the arts and crafts of man ripen—and rot. An America which has made the full shift from a rural to an urban economy cannot avoid the delights and the dangers of urbanization, and suburbanization. For this reason it would be good for a modern city to play host to a disturbing rustic from the Judaean countryside, the same rustic who invaded Jerusalem seven hundred years before Christ and spoke the telling words recorded in the Book of Micah.

I. WORKING YOUR WAY INTO THE BOOK

HISTORICAL SETTING

According to the Book of Jeremiah, the prophecy of Micah occurred during the reign of King Hezekiah of Judah:
Read Jeremiah 26:18–19.
Hezekiah's reign lasted from 715 to 687 B.C. The title to the Book of Micah—not a part of the original book but added centuries later, in all probability—assigns Micah a slightly longer range:
Read Micah 1:1.
The three kings mentioned, Jotham, Ahaz, and Hezekiah, had combined reigns extending from 742 to 687 B.C. These dates cover the period of Assyrian resurgence in the west under the military emperors Tiglath-pileser III, Sargon II, and Sennacherib. Before their onslaught Damascus fell in 732 B.C., Samaria in 722 B.C., a Palestinian coalition (not including Judah) in 711 B.C., and Judah herself almost fell in 701 B.C. Thus the critical dates for Judah are

711 B.C. and 701 B.C.; it is thought that Micah did most of his preaching just before these two dates. For a biblical account of the events of 701 B.C.:

Read 2 Kings 18:13—19:37; Isaiah 36, 37.

Sennacherib recorded this campaign himself on the six-sided Prism of Sennacherib (now in the Oriental Institute of the University of Chicago); he said that he besieged and captured forty-six strongholds of Judah, which he placed under the puppet kings of Philistia. And then he shut up Hezekiah "like a bird in a cage in the midst of Jerusalem, his royal city." The siege of Lachish, one of the forty-six strongholds, was memorialized in an impressive Assyrian bas-relief now in the possession of the Palestine Archaeological Museum in Jerusalem, Jordan. The Greek historian Herodotus reports that the Assyrian army was decimated on this campaign by a plague of mice— that would have been the bubonic plague—and that for this reason Sennacherib pulled out of the region without invading Egypt. Piecing together the information from these three sources—the Bible, the Assyrian archaeological record, and Herodotus—we arrive at an outline picture something like the following: Sennacherib invaded Palestine to put down a pro-Egyptian, anti-Assyrian coalition; in process he stormed and took the villages and cities of Judah, whereupon Hezekiah sent him a heavy tribute, thinking to avoid the siege of Jerusalem. Sennacherib accepted the tribute and then, perversely, laid siege to Jerusalem anyway.[1] But disease decimated the Assyrian ranks and delivered the city. Judah was saved by a hairbreadth to live for more than a century.

The Man Micah

Micah was a native of Moresheth, a town of the Shephelah bordering on Philistia and looking toward Egypt. Life in this frontier village may have made the prophet unusually sensitive to the precarious international situation, which turned the Palestinian states into pawns in the tug of war between Assyria and Egypt. Micah curiously combined a world view with a stout loyalty to the country

[1] Some scholars have suggested that the mention of Tirhakah in 2 Kings 19:9 indicates the possibility of another Assyrian invasion, to be dated between 689 and 686 B.C. This would eliminate the charge of treachery against Sennacherib.

and the village and its common people. City life was repulsive to him. He was much like Amos, his older contemporary who lived some twenty miles to the east. Two centuries earlier, Micah's home town had produced the prophet Eliezer, who had spoken against king Jehoshaphat:

Read 2 Chronicles 20:37.

Micah was contemporary to Hosea and Isaiah as well as to Amos. There is no indication that he ever met any of them, though he is enough like Amos to have been influenced strongly by him or his writings, and in his social preaching he was solidly in agreement with Isaiah. It seems not unlikely that Micah and Isaiah should receive the credit for Hezekiah's change of heart as recorded in 2 Kings 18–19, and for the religious reforms which followed. The elders of Jerusalem a century later attributed great influence to Micah (Jer. 26:17–19).

MILITARY CONTAGION

In the light of the background just given, we may read the first chapter of Micah with quick discernment:

Read Micah 1:2–16.

Micah foresees a military invasion of Judah like that which destroyed Samaria and ended Israel's national history in 722 B.C. He represents conquest as a kind of epidemic, fatal in the north and now spreading south. The roll call of Judaean cities in verses 10–15 lists some of the towns falling under Sennacherib's sword in 701 B.C. This poem contains a series of Hebrew puns, somewhat obscured through copying, and altogether lost in most English translations. For a hint at the original force of the play upon words, read the poem in Moffatt's translation.

SOCIAL CAUSES

But the military calamity about to befall Judah did not root in militarism and politics, except as these reflected a deeper cause. It rooted in social injustice, and this in turn grew in the soil of the big city: "What is the transgression of Jacob? Is it not Samaria? And what is the sin of the house of Judah? Is it not Jerusalem?" (Mic.

1:5b). As the city was divorced from the country, so its leaders were separated from the common people, turning them from fellow citizens into subjects, and from subjects into victims:

Read Micah 2:1–2.

The greedy rich make themselves richer at the expense of their fellows. The princes join these rich exploiters:

Read Micah 3:1–4, 9–11.

Nowhere in the Bible, and perhaps nowhere in all literature, will you find social injustice denounced with stronger invective. Here are shepherds who turn into wolves, devouring the flocks they are sworn to protect.

The prophets have deserted their calling as spokesmen of God and have become high priests of vested interest. They are themselves corrupted by wealth:

Read Micah 3:5–8.

Thus, social criticism all but ceased in Jerusalem. And the rightful leaders of the people—the leading property holders, the princes, and the prophets—had become public enemies.

Micah did not belong to the "prophets' guild," nor to their way of thinking. He did not subscribe to the cult of assurance. Consequently, against much official opposition he spoke his burning words of social criticism:

Read Micah 2:6–11.

Nevertheless, through irresistible conviction Micah felt compelled to speak. Micah's word was doom, judgment.

JUDGMENT AT GOD'S HOUSE

Read Micah 2:3–5; 3:12.

The fate of Israel, now dispersed in Assyrian captivity, was about to fall upon Judah. Micah thought his native country was living its last hours. His contemporaries, the comfortable prophets, taught that this could not come to pass because Judah was a chosen nation and God would be discredited if anything happened to them. But Micah did not see God as dependent on Judah; he was universal Lord of righteousness, ruler of history who had to judge his Chosen People with special severity if they flaunted his justice. The death of Judah would not discredit God under such circumstances; it would only vindicate and exalt him.

The fate of the big city, as pictured in the last verse of chapter 3, is the irony of history. The big city disdained the country, used it as its market and its food bin, its slave mart; but in the end, the country reclaimed the city: grass grew in the streets, saplings thrust up through the pavements and became the trees of a forest; and its citizens were birds and wild animals.

MAIN THEMES

We have already discussed the main themes of the first three chapters—those of the prophet Micah himself. It remains only to list them by way of summary.

1. *The crime of the big city.* Micah saw Jerusalem as the exploiter of the country.

2. *The injustice of the leaders.* Both princes and priests exercised power to their own advantage and at the expense of the people.

3. *The judgment of God.* This judgment would take the form of destruction to Jerusalem and its Temple. Judah, like Israel before her, would be dispersed in captivity.

KEY VERSES

The whole message of Micah up to this point seems to be gathered into a few verses, 3:9–12.

ADDITIONAL THEMES

A careful reader of the present Book of Micah may well feel that the prophecy of Micah of Moresheth must have ended with Micah 3:12. The atmosphere of the rest of the book is so different, as though later passages had been added by many hands over a long period of time, even beyond the Babylonian Exile. These additions may be catalogued under four main headings.

1. *An extension of Micah's words of indictment and judgment.* Scattered through the second half of the book are several passages which are soundly in keeping with the first three chapters. The words enlarge our picture of general injustice and corruption, and reaffirm the inevitability of judgment:

Read (in this order) Micah 6:9–16; 7:1–7; 5:10–15.

We cannot deny that these words could have come from the original prophet, but as is the case with some other biblical books, they may have been added by a disciple. At any rate, they have the authentic ring.

2. *Judah on trial before God.* There is a passage in which Judah is represented as the defendant in a court trial in which God himself is the plaintiff:

Read Micah 6:1–8.

This is a sublime passage. In spite of the courtroom metaphor, there is a winsomeness, a tenderness here not discerned in the rest of the book. The thought seems more nearly akin to that of Hosea. God pleads, reveals his love, begs for his people to repent. God shows himself not only as Judge but as Redeemer. There is demand in this passage but there is also implicit promise. Although there is nothing here that contradicts Micah 1–3, the mood is different. The passage constitutes an enlargement of the spirit and thought of the book. And the lyrical words of 6:8 appeal so deeply and so truly to most readers that these readers at once nominate them as the golden text of the whole book.

3. *Visions of the future.* The bulk of material in chapters 4–7 deals with the restoration of Judah following the Exile; they paint a picture of God's universal kingdom in a world at peace. But they do not all derive from the same mood. Some are vindictive and imperialistic; others are much more universalistic and humanitarian. It seems wise to make some analysis.

Read Micah 4:9–10.

These words picture the Babylonian captivity begun and ended. And they are followed in the text by a stentorian call for vengeance:

Read Micah 4:11–13.

These words are nationalistic, even chauvinistic in spirit. They call for a vast, punitive war against all the nations of the world, with Judah emerging as victor and ruler. This same spirit is discerned in other passages:

Read Micah 5:5–9; 7:8–10.

This pictures a world at peace because it has suffered a knockout blow from the mailed fist of Judah. Other passages envision Jerusalem as a world capital, but on a very different basis:

Read (in this order) Micah 7:11–13, 16–17; 4:8.

The nations here are drawn to Judah; they are won, not conquered by force. Persuasion rather than coercion assures a spiritual kingdom.

The theme of the remnant is also sounded, and with it the theme of restoration:

Read Micah 2:12–13; 4:5–7; 7:14–15.

Quite naturally coupled with such visions of restoration and universal kingdom is the vision of the future king, the Messiah:

Read Micah 5:1–4.

This passage was familiar to the early Christians and was much quoted by them. And this, in turn, is surely in keeping with a vision of universal peace:

Read Micah 4:1–4; Isaiah 2:2–4.

Curiously enough, the same lyrical addition was made both to the Book of Micah and to the Book of Isaiah. This vision of a warless world under God is still too great for our small hearts. Through wars and armistices, through League of Nations and United Nations, it beckons us and we follow on, still seeking.

4. *The forgiving mercy of God.* The final addition, in our analysis, is also the final passage of the book. It is a kind of doxology:

Read Micah 7:18–20.

The accent here is upon the grace of God in forgiveness and redemption. As it was God's first word to his Chosen People in the deliverance from Egypt, so it is the final word of the book. God's grace surrounds his people as past experience and as future promise.

OUTLINE OF THE BOOK OF MICAH[2]

I. Background of Micah's prophecies, 1:1–4
   A. Introductory heading, 1:1
   B. An eschatological psalm, 1:2–4
II. Discourses on the Assyrian crisis, 1:5–16
   A. The wailing prophet, 1:5–9
   B. The alarm, 1:10–16
III. Prophecies of ethical concern, 2:1—3:12
   A. The Jerusalem men of wealth, 2:1–10
   B. Love for false prophets, 2:11
   C. Dreams of restoration, 2:12–13

[2] Rolland E. Wolfe in *The Interpreter's Bible,* Vol. VI, p. 900.

D. Appeal to the leaders of Judah, 3:1–12

IV. Visions of a glorious future, 4:1—5:15
   A. Universal religion and perpetual peace, 4:1–8
   B. The way of monarchy, militarism, and vengeance, 4:9—5:6
   C. A world of purity, blessing, and benediction, 5:7–15

V. Adversity that triumphs in hope, 6:1—7:20
   A. God's controversy with his wayward people, 6:1–5
   B. Incidentals or fundamentals in religion, 6:6–8
   C. The Deity's final plea to Jerusalem, 6:9–16
   D. The pessimism of despair, 7:1–6
   E. The invincible triumph of faith, 7:7–20

KEY VERSES

A key passage, appropriate to the second cardinal idea below, is 6:6–8, the acknowledged golden text of the Book of Micah.

II. PREPARING YOUR BOOK SERMON

The most difficult problem facing the preacher is the problem of the book's unity. The word of Micah of Moresheth seems to have been one of judgment. This word was later enlarged, principally by visions of restoration and universal kingdom. How shall we present Micah, in terms of the living prophet or on the basis of the present book? We suggest that either approach is both legitimate and rewarding.

CARDINAL IDEA

1. Of Micah the prophet: *The shame of the big cities spells death; God's righteousness cannot be flaunted.* A civilization ripens in cities; but this is where a civilization also begins to rot. God seems more remote from city people, but he is really in the midst of the city judging her life by his righteous standards.

2. Of the present Book of Micah, expanded by editors and disciples: *A society of injustice and war with its deep inhumanities and its serious cataclysms can give way to a new order of peace and justice when all men acknowledge the prior claims of a righteous God.*

SHAPING A PREACHING OUTLINE

Seeking key passages for the two differing emphases just traced in the two cardinal ideas given above, one finds Micah 3:9–12 perfectly suited to the first and Micah 4:1–4 just as well fitted to the second. Also suited to the second cardinal idea (presenting the whole Book of Micah) is a combination of passages, 3:1–12 and 6:6–8.

A sermon on the whole Book of Micah should have two parts: (1) the shame of the big city leading to decay and downfall; (2) the resurrection of that same big city as the center of faith, justice, and world peace. Micah's vision may be made the basis for a searching sermon on the life of a modern city. To what extent is it liable to Micah's indictment? To what extent responsive to his vision?

A sermon on the original message of Micah the prophet (as differentiated from the whole book) might follow a suggestion of Carl Hanley, a former student of mine: (1) the city eats up the country; (2) then the country reclaims the city. Urbanization and suburbanization spell out real dangers to a nation. There are primitive heritages in the soil and in the rural economy that may be lost, to the moral peril of a people and to their ultimate ruin.

A sermon on the whole book might be developed with the five main themes as separate divisions. These are (1) the corruptions of the cities; (2) the call for justice and true religion; (3) the judgment of God upon Judah; (4) the restoration through a remnant; (5) the vision of a world at peace.

A MODERN TITLE

"Of Pride and Privilege," "Darkness at Noon," "Internal Enemies" and "The Shame of the Cities" come to mind as possible titles.

30

CORPSE IN ARMOR

The Book of Nahum

Assyria fell at the zenith of her military power. The deathblow was struck in 612 B.C. In June of that year Cyaxares of Media and Nabopolassar of Babylon joined forces to attack Nineveh, the Assyrian capital; in August, the city fell. Assyria was a spent force, a victim of her own militarism. Arnold J. Toynbee pictures the fall in an unforgettable figure: "The indomitable warrior who stood at bay in the breach at Nineveh in 612 was 'a corpse in armour', whose frame was only held erect by the massiveness of the military ac-coutrements in which this *felo de se* had smothered himself to death."[1]

The biblical Book of Nahum is a gleeful Jewish shout of triumph over the fallen corpse of a defeated Assyria. As such it probably reflected the pent-up feelings of the entire civilized world; all could join Nahum's exultant song:

> All who hear the news of you
> clap their hands over you.
> For upon whom has not come
> your unceasing evil?
> [Nah. 3:19]

I. WORKING YOUR WAY INTO THE BOOK

Occasion

Assyria had ruled the world for two and a half centuries, half of

[1] Arnold J. Toynbee, *A Study of History*, abridged by D. C. Somervell (New York: Oxford University Press, 1947), p. 342.

that time through terrorism. In her heyday, it was "Assyria over all."

> Multiply yourselves like the locust,
>   multiply like the grasshopper!
> You increased your merchants
>   more than the stars of the heavens.
> [Nah. 3:15b–16a]

And the Assyrian dominion was a bloody one: siege, capture, sacking and burning, captivity, the pulverization of resistance through the mixing of peoples. Ten tribes of Israel were obliterated from history by this means. This last policy is vividly reflected in the Assyrian action after the overthrow of Samaria in 722 B.C.:

Read 2 Kings 17:23b–24.

Nahum pictures the Assyrian reign of terror in several lines of his poem:

> The lion tore enough for his whelps
>   and strangled prey for his lionesses;
> he filled his caves with prey
>   and his dens with torn flesh.
> [Nah. 2:12]

> Woe to the bloody city,
> all full of lies and booty—
> no end to the plunder!
> [Nah. 3:1]

Let us turn again to Arnold J. Toynbee's fascinating account of this predator in *A Study of History:*

When we gaze back over the century-and-a-half of ever more virulent warfare . . . the historical landmarks which stand out at first sight are the successive knock-out blows by which Assyria destroyed entire communities—razing cities to the ground and carrying whole populations away captive: Damascus in 732, Samaria in 722, Musasir in 714, Babylon in 689, Sidon in 677, Memphis in 671, Thebes in 663, Susa *circa* 639. Of all the capital cities of all the states within reach of Assyria's arm, only Tyre and Jerusalem remained inviolate at the time of the sack of Nineveh herself in 612.[2]

The sack of Thebes is explicitly mentioned in Nahum's poem.

[2] P. 341.

Through this allusion to a past act of destruction done by Assyria, the prophet is saying, "The evil that you have done to others has now come upon you."

Read Nahum 3:8–13.

Toynbee tells us that all of Assyria's victims "struggled back to life, and some of them had great futures ahead of them. Nineveh alone fell dead and never rose again."[3]

DATE AND AUTHOR

Nahum seems to have written his poem in the very midst of the siege, though the fall of Nineveh was still in the future (Nah. 2:13; 3:5–7, 11, 15). Thus the book may be dated about 612 B.C. This makes Nahum a contemporary of Zephaniah, Habakkuk, and Jeremiah. Unfortunately we know nothing about him except what is shown by the book itself, for he is not mentioned outside his own writing.

COMPOSITION

The Book of Nahum is composed of two poems. The longer of the two, chapters 2 and 3, is directly related to the siege of Nineveh. This longer poem has no chronological structure, but it does dwell upon a few major themes: the attack, the crimes of Nineveh, the flight and capture of the armies and people, the destruction of the city. By a slight rearrangement of verses these may be read in an order of approximate sequence:

1. The attack: Nahum 2:1–5; 3:1–3.
2. The crimes of Nineveh: Nahum 2:11–13; 3:1, 4.
3. The flight and capture of the people: Nahum 2:6–10.
4. The capture and destruction of the city: Nahum 3:8–17.

Here we have the picture of the self-defeat of triumphant militarism, the end of an empire without moral reason to continue—weak in its panoply of power:

> All your fortresses are like fig trees
>   with first-ripe figs—
>   if shaken they fall

[3] *Ibid.*

into the mouth of the eater.
Behold your troops
are women in your midst.
[Nah. 3:12–13]

The second poem in the book, in point of composition, is chapter 1. This preface to the main part of the book was apparently constructed by reworking an earlier acrostic (alphabetical) poem on the wrathful vengeance of God; in subject matter it includes not only war but calamities of Nature like whirlwind, storm, earthquake, and flood (Nah. 1:3b, 6b, 8). Moreover, it dwells not alone upon the wrath of God against his enemies but includes some lyrical passages on the mercy of God toward his friends (Nah. 1:7, 12, 15).

Although there are clear indications of the reasons for Nineveh's fall in the long poem, the cause becomes still more explicit in the short one. It is ethical:

Read Nahum 1:2, 3, 9, 14.

To put it bluntly: Assyria perished because her life became a moral stench in the nostrils of the Almighty.

MAIN THEMES

1. The weakness of militarism when it becomes the foremost concern of national policy.

2. The sovereignty of God over nations.

3. The judgment of God upon predatory nations.

Nahum is honest in his emotion. He allows himself to feel glee over a fallen foe; and then he has the courage to relate this genuine emotion to his religion. Certainly he is right, as far as he goes. Assyria perished under God's judgment for her manifold crimes. But it did not follow that Israel's problems were solved by the fall of Nineveh. Jerusalem does not stand because Nineveh falls; in less than a quarter of a century Jerusalem would lie in ruins. Israel is not approved at the bar of justice because Assyria is condemned. The chastisement of exile for Judah was even then in the making. "Judgment begins at the house of God." It is not the vocation of a godly people to stand forever pointing blame at others. Nor is it their place to fight the enemy with his own weapons.

There is much in Nahum that makes it difficult for us to see his positive message. He is nationalistic, even chauvinistic. Certainly his poem is no lofty peak of the Bible; but it is a genuine foothill of God's truth. From the eminence of the Sermon on the Mount we need to see that truth clearly, and then, with the Teacher of the Mount pointing the way, we need to see farther.

KEY VERSES

Woe to the bloody city,
all full of lies and booty—
no end to the plunder!

. . . .

There is no assuaging your hurt,
    your wound is grievous.
All who hear the news of you
    clap their hands over you.
For upon whom has not come
    your unceasing evil?
                    [Nah. 3:1, 19]

II. PREPARING YOUR BOOK SERMON

CARDINAL IDEA

Military prowess becomes suicidal to a nation bent upon conquering and victimizing its neighbors; God, in moral righteousness, will overthrow such a power.

SHAPING A PREACHING OUTLINE

Most Christian preachers will want to speak on "the message and the silence of Nahum." They will want to deal with the message *of* the book and then add their own Christian message *about* the book. This should make a good two-point sermon. Assyria was a Great Power, the most frightening military power in antiquity. She spread her rule over the world, holding nations as securely and cruelly as Russia holds her satellites today.

Nevertheless, Assyria fell; and she fell not when her military machine was in decline but when it was at the apex of its efficiency. Arnold J. Toynbee assures us of this: "The Assyrian war-machine

. . . was continuously overhauled, renovated and reinforced right down to the day of its destruction."[4] Here we have history's repudiation of the dictum that God is on the side of the largest battalions. Rather, this slice of history underscores two contrary dictums: (1) "Whom the Gods would destroy they first make mad."[5] (2) "Though the mills of God grind slowly, yet they grind exceeding small."[6]

When we look at world politics, we need the assurance that God is in history; and that "God will not always chide; neither will he hold his anger forever." At the same time—and here the Christian preacher will speak where Nahum is silent—we may well be worshiping the gods of our enemies. Militarism looks very different from our side of the curtain: in us it is "national defense," "national security"; but in our enemies it is "warmongering." The United States has not yet overcome the surprise of Sputnik I and Sputnik II. Before that time we had supposed that our superior military might would induce the Soviets to abandon their race in armaments. We still seem to feel that our might should make them trust us and feel peaceful and secure. But what effect did the specter of their military superiority have on us? It activated us into a militaristic frenzy. We did not rest until we had thrust a rival moon into orbit and had begun a race for the first rocket to the moon. Military cutbacks ceased; the armament race was renewed. Increasingly, since World War II, our national policy has been evolved out of expediency rather than from principle. Our intervention in the Suez crisis, in spite of our responsibility for helping to create the crisis, was a welcome deviation from this policy of bolstering French imperialism and winking at Spanish fascism. A nation more concerned with the balance of power than with international justice is a weakening nation, even if that nation is our own country. It is easy for us, looking across curtains and boundaries, to see the weaknesses of militarism and power politics. We can even see God at work in the judgment of other nations. When will we have the Christlikeness and the courage to apply those lessons to ourselves?

A second approach to sermon outline will follow the topics of the

---

[4] *Ibid.,* p. 338.

[5] Henry Wadsworth Longfellow, *The Masque of Pandora,* VI.

[6] Longfellow, *Poetic Aphorisms: Retribution,* translated from *Sinngedichte* by Friedrich von Logau.

Book of Nahum, arranging them in some such fashion as the following: (1) the power and dominion of a "great" nation; (2) the crimes of the "great" nation; (3) God against the "great" nation; (4) the judgment and downfall of that nation.

A third approach will use one of the best-known sayings of Jesus as the basis of outline: ". . . for all who take the sword will perish by the sword." The sermon will have two points: (1) taking the sword; (2) perishing by the sword.

A Modern Title

"The Mills of God," "Worshiping the Gods of Our Enemies," "How Are the Mighty Fallen!" and "The Nemesis of Militarism" are among the titles that may occur to you.

31

MAN'S DOUBT AND GOD'S ANSWER
The Book of Habakkuk

DOES it pay to be good? Faith says Yes; but there is a mountain of evidence to the contrary. The Psalmist proclaims the affirmation of faith:

> Truly God is good to the upright,
>   to those who are pure in heart.
> [Ps. 73:1]

Nevertheless, there is a huge stumbling block in the way of his faith:

> But as for me, my feet are almost stumbled,
>   my steps had well nigh slipped.
> For I was envious of the arrogant,
>   when I saw the prosperity of the wicked.
>
> . . . .
>
> Behold, these are the wicked;
>   always at ease, they increase in riches.
> [Ps. 73:2, 3, 12]

And so the doubt which is hurled aside by the affirmation of faith returns and will not be vanquished:

> All in vain have I kept my heart clean
>   and washed my hands in innocence.
> [Ps. 73:13]

This theme—the prosperity of the wicked and the suffering of the righteous in God's world—is well known to Scripture. We find it in Psalms 37 and 49 as well as in the psalm we have just been quoting. We find it in Jeremiah's complaint (Jer. 12:1-6) and in the cosmic drama of Job. The question will not die. Whether we ask it on the

223

domestic scene with individuals in view or on the world scene with nations in mind, we seem unable to escape it. All of us—each man in his own place and time—must face the issue and grapple with it; for this is the ultimate testing of faith, man's deepest encounter with himself and with his God.

Prophet Habakkuk asks the question, honestly and persistently. He does not find the whole answer; that will have to wait upon the vision of the Suffering Servant and upon the cross of Christ. Nevertheless, Habakkuk does find an answer which is universal and valid. Let us acquaint ourselves with it.

I. WORKING YOUR WAY INTO THE BOOK

THE FIRST QUESTION

The Book of Habakkuk is cast largely in the form of a dialogue between a doubting prophet and his God. The prophet begins with a question which amounts to a complaint:

Read Habakkuk 1:1–4.

Violence, wrongs, destruction, injustice—against the righteous. That is the situation. The prophet cries to his God for help to right these wrongs, but no help comes; God does not answer. So great is the prophet's courage and his candor: he complains to his God for this seeming flaw in the divine justice.

What is the scene? We are not told exactly. It may be domestic or international. Habakkuk may be complaining about the injustice of the wealthy against Judah's poor, repeating the charges of Micah; pleading on behalf of the downtrodden Jew, suffering at the hands of his own greedy brother. Or he may have been complaining about the tyranny of some foreign power over his beloved homeland. Time after time Judah writhed under the heel of an oppressor—Egypt, Assyria, Babylon, Persia, Greece, Rome. The injustices of foreign occupation and alien rule are notorious in any age, and more cruel in some quarters than in others. Most commonly it has been supposed that Habakkuk was writing as the seventh century B.C. turned into the sixth, when Assyria was going down and Babylon was rising. But there is some evidence that the book, or parts of it, may have come after the lightning conquests of Alexander the Great, late in the fourth century.

Whatever the period, there was domestic injustice enough and foreign tyranny aplenty. Almost any period in the history of the Jews reflects conditions against which a prophet could lift his cry. And not in Judah alone. Jewish synagogues have been dynamited in Jacksonville, Florida, and Nashville, Tennessee. A Negro youth has been castrated in Alabama. Delinquents turn schools into "blackboard jungles" in New York City. Russia has crushed tiny Hungary like a bear swatting a fly. Habakkuk's question is for all times and all places—for this time of prejudice and tyranny most of all, perhaps:

> O Lord, how long shall I cry for help,
>   and thou wilt not hear?
> Or cry to thee "Violence!"
>   and thou wilt not save?
>   [Hab. 1:2]

THE ANSWER

God's answer comes. He is preparing an instrument of his justice who will sweep down upon the wicked and punish them.
Read Habakkuk 1:5–11.

This is not a new idea. Isaiah had expressed an identical thought regarding Assyria:
Read Isaiah 10:5–7.

It had been furthest from Assyria's intention to serve God. Assyria had been, in fact, a godless nation. But even so, Assyria had served as a rod in God's hand, used by the Almighty to deal out his judgment in history upon the unrighteous. Now, Habakkuk is learning, what God had done with Assyria in the day of Isaiah, he is again doing with another nation.

The nation is named—Chaldea. This would be Babylon. But we must remember that the names of nations are sometimes used covertly in the Bible. Both 1 Peter and Revelation use the name of Babylon, as a cryptogram for Rome. Perhaps something of the same thing is happening in the Book of Habakkuk. At any rate, the authors of the commentary on Habakkuk that was found among the Dead Sea Scrolls understood him to be referring to the Greeks. Moreover, the text of Habakkuk 2:5 is uncertain; the word which is rendered "wine" could, with a very slight change of letters, become "the Greek." Then the meaning would become quite clear, more consistent than it now appears to be. Charles L. Taylor, Jr., renders the verse as follows:

> How much more treacherous is the Greek,
>   the arrogant one, who stays not at home!
> Greedy as hell,
>   insatiable as death,
> Who gathers to himself all nations
>   and collects to himself all peoples.[1]

Whether it is Nebuchadnezzar or Alexander the Great, God is taking this godless conqueror in hand and using him as an instrument of his divine judgment in history. In the same way, we shall have to say, he has used Caesar and Napoleon, Hitler, and Stalin.

The Second Question

Such an answer leaves the questioner more deeply unsatisfied than ever. And it gives rise to a more painful question, probing even deeper:

Read Habakkuk 1:12–2:1.

Men who are drunk with empire, thirsting for still more blood, perpetrate unspeakable cruelties. How can we think of them as God's instruments? Granted that a man or a nation needs to be punished, what if the punisher is more evil than the one he chastises? Suppose he perpetrates wrongs more magnitudinous than any we have done? Where is the justice in that? Where is the work of God in such an apparent anomaly?

A man can be so submerged in his own outraged sense of justice, in such a plight that he will see nothing, hear nothing of God. He must somehow keep his head, rise sufficiently above his predicament to listen for an answer; this is his watchtower. "O Lord, I believe. Help thou my unbelief!"

The Answer—Negative

Read Habakkuk 2:2–20.

The heart of God's answer to Habakkuk's second question is a single verse:

[1] *The Interpreter's Bible*, Vol. VI, p. 991.

Behold, he whose soul is not upright in him shall fail,
but the righteous shall live by his faith.
[Hab. 2:4]

This verse has both a negative and a positive side. The negative is elaborated in the verses that follow and takes the form of five *woes* upon the wicked conqueror:

1. The first woe: crushed to earth, the victims finally rise in revolt (Hab. 2:6–8).

2. The second woe: predatory security will crumble, no matter how it fortifies itself (Hab. 2:9–11).

3. The third woe: fire will beget fire, for there is a moral order in the universe; God alone is sovereign (Hab. 2:12–14).

4. The fourth woe: tyranny degrades the tyrant even more than it degrades the slave; cruelty is ultimate suicide (Hab. 2:15–17).

5. The fifth woe: He who worships the gods he has manufactured will discover that his gods have no power to deliver him from his own time of troubles (Hab. 2:18–19).

These five woes are summarized in one dynamic principle: the self-destruction of tyrannical cruelty. Evil is broken on the rock of God's rule. Such an answer is reassuring to faith; but it is not easily accepted. It is a justice which "seems slow" (Hab. 2:3). We wait so long for it. Moreover, realism teaches us that one tyrant gives way to another; and the weary cycle is again repeated. Assyria dies a military suicide of her own successes; but Babylon rises and makes the Chosen People captives and exiles. Persia comes as a deliverer to set these people free; but Greece boots Persia into oblivion and becomes the new master. Stalin helps us dispose of Hitler; then Stalin and his successors become more evil than many Hitlers. Yes, we wait; the vision awaits its time.

THE ANSWER—POSITIVE

The positive part of God's answer is brief, almost enigmatic: ". . . the righteous shall live by his faith." Martin Luther turned this verse into the Protestant doctrine of justification by faith. It seems clear that he was reading his own meanings into the verse, at least to some extent.

The righteous man looks forward to the time of vindication; it is only human for him to do so, and it is just. But he must live in the meantime, and he discovers that not all is lost. He can live, though ridden by injustice and evil; he can live to the extent that God becomes real for him. And so the chapter ends, appropriately, in the temple:

> But the Lord is in his holy temple;
> let all the earth keep silence before him.
> [Hab. 2:20]

This is where the original book ended. The third chapter, added later to amplify the positive answer of chapter 2:4, is a psalm of praise in which the poet sees God with the eye of faith and comes to accept fellowship with his God as a benefit greater than prosperity. We end with a picture of one who is "poor, yet making many rich." We are on the threshold of the great insights into the redemptive role of suffering for righteousness' sake. We glimpse the reason why the spiritual highlights in a war of conquest are found not on thrones or even on battlefields but in prisons and concentration camps. The man who has the courage to go there for his convictions, like a Martin Niemöller or an Eivind Berggrav, has found something more precious than success and dominion.

If we follow out the road on which Habakkuk has set our feet, it will bring us finally not to the throne room but to the cross. And the cross will bring us to God.

OUTLINE OF THE BOOK OF HABAKKUK

I.   Title, 1:1
II. The first question: Why does God permit injustice?
     A. The question, 1:2–4
     B. God's answer, 1:5–11
III. The second question: Granted that Judah needs correction, how can God justify his use of a still more evil nation (Chaldea) to administer the punishment?
     A. The question, 1:12—2:1
     B. God's answer, 2:2–20
          1. The answer in essence, 2:2–4
          2. Introduction to the woes of judgment, 2:5–6a
          3. The five woes of judgment upon the cruel tyrant, 2:6b–20
IV. A psalm of praise to God for his Majesty

A. Title, 3:1
B. Introduction, 3:2
C. A vision of God's coming in power, 3:3–15
D. Joy in the midst of adversity, 3:16–19

KEY VERSES

Some verses from Habakkuk stick in the memory. Among these, find: Habakkuk 2:3, 12, 14, 20. The central, key passage of the book can be no other than Habakkuk 2:4.

II. PREPARING YOUR BOOK SERMON

CARDINAL IDEA

In the midst of injustices and even in the midst of violence which injustices beget and multiply, God is the ruler, and the man of faith can find life in a new dimension, a joy in the very midst of adversity.

SHAPING A PREACHING OUTLINE

One thing that makes the modern application of Habakkuk difficult for an American preacher is that he lives under one of the world's two great political powers; the book is addressed to the members of a tiny nation, which had long been a victim of Great Powers. This sermon might better be preached by a citizen of one of the European countries, even of one of the Iron Curtain countries. Yet, at a deeper level, it may be possible for us to see the dialectic of history—righting injustices and doing so by violent means. The Bolshevist Revolution was a fearful evil, even though it had its part in ending the fearsome evil of Czarism. Nevertheless, it brought injustice to light on a global scale and forced a crisis in human relations which Western colonialism had long tolerated, unblinking. This is a time of turmoil and of crisis, a time in which great moral issues are at stake; and no one can read this time aright if he leaves God and his justice out of it. Neither can he face it or make sense of it without that deepening of individual justice and integrity which comes to him through those who find God, through those who see more in the human spirit than the hunger for bread and power.

The issues of Habakkuk are as real now as they were in antiquity. What are we to make of injustice and violence spread abroad and multiplied upon the face of the earth—the cruel, demonic, imaginative inhumanity of man to man, the racial wrong, the political tyranny, the economic want? Does God care about all this? What is he doing about it? Dare we read the apocalyptic events of purges and revolutions, of strikes and boycotts as a message from the Eternal? Is there any watchtower which will lift us high enough above the battle for us to see a vision from God relating to the strife? And, once we see it, are we willing to follow that vision where it leads us—beyond success, prosperity, even beyond concern for our own rights? Are we willing and able to turn to the inner resources which spell suffering rather than dominion, truth rather than power? Or do we, perhaps, long for our redemption without a Calvary?

One way of outlining the sermon on Habakkuk is to follow the development of the present chapter: (1) the prophet's question about injustice and violence, together with God's first answer; (2) the deeper perplexity which God's answer creates: How can God use the cruelty of a Babylon or a Russia to serve the cause of his justice? (3) God's double answer to this deeper question: (*a*) the impermanence of power-drunk peoples, and (*b*) the deep inner resources of real faith in God. This is essentially the way in which the Book of Habukkuk unfolds.

Another way of outlining the sermon would gather Habakkuk's two questions into one: (1) The question: (*a*) as first stated, and (*b*) as restated in the light of deepened understanding; (2) the social answer: (*a*) strife between nations and peoples as an arena of divine judgment, and (*b*) the self-destruction of power-drunk empires and societies; (3) the personal answer: (*a*) goals beyond immediate success and power, (*b*) the ability to tolerate crisis and chaos without disintegrating, and (*c*) abiding in God's presence and power.

A third approach could take its standpoint on the tower of Habakkuk 2:1, and envision what Habakkuk saw from that vantage point: (1) the injustice; (2) the punishment; (3) the new and more complicated injustices; (4) the final collapse of unjust powers; (5) the majesty of God in Nature and among nations; (6) the role of the faithful man.

A MODERN TITLE

Possible titles include: "How Does God Deal with Evildoers?" "Standing when the World is Falling" "Man's Doubt and God's Answer."

32

NO FAITH BUT FASHION

The Book of Zephaniah

Wearing foreign clothes and following foreign gods, Judah in the seventh century B.C. had turned its religion into a question of fashions. What are you believing this year? Judah's fashions in religion were borrowed from all her neighbors: Assyria (predominantly), Philistia, Ammon, Canaan. The result was an undermining skepticism with attendant corruption of morals: religion, religion everywhere, and not a thing to believe!

I. WORKING YOUR WAY INTO THE BOOK

AUTHOR

All that we know about the author is contained in the title (Zeph. 1:1). He was the great-great-grandson of King Hezekiah of Judah. This would make his contemporary, King Josiah, his second cousin. In other words, our prophet was a prince. He would also have been contemporary to Jeremiah.

DATE

The title tells us that Zephaniah preached "in the days of Josiah." Josiah's reign spanned the years 639–609 B.C. But we are able to narrow that date considerably. First, the conditions which Zephaniah attacked could have existed only before Josiah's reforms of 621 B.C. These are described in 2 Kings 22–23. Second, our extrabiblical knowledge of contemporary history draws our attention to the

Scythian invasions of 626 B.C. According to Herodotus, these bar-
barians swept down on horseback from their homeland north of
the Black Sea into the Middle and Near East, and in their ancient
version of blitzkrieg, killed, burned, and plundered everywhere.
They took the coastal route through Palestine to Egypt, but Pharaoh
Psamtik I bought immunity by bribing them heavily. (Does Zephaniah 1:18 contain an allusion to this bribery?) As it turned out,
the Scythians left Judah untouched; but while the raids were taking
place there could have been no assurance in Jewish hearts that Judah
would escape. It is possible that the Scythian invasion of 626 B.C.
lies in the immediate background of our book. Of late, some scholars
have questioned this.

THE TIMES OF ZEPHANIAH

Assyria was in control of Palestine. She was a harsh mistress.
Zephaniah's time, according to his own words, was characterized by
a religion adulterated with foreign admixtures from Canaanitish Baal,
from Assyria, and from Ammon and Philistia. This compounding of
a religion from many religions is known as syncretism. Note the
evidence of it:

Read Zephaniah 1:4–6, 9a, 12.

The "remnant of Baal" and "the idolatrous priests" are Canaanitish.
The "host of the heavens" refers to Assyrian star worship, and Mil-
com is an Ammonite deity. Leaping over the threshold is an element
from Philistine religion; see 1 Samuel 5:5. Syncretism usually results
in skepticism, reflected so well in Zephaniah 1:12. When there are
many faiths, the people tend to have little faith.

Apparently, along with the adoption of foreign religions, there
was a general tendency to assimilate the culture of Assyria. In other
words, there was cultural as well as political collaboration with the
Assyrian masters of Palestine. This showed up in the realm of
fashions:

Read Zephaniah 1:8.

In addition to the religious and cultural defection of Judah, there
was social corruption:

Read Zephaniah 1:9b, 12; 3:1–5.

Violence, fraud, oppression, profanation—such accusations are laid at the door of the princes and the priests. It is a time of injustice and immorality.

Until the reforms of Josiah in 621 B.C., the conditions created by King Manasseh's collaboration with the Assyrians prevailed in Judah. For a quick picture of these:
Read 2 Kings 22:1–9, 16.

Main Themes

Zephaniah's preaching was a fiery denunciation of the abuses we have just noticed, and the annunciation of an imminent judgment which would fall not just upon Judah but upon all nations. This judgment centers in the Day of the Lord:
Read Zephaniah 1:14–18.

We seem to have here an elaboration of the idea first presented to Israel in Amos 5:18–20. Clearly, Zephaniah envisioned a world cataclysm in which God would thresh the nations, saving the wheat and destroying the straw and chaff.
Read Zephaniah 1:2–3; 2:1–2.

The divine judgment upon Judah and the other nations will be so complete that it will mark nothing less than the end of the old order. This will necessitate a new beginning. A remnant will be saved from Judah:
Read Zephaniah 2:3, 6–7, 9c; 3:11–13.

This idea of the faithful remnant who will be saved is not new with Zephaniah, of course; Isaiah had it, and may have originated it. To the idea of the faithful Jewish remnant is added the idea of the universal remnant from among the heathen nations:
Read Zephaniah 3:9–10.

The international revolution thus described is a kind of reversal of Babel. All of this will be followed by a new, golden age in Jerusalem:
Read Zephaniah 3:14–20.

Some scholars attribute to Zephaniah's original preaching only the gloomy predictions of doom, making these predictions of a saving remnant and a New Jerusalem later editorial additions. Be that as it may, the book as it now stands includes them.

Thus, to summarize, the message of the Book of Zephaniah includes: (1) judgment upon Judah and all nations for their irreligion and injustice; (2) the deliverance of a saving remnant; (3) a new, golden beginning.

Regarding this total message, we shall have to say that Zephaniah was wrong if he thought judgment would fall at the hand of the Scythians, for the menace from that quarter vanished. But he was right in that disaster did visit Judah only a few years later, and in that all the nations of antiquity suffered calamity in their time. He was also right about the emergence of a Jewish remnant, though this remnant was not always as religiously perceptive or as morally pure as he had dreamed. There was a restoration and new beginning; in this he was right. But he was wrong in expecting it to be a golden age.

So Zephaniah emerges chiefly as an authenticated prophet of judgment. As we have said elsewhere in this book, judgment is not God's only word, nor is it his final word, but it is a word of God, nonetheless. Zephaniah declared it.

The heart of the social problem that evoked Zephaniah's ringing denunciation was Jewish collaboration with Assyria, collaborationism of the sort that characterized Vichy France after the collapse of the Maginot Line in World War II. A whole society is corrupted when the people can do nothing from their own free conviction, but must live by expediency, terrorized into a faith and a way of life that they hate. Revolution and catastrophe circle above such a society like watching vultures.

OUTLINE OF THE BOOK OF ZEPHANIAH

   I. Title, 1:1
  II. World-wide judgment, 1:2–3
 III. The judgment of Judah, 1:4–18
     A. Judah's sins and their punishment, 1:4–13
     B. The Day of the Lord, 1:14–18
 IV. The judgment of the nations, 2:1–15
     A. The gathering, 2:1–2
     B. A chance for the just, 2:3
     C. Neighboring nations, 2:4–12
     D. Assyria, 2:13–15
  V. Warnings and promises, 3:1–20
     A. Jerusalem's sin, 3:1–5
     B. Unlearned lessons of history, 3:6–7

C. Punishment of all nations, 3:8
D. Babel reversed, 3:9–10
E. The remnant, 3:11–13
F. Jerusalem the Golden, 3:14–20

II. PREPARING YOUR BOOK SERMON

CARDINAL IDEA

Doom awaits a people who put their way of life together from scraps of other cultures upon the basis of expediency rather than developing it from a kernel of genuine faith which is their own.

SHAPING A PREACHING OUTLINE

The real subject of this sermon is the peril of syncretism. As Zephaniah saw it, the nation of Judah in his time had lost the seamless robe of its own true faith and was trying to cover its spiritual nakedness with a tattered cloak, patches upon patches, which it had begged from its neighbors. There are, of course, two kinds of syncretism: the kind that comes from political pressure (like Judah under Assyria); and the kind that comes in a time of civilization's decadence (like that which overtook ancient Rome). Our age is no stranger to either variety. Following this line to its logical outcome, the sermon would unfold in the following manner: (1) syncretism; (2) the weakness which it evokes in a people: (*a*) a basic skepticism, and (*b*) a pervasive corruption; (3) the judgment that must inevitably come. If we wish to give Zephaniah's original message before it was edited, we will stop at this point, on the note of warning. If we want to include the message of the book as we now have it, a fourth point may be added: (4) our only hope: a saving remnant and an entirely new beginning.

Zephaniah may be treated as the voice of conscience that stands between two kings, Manasseh the corrupt collaborationist, and Josiah the zealous reformer: (1) Manasseh symbolizes both syncretism and the weaknesses which it evokes in a nation; (2) Zephaniah is the voice of doom calling to repentance: God putting his evaluation on the situation; (3) Josiah is the response of repentant faith. These main elements may be universalized and applied to contemporary situations.

A Modern Title

Thomas of Celano wrote the hymn *Dies Irae* under the inspiration of the Book of Zephaniah. The first line is translated: "Day of wrath! O day of mourning!" Either the Latin or the English makes an appealing title. "No Faith but Fashion" attempts to convey the meaning of syncretism without using the word. "Prophet of Doom" and "When the Vultures Gather" reflect the gloom of the book, and may have some merit.

33

O'ER CRUMBLING WALLS

The Book of Haggai

THE people of Judah were living indoors; they had rebuilt their own houses. But God was camping-out in the ruins of his Temple. And then the voice of a prophet rose and re-echoed "o'er crumbling walls."

I. WORKING YOUR WAY INTO THE BOOK

This slight book of two chapters contains four oracles from the prophet Haggai exactly dated as to month and day in the year 520 B.C., sixteen years after the end of the Exile. The book also gives us the people's reaction to Haggai's preaching. The book is a report in the third person, not by Haggai but about him.

From Ezra 4:24; 5:1–2 and 6:14–15 we learn that Haggai was associated with another prophet, Zechariah, and that these two inspired the returned exiles to rebuild the Jerusalem Temple. This was done in five years, 520–515 B.C. Haggai and Zechariah had a limited but very specific objective—simply to arouse the people to restore the Temple. They achieved it.

The Temple had lain waste since 587 B.C. when the Babylonians sacked and fired it. We may picture it as a semiruin, not in total demolition. We must also remember that even in its ruined condition, it was in use for the Temple cultus. Remembering services conducted in bombed-out churches of Britain and Europe in World War II, we do not require a great deal of historical imagination to reconstruct the situation of the returning Jewish exiles.

The Jews felt unable to do any better than this by their Temple because they themselves were in dire economic straits:

Read Haggai 1:6, 9–11; 2:16, 17.

First Oracle

From the same circumstances, Haggai argued that they could delay the restoration of the Temple no longer. Their economic depression was caused by their spiritual depression. The Temple lay in ruins at the center of their national life, and their whole existence was necessarily a shambles. Let them begin to rebuild from the spiritual center, and they would change the material situation. So he argued:

Read Haggai 1:2–11.

These verses constitute Haggai's first oracle. They vividly picture the depressed condition of the Jewish community. Where, for example, could you find a better symbolization of financial inflation than 1:6: ". . . he who earns wages earns wages to put them into a bag with holes."

Haggai's arguments (buttressed by those of Zechariah, no doubt) proved to be very persuasive:

Read Haggai 1:12–14.

No sooner had the work on the Temple got under way than some people began to make discouraging comparisons between their work and the glory of Solomon's Temple. This evoked the second of Haggai's oracles.

Second Oracle

Read Haggai 2:1–9.

Haggai had to admit that the rebuilt Temple would not match Solomon's in splendor. But a man is not confined to the present; he has a future, and he has dreams for that future. The past was glorious, and though the present is a time of plight, the future will be filled with hope. Haggai's hope is eschatological: God himself will shake the nations and bring about a reordering of international life, presumably with a world capital at Jerusalem in a Temple even more glorious than Solomon's. Perhaps the recent upset of Babylon by Persia (539 B.C.), and the disorders attending the ascent of Darius I, led Haggai to expect an imminent, cataclysmic judgment and the ushering in of the kingdom of God.

THIRD ORACLE

Haggai's third oracle may be somewhat confusing to the average Bible reader:

Read Haggai 2:10–19.

The oracle seems to contain two sections, verses 10–14 and verses 15–19. This has led some commentators to treat 2:15–19 with 1:15a as a separate oracle. In any case, the thought in this second part of the oracle is a simple continuation of the thought of the first oracle. That first oracle pictured the economic devastation resulting from neglecting to rebuild the Temple; these present verses (2:15–19), the second part of the third oracle, picture the prosperity to be expected when the Temple is rebuilt. This much of the third oracle is clear; it presents us with no difficulty.

It is when we read the first part of the third oracle (2:10–14) that we seem to be in a foreign thought-world: Touch a dead human body, then touch any article of food and it automatically becomes unclean. That is the effect of unclean flesh, of a corpse. In contrast to that, consider the effect of touching the holiest of all flesh, that of a sacrifice just offered on the Temple altar; that touch does not purify. The prophet seems to be saying that wickedness is more contagious than holiness. All the more reason, therefore, to make the sacramental impact of the Temple as pure and as strong as possible. In Haggai's words this idea remains in the realm of ritual. While it remains there it leaves most modern readers cold. If we are allowed to extrapolate Haggai's argument to include the moral realm we can assent to it readily: Moral wrong is a more virulent contagion than the right. Therefore it is all the more imperative to work at the constructive task of building up positive moral influences. But, while the institution of religion should radiate moral health to a community, it must be more than an ethical culture society. It must be in some sense a sacramental society mediating the grace of God to men.

FOURTH ORACLE

The fourth oracle is concerned with Haggai's dream for the future:

Read Haggai 2:20–23.

In these words Haggai expresses the hope that Zerubbabel, the governor of Judah by appointment of Persia, will become king of Israel, re-establishing the Davidic line (for he is of Davidic descent) and ushering in the messianic age. This dream was fated for disappointment; the Davidic line was never re-established. Perhaps the Persians became suspicious of Judah's reviving political ambitions and nipped them in the bud by removing Zerubbabel from the governorship and whisking him away to exile or to death. There are hints in Ezra and Nehemiah that something of the sort may have happened. See Nehemiah 6:7 for one such hint.

In spite of the literal failure of Haggai's dream of a Messiah in that immediate situation, Christians will find great validity in the general outline of his vision. A completed temple is God's house and it waits for the divine host to come and occupy it. Only as he comes and makes himself manifest there does the temple come to be the source of power and light to the people.

Key Verse

"Go up to the hills and bring wood and build the house, that I may take pleasure in it and that I may appear in my glory, says the Lord" (Hag. 1:8).

II. PREPARING YOUR BOOK SERMON

Cardinal Idea

When in disrepair through disaster or neglect, a church building must be rebuilt—to save the whole life of the community from demoralization and to point it toward its destiny.

Shaping a Preaching Outline

A good deal will depend upon finding a relevant situation for this sermon. It will fit quite naturally into communities which have suffered the devastation of war or natural calamity. I have vivid memories of preaching for several months in a temporary chapel of rough timber and sheet metal erected on the cement foundations and floors of a bombed-out church in Manila, the Philippines. The congregation had drawn up plans for its new, permanent building, and was giving out of its poverty toward the building fund. Or, to take another example of an equally relevant situation, the churches in Pikeville, Kentucky, following the floods of 1957, had to be rebuilt by members who had also suffered the flooding of their homes with consequent loss of possessions and great damage to property. In either of these situations, or in comparable ones, the message of Haggai would be relevant and timely.

There is a sociological calamity now occurring in American cities on a phenomenal scale: the rising of new subdivisions in urban societies which are building swank residential and shopping communities—consumer neighborhoods—often without any plans for churches. Between these new subdivisions and the early American pioneer communities the contrast is sharp and instructive. Early villages rose as cultural unities with a church, a school, a store, and a government building at the center. And the same people who built the houses undertook responsibilities for the other buildings, which were organs of their corporate life; in fact, they often built for the community before they built for themselves. Modern subdivisions are the product of contractors, real estate dealers, and individual home owners who are interested largely in financial profit and domestic comfort. Little thought is given to the making of a cultural community; little responsibility is accepted locally for schools, for civic and political integrity, and for churches. When churches come to such communities, they are often placed there as missionary projects organized and paid for from the outside. Unless we can create a new sense of religious responsibility in the minds of millions now moving into the suburbs, suburbia has become a vast, foreign-missionary field. One could hardly find a more apt situation for the words of Haggai: "Is it a time for you yourselves to dwell in your paneled houses, while this house lies in ruins?" (Hag. 1:4). The ruins here are sociological, of course, not physical; but the problem is the same. Will the church question lie fatally neglected?

We shall have to admit, of course, that the answer to the church question cannot be found in the past. Neither in postexilic Judah nor in Puritan America was there any real freedom of worship. Non-Jews were driven from Jerusalem. Quakers were not welcome in Massachusetts. Baptists had to establish Rhode Island for this reason; and Roman Catholics, Maryland. We should not care for modern subdivisions to perpetuate these patterns of intolerance.

Nevertheless, we are now confronted by these and other patterns of discrimination which seem to defy solution. Restrictive covenants draw religious, racial, and financial lines; and even without such covenants, subdivisions tend to become expressions of caste and class. When churches do arise in such status-communities they tend to become class churches; they frequently do not solve but, rather, aggravate the social problem.

Against this modern background, it will be helpful to notice that the thought of Haggai moved through three phases. First, he dealt with the objection of the people: they were too poor to build at that time. In spite of their need and poverty, they were nevertheless the ones who had to do the building. The very health and prosperity of their new life depended upon it. To build homes and not to build the church is fatal shortsightedness. Second, he faced the discouraging comparisons between what his people could do and what Solomon had done in his former glory; but he refused to be imprisoned in the past. Third, he refused to be cowed by the limited horizons of his present situation. Lifting his eyes to the future, he saw a nobler Temple. All of this he related to the central object: to make a home, in the midst of the homes of the people, for the living God.

In some communities, the two basic objections of the people might serve as the main foci of the sermon: (1) how can we be expected to build when we are so poor? (Hag. 1:2); (2) how can we do it when our tiny chapel will compare so unfavorably with the big city churches from which we all came? (Hag. 2:3). Haggai's answers are four: (1) we will be poorer still if we do not build; (Hag. 1:9); (2) the church of the future will be more glorious (Hag. 2:9); (3) the forces of evil are so virulent (Hag. 2:10–14); (4) we must acknowledge the living presence of the living God (Hag. 2:5b).

A MODERN TITLE

"Rebuilding the Temple" is an accurate if prosaic title. "Temples Still Undone" is one phrase from the hymn by Purd E. Dietz, "We Would Be Building," which offers in its own name a good title, and in phrases of the hymn, a number of good titles.

34

BETTER THAN STANDING ARMIES

The Book of Zechariah

ZECHARIAH believed that a flourishing life of faith and worship in the heart of a nation is better than standing armies and fortresses. Americans used to believe that too. We gave the prophet more than lip service when we quoted: "Not by might, nor by power, but by my Spirit, says the Lord of hosts" (Zech. 4:6). But do we believe it now? Upon which will we rely the more readily, Pentagon or Cathedral? Sometimes it seems that we may be trying to shoot ideas with bullets and capture the minds of men by flying fleets of airplanes over their heads. Zechariah would have little faith in such a course. To his mind the defenses of a nation and its guarantees to peace were inward matters of loyalty to God and justice to men. A city fortified by stone walls could be laid in ruins, but a city ringed by a wall of God's fire would prove invulnerable (Zech. 2:5).

I. WORKING YOUR WAY INTO THE BOOK

HISTORICAL SETTING

The historical background of Zechariah is the same as that of Haggai (see the preceding chapter, p. 239). Zechariah's objective was the same as Haggai's, and his viewpoint was essentially the same. He differed from Haggai by preaching over a period of two years, 520–518 B.C. in contrast to Haggai's few months of preaching in the one year, 520 B.C. His message differed from that of Haggai not so much in essentials as in extent and intensity: (1) the historical perspective, showing Israel among the nations, is wider and more detailed; (2)

the ethical aspect of religion is more emphatic; (3) the reality of the unseen spiritual world is much more vivid, and the Day of the Lord becomes much more violent and cataclysmic. To convey the fervor and intensity which he felt, Zechariah employed allegory and the bizarre imagery of apocalyptic. We find ourselves in an atmosphere not unlike that of Revelation and Daniel.

The book falls naturally into two major divisions, the visions and oracles of Zechariah (chaps. 1–8), and the apocalyptic visions of Deutero-Zechariah (chaps. 9–14). Deutero-Zechariah is composed of two appendices to the book, chapters 9–11 and chapters 12–14. They reflect backgrounds from the Persian and Greek periods and seem to have come after the fall of Alexander the Great. In the first eight chapters of the book, Zechariah placed great hope in the restoration of the high priesthood of the Temple and in the re-establishment of the Davidic kingdom; Joshua, the high priest, was to bring an entirely new cultus to a reformed Israel; Zerubbabel was to be a political Messiah. In these respects, Zechariah and Haggai were in complete agreement. But Deutero-Zechariah, writing two or three centuries later, had given up hope in the power of men—either high priests or kings; and, like the Seer of Patmos long afterward, he looked through the haze of history to the final judgment and ulti-mate sovereignty of God over history. In Zechariah, it is man who acts as God's agent; in Deutero-Zechariah, it is God who acts, directly and decisively. In our analysis we shall deal with these two divisions of the book separately.

ZECHARIAH: CHAPTERS 1–8

The first eight chapters, constituting the preaching of the prophet Zechariah, 520–518 B.C., are composed of eight visions and a number of related oracles. The visions are highly allegorical, but their mean-ing in general is not difficult to penetrate.

EIGHT VISIONS

1. A World at Peace.
Read Zechariah 1:7–17.
These four horsemen of Zechariah are very different from the four horsemen of John's Apocalypse. They symbolize peace in four

directions, in other words, enveloping the earth. Some Jews were waiting for a revolt against Persia to provide them with the opportunity of restoring the Davidic dynasty and the kingdom of Israel in Jerusalem. So the Persian peace was distasteful to them. We should have no difficulty understanding these ancient Jews. For the past several years we have been waiting for news of revolt in Russia, thinking such a disintegration of our enemy would solve all our problems. We are much like Judah waiting for news of revolt in Persia. The meaning of this vision, then, is quite clear: Do not expect your good to come from the downfall of your enemies; don't count on their collapse. Learn how to build positively in your time and where you are.

2. A Doomed Imperialism.

Read Zechariah 1:18-21.

Judah seemed to be hemmed in by imperialism from every side (the four horns), but God would in his own time break this imperialism down (the four smiths) and set his people free. Thus the Jews were entitled to the long-term faith that international evil was essentially an impermanent structure. An evil imperialism carries its own seeds of destruction. Its downfall may be counted on ultimately. But this makes the positive task of a holy nation moral not military.

3. A City without Walls.

Read Zechariah 2:1-5.

Zechariah, in contrast with Nehemiah's later view, held that the walls of Jerusalem should not be rebuilt. Jerusalem had a better defense in complete reliance upon God. The point of the vision: Your security is from God, not from fortresses.

4. A Worthy Priesthood.

Read Zechariah 3:1-10.

Priests must not be pagan. But they cannot depaganize themselves. This requires God's redemptive work of forgiveness in the life of the priest, and it depends upon the priest's full commitment to God.

5. God over Church and State.

Read Zechariah 4:1-6a, 10b-14.

The seven candlesticks represent the watchful presence of God. The two olive trees symbolize Joshua, the high priest, and Zerubbabel, the would-be king. These symbols seem to say, "The eyes of God are upon both church and state."

6. The Flying Scroll.

Read Zechariah 5:1–4.

This is a symbolic picture of God's judgment upon the wicked.

7. The Removal of Wickedness.

Read Zechariah 5:6–11.

Before the Messiah can come, Judah must be freed of wickedness. Wickedness is worshiped in Babylon, but not in Jerusalem. Israel must be holy.

8. The Four Chariots.

Read Zechariah 6:1–8.

The four chariots going in all four directions symbolize the omnipresence of God and his universal sovereignty. God rules over all the earth, and his will ultimately triumphs.

SIX ORACLES

1. The Need of Repentance.

Read Zechariah 1:1–6.

Let Judah return to God, that he may turn to her; let her not be rebellious and unrepentant, as she was before the Exile.

2. Security and Insecurity.

Read Zechariah 2:6–13.

Babylonian Jews are asked to give up their material security in Babylon and return to Judah, for Babylon is a hollow shell which will shortly crash to earth.

3. Zerubbabel to Build.

Read Zechariah 4:6b–10a.

Zerubbabel has laid the foundation of the Temple and he will go on to complete it.

4. Zerubbabel to be Crowned.

Read Zechariah 6:9–15.

The language of this oracle is slightly disguised—probably to deceive any Persian official who might chance to read it. But the "branch" is Zerubbabel. Zechariah is calling for the speedy coronation of Zerubbabel (of David's line) and the restoration of the Jewish monarchy.

5. Social Justice.

Read Zechariah 7:1–14.

God requires much more than ritual purity; he demands moral

obedience and social justice. These two oracles are in the best tradition of the eighth-century prophets.

6. The New Jerusalem.
Read Zechariah 8.

This chapter contains three oracles. Their message may be summarized as follows: True worship in Jerusalem will not only rally Judah and bring her glory; it will bless all the nations.

DEUTERO-ZECHARIAH: CHAPTERS 9–14

This section of the book presents us with two collections of oracles picturing the coming of the Messiah as the Prince of Peace, the final eschatological war, and the ultimate establishing of a war-less world of justice and holiness with Jerusalem as world capital.

There are several passages of this section which are echoed in the New Testament:

Read (in this order) Zechariah 9:9; *Matthew* 21:5; *John* 12:15; *Zechariah* 11:12–13; *Matthew* 26:15; 27:9; *Zechariah* 12:10; *John* 19:37; *Zechariah* 13:7; *Matthew* 26:31; *Mark* 14:27; *Zechariah* 14:8; *Revelation* 22:1–2; *Zechariah* 14:11; *Revelation* 22:3.

There is great beauty here, but much cruelty and narrowness as well:

Read Zechariah 9:15; 10:5; 11:6, 9; 14:12.

We must remember, however, that we are reading apocalyptic and that the language is highly figurative. The basic meaning is that God rules nations and judges them and that there will be a final accounting upon righteous principles.

OUTLINE OF DEUTERO-ZECHARIAH[1]

    I. Triumph of the messianic king, 9:1–12
   II. Victorious war against the tyrants, 9:13–17
  III. God alone gives the rain, 10:1–2
  IV. God's anger against his people's oppressors, 10:3–12
   V. Fall of the tyrants, 11:1–3
  VI. God's judgment upon an ungrateful people, 11:4–14
 VII. Doom of a wicked governor, 11:15–17
VIII. Victory of God's people over the heathen, 12:1—13:6

[1] D. Winston Thomas in *The Interpreter's Bible*, Vol. VI, p. 1091.

IX. National purification, 13:7–9
X. The last days, 14:1–21

KEY VERSE

No one verse can stand duty for the complexity of the whole book, but perhaps this one comes nearest: "Be silent, all flesh, before the Lord; for he has roused himself from his holy dwelling" (Zech. 2:13).

II. PREPARING YOUR BOOK SERMON

CARDINAL IDEA

When we give true worship its central place, we will bring peace and prosperity not only to ourselves but to all mankind.

Since the cross, it is no longer possible to believe that perfect obedience to God will bring success and peace. Sometimes, to use the words of Jesus, it brings "a sword." For this reason we need to be very careful in presenting the teaching of Zechariah today. We seem to be on safest ground when we think of the book as addressed to the covenant community—to the church and to us as church members. The concern of the church is not self-defense or power but full commitment to God. "But seek first his kingdom and his righteousness, and all these things shall be yours as well" (Matt. 6:33). Put these things first, and leave the outcome to God.

SHAPING A PREACHING OUTLINE

Zechariah, in the first of the visions, affords a startling connection with modern events. We, too, think largely in terms of the threat to our life which comes from misbehaving enemies. Therefore we plot our security in military terms rather than in terms of righting our own house morally, socially, and religiously. We depend for our health upon the sickness of Russia or of some other enemy, social or personal—a perverse notion. We need to begin to think of waging peace instead of war—hot or cold.

One approach to a sermon outline might unfold somewhat as follows:

1. The folly of expecting our good to come from the downfall of our enemies (1:7–17)
2. The folly of expecting our good to come from our own unrepentant strength (1:1–6; 4:6b)
3. The wisdom of turning to God
    a) The impermanence of evil; the ultimate victory of God (1:18–21)
    b) God, the real life of both church and state (4:1–14)
4. The outcome: worship at the center of life
    a) Repentance and cleansing (1:3; 3:1–10; 5:1–11)
    b) Worship as moral service (chap. 7)
    c) The prosperous and peaceful nation, blessing all nations (8:22, 23)

Although ordinarily it seems inadvisable to plan a sermon with more than five points, a book sermon might be organized around the eight visions of Zechariah, discussed earlier. The visions are so vivid and can be re-created by the preacher in such clarity that their number may be a secondary consideration. Contemporary relevance will be sought at each point, together with modern illustrations. A striking illustration of the third vision, for example, may be taken from the history of international defenses along the Canadian border since 1812. The United States and Canada moved from an early policy of armed watchfulness to the present one of trusting neighbors. Zechariah's insights apply, of course, not only in politics but in every realm of group and personal life.

A MODERN TITLE

"Not by Might, Nor by Power" and "A City without Walls" come from the Book of Zechariah. Titles appropriate to Haggai would also be fitting here. Martin Luther's hymn, "A Mighty Fortress is Our God," offers itself as a good title.

35

RELIGIOUS RECESSION

The Book of Malachi

MALACHI is a transliterated Hebrew word meaning "my messenger." It is not a proper name. Thus the twelfth of the books of the Minor Prophets is anonymous. The book was written in a time of religious recession and national discouragement.

I. WORKING YOUR WAY INTO THE BOOK

HISTORICAL SETTING

The Book of Malachi sheds a great deal of light on its own date. Notice some of the evidence:

Read Malachi 2:8, 9; 1:7, 8, 13, 14; 3:8–10.

The Temple was standing, but the Temple service was badly neglected. The priests were perfunctory and negligent in their duties. The people were offering defective sacrifices to God, and they were withholding their tithes. The situation was, to say the least, spiritually lukewarm.

From the Books of Haggai and Zechariah we know that the Temple was rebuilt following the Exile, during the five-year period 520–515 B.C. Although there were older people who wept then because the new Temple fell so far short of the glory of Solomon's celebrated shrine, the people as a whole were happy and exultant when it was completed. The neglect of the Temple pictured in Malachi would surely not have followed immediately upon its dedication. Some years, possibly several decades, were needed to bring about such a degeneration of religious morale. If a whole generation of returning exiles had passed from the scene, and their children and grandchildren were left to carry on the discouraging work of reconstruction amid scant signs of progress, we could reasonably expect the decline of religious zeal so clearly reflected in the book.

There was not only neglect of the Temple; there was also a great deal of moral laxness:

Read Malachi 2:10; 3:5.

Such moral laxness is to be expected in a time of poor and perfunctory church attendance. Both the neglect of the Temple and the decline of morals, in fact, may have sprung from other roots:

Read Malachi 2:17; 3:13–15.

There was a general disillusionment, a moral cynicism. "What's the use? Nothing we do turns out right. The righteous fail. The wicked prosper. God pays no attention to us."

Life in the restored community of Judah following the Babylonian Exile had fallen far short of the dream of Isaiah, chapters 40–55. The returning exiles had been few in number and poor. They had been able to occupy a tiny territory, little bigger than Jerusalem. Their former Jewish neighbors and kinsmen who had remained in Babylon far outnumbered them, and had a much better lot. In Palestine, "the people of the land," their new neighbors, harassed and threatened them at every opportunity. Their lot was hard, their prospects were unpromising.

In the face of these discouragements, disillusionment and cynicism crept in. The Jews lost their sense of mission. The dream faded.

Read Malachi 2:11, 14–16.

One result of the attrition of the discouraging circumstances and of the pressure from "the people of the land," who far outnumbered the Jews, was the divorcing of Jewish wives and remarriage to Gentile women. Homes resulting from such unions would have had little interest in the ancestral religion of the Jews. To many observers it seemed that the national existence of Judah was doomed and that the very faith of Israel was threatened.

Such was the situation as Nehemiah found it in 444 B.C.

Read Nehemiah 1:3; 13:10–30.

In a word, all the conditions pictured in the Book of Malachi could be found in Judah just prior to the reforms of Nehemiah and Ezra.

There are two other indications of date:

Read Malachi 1:8.

Judah was ruled by a governor, a clear indication of postexilic date; prior to the Exile, Judah was ruled by kings of the Davidic line.

Read Malachi 1:2–5.

Edom (the nation descended from Esau, and therefore the close kin of the Jews, who were descended from Esau's twin, Jacob) had recently been driven from its homeland in the Sier range by invaders. From secular history we know these invaders to have been the Arabs who set up the Nabataean kingdom. Unfortunately, we do not know the exact date of this displacement of Edom, but it may have occurred after 500 B.C.

Putting all the strands of evidence together we conclude that the Book of Malachi records the prophecy of a man addressed to the discouraged community of Judah sometime near 450 B.C., just before Nehemiah and Ezra, with their great burst of energy, lifted the nation out of the doldrums.

MAIN THEMES

In general, the Book of Malachi takes the form of a dialogue between God and his people. Much can be learned from the questions and complaints of the people:

Read Malachi 1:2, 6, 7, 13; 2:10, 14, 17; 3:7, 8, 13–15.

These questions and complaints may be summarized somewhat as follows: "If God loves us, why are we so poor and so harassed?"

God's answers to these complaints form the bulk of the book, but they may be summarized under three headings:

1. Judah's condition is in great part the result of covenant faithlessness:

Read Malachi 1:6–2:9; 2:17; 3:7–12.

The Jews could not hope to reap grapes from the thistles they had been sowing. Their moral indifference and their religious neglect resulted in a decline of the whole civic life.

2. God had not been as neglectful of Judah as the Jews had supposed. He had granted them a revival and continued existence following the Exile. In contrast to this, he had allowed Edom, close kin to Israel, to be driven from its homeland:

Read Malachi 1:2–5.

Since the Edomites had turned out to be such bitter enemies of the Jews and had done so much to heap insult upon injury at the fall of Jerusalem in 587 B.C., the national misfortune of Edom should have proved reassuring to the Jews—as reassuring as the fall of Hitler and Tojo in A.D. 1945 to the Western powers.

3. There is a future in which God will level out his justice by granting rewards to the righteous and punishments to the wicked: *Read Malachi 3:1–5, 16–18.*

With these reassurances of God's love and faithfulness as support, the Jews are to face their moral and religious duty. This duty is to come heartily to Temple worship, to support it generously and loyally; from this center of renewal, they are to renew their whole national life, their home life, and their morals. The result will be a new blessing and vitality, a final upturn from their long depression.

OUTLINE OF THE BOOK OF MALACHI

    I.   Title, 1:1
   II.   The fate of Edom, 1:2–5
  III.   Faithless priests, 1:6—2:9
  IV.   Faithless people, 2:10—4:3
       A. Divorce and remarriage to Gentiles, 2:10–16
       B. Doubt of God's justice, 2:17—3:5
       C. Decline in stewardship of money and goods, 3:6–12
       D. Disillusionment and cynicism, 3:13—4:3
   V.   Appendix, 4:4—6

The appendix appears to have been written as the conclusion not merely to the Book of Malachi but to the whole collection of the twelve Minor Prophets.

KEY VERSES

There is no single passage that summarizes the whole message of Malachi, but 1:10–11 seems to come closest. This passage represents both the negative and the positive side of the book. It were better to shut the doors of the Temple than to conduct an unworthy service of worship within; for God is not dependent on his Temple for his existence; he is the living God of all nations, and their spiritual health is dependent upon the purity of their worship and loyalty to him.

II. PREPARING YOUR BOOK SERMON

CARDINAL IDEA

A neglected church at the center of community life indicates decay and decline throughout the whole society; but genuine worship of God at the center of community life pervades and saves the whole corporate life of a people.

SHAPING A PREACHING OUTLINE

It is possible to work from the two key verses given above, taking them as the text of the sermon. The church that stands in the midst of a community in a perfunctory way were better closed, for it is an index of decaying community life and an affront to God. God is living and real, and our life and reality depend upon our loyalty to him.

In much the same way, the statement of the cardinal idea given above may be analyzed for the main divisions of a book sermon: (1) neglected church, declining community; (2) vital church pervading community life; (3) loyalty to God as a saving force in the community.

A topical treatment of the main phases of thought in the book might develop along the following lines: (1) a national or local depression resulting in discouragement and disillusionment; (2) a loss of faith in God and a neglect of corporate worship; (3) a general decline in morals; (4) a reminder of God's universal sway over nations and of his ultimate justice; (5) a renewal of loyalty to God, centering in worship but affecting the whole of life.

Another good approach to the sermon will be through the dialogue form of the original book. Let God and people question each other and reply to each other. This will require a phrasing of the main questions and complaints of the people so that they will have modern relevance. It could be done as a paraphrase of the book. At the beginning, for example, the sermon might open like this:

GOD: I have loved you.

PEOPLE: How hast thou loved us? Are we not in a business recession? Is not crime on the increase? Are we not hated and distrusted among the nations?

GOD: You forget that I did not allow the Axis armies to defeat you and occupy your country in the last war. Hitler and Tojo dreamed of world dominion but they are dead; their empires have died aborning. Should you not praise me for V-E Day and V-J Day? And, yet, in spite of all this, you despise my name.

PEOPLE: How do we despise thy name?

GOD: By the perfunctory way in which you approach my altars!

The dialogue sermon could be delivered by two preachers, one at the pulpit, the other at the lectern. Or, of course, a single preacher could take both parts.

The life situation to which the Book of Malachi was originally addressed was a neglected Temple in the midst of a general depression of Jewish national life. This double difficulty may be duplicated upon a national or local scale in some modern period. Or either difficulty may appear separately. To be relevant and helpful, the book sermon on Malachi should not be addressed to a boom town in a time of prosperity when church-attendance statistics are at an all-time high. A sermon of challenge may be needed in such a situation, but it will be a different sermon.

A MODERN TITLE

A few of the possibilities suggested by phrases in the book, or ideas about it, are as follows: "Robbing God—and Ourselves," "God Says, 'Shut the Church Doors,'" "What is the Good of Church-going?" "God Calls for Loyalty," and "Religious Recession."

36

HOW PREACHERS MAY USE THIS BOOK

SHORTLY after the publication of my earlier book, *Preaching on the Books of the New Testament*, I received letters from several ministers indicating that they were announcing long series of sermons on the New Testament books, one to a Sunday for periods ranging from several weeks to several months. This is certainly one way to do such preaching, but it was not what I had in mind when I sent the book out into the world. And, while a book is independent of its author once it has been published, and has complete license to speak its own message to each reader, perhaps the author will be permitted a quiet word in defense of a different way of working.

What I propose as a workable program for the hard-pressed parish minister is something approaching the plan followed by students in my seminary class, "The Use of the Bible in Preaching." Each student selects a major biblical book. He makes a study of it during the whole three months of the quarter, devoting most of his out-of-class preparation to it. From this study, he extracts four papers which are written by way of a report to his professor and his fellow students. They unfold in the following manner:

First Paper: The student's own review of the book based simply upon his reading of the book itself in at least three versions. He merely lets the book speak to him in its own way, as far as he is able to listen. Then from this first hand encounter, he tries to answer several questions—seeking aid from no expert, but using his own impressions as his sole guide: (1) What is the main theme of this book? Can you state it in a sentence? If you were giving the book a modern title indicating its contents, what would you call it? (2) Are there any significant subordinate themes? What are they? Are there special points of interest, peculiar emphases? (3) How is the book organized? Outline it in your own way. (4) What is your reaction to the book? Aside from what the book tells you, what kind of personal response does it stir up in you? This is hard to put into words, but at least make an attempt to indicate your part of the dialogue which took place between author(s) and reader.

Second Paper: Now the student goes to the experts and reads all he can find about this book. He reads "Introductions" to the books of the Bible concerned, not one, but several. He reads the introductions to several commentaries, all in an effort to discover what the scholars have said about the biblical book he has under study. Then he prepares a brief report summarizing his findings, comparing and contrasting the points of view as he tries to answer the following questions: (1) When was this book written? (2) To what readers was it addressed? What was their situation (historically, sociologically, religiously)? (3) Who wrote it? (4) For what purpose was it written? (5) What is its main message? (6) How is it organized?

In preparing this second paper, the student will find himself elated to discover that he has already seen some things as clearly as the scholars who have devoted special gifts and years of study to their work. But he will also discover that his reading has been shallow or perhaps even mistaken in some respects. In any event, it was highly desirable for him to begin with a firsthand encounter with the book itself and with his own impressions; for it is not the experts that we need to understand, but the book itself which all of us, amateurs and experts alike, are reading. Putting our own study ahead of the study of the experts will make us remarkably sensitive to their insights. But, of course, any man would be a fool to refuse this help.

Third Paper: This is a catalogue of sermon starters. Any biblical book abounds in sermon ideas for any thoughtful minister, and the possibilities are so rich and varied at different times in his life that he may well regard it as an inexhaustible mine of treasure. Every time he comes back to it he will see things he failed to see before; there is always new light breaking from its pages. Therefore, a man should write down only those striking ideas that seek him out, ideas that cry to be preached. But it will help to keep these in some kind of order, arranging them by categories, somewhat as follows:

1. Personalities of the book (individually or in groups).
2. The ruling ideas of the book.
3. Striking texts.

4. Expository sections: incidents; narratives, parables, allegories; units within the book as paragraphs, chapters, and groups of chapters.

5. Ideas for sermons on the whole book (there may be several of these).

6. Illustrations for use within sermons.

What is a sermon starter? It is not merely a text or a paragraph of Scripture, innocently listed on a paper. It is the minister's own personal dialogue with that Scripture—the reasons why it arrested his attention. Therefore, a sermon starter, if it is to give real promise for some future development, will probably include: (1) the Scripture itself; (2) a topic of some kind; (3) the beginnings of a proposition, which in this case may be stated not in a single sentence but in a brief paragraph; (4) the aim of the sermon (why this sermon is needed). Each sermon starter, consequently, will be a note of 75 to 150 words—the minister's memorandum to himself for possible use in the future.

Any minister who will follow some such plan as we have just sketched will find himself embarrassed with homiletical riches. He will have hundreds of sermon ideas in a short while, more than he can preach in a lifetime. Then he can begin to be selective, choosing the big themes and the important objectives. He will preach out of an overflow; every sermon will say much, but it will suggest even more.

Fourth Paper: This is a book sermon. This sermon is admittedly difficult to come by, and it will come only after a complete immersion in the book itself. It comes at the end not at the beginning of a long study. Thus, although a minister may decide to preach a series of sermons from a given book and may begin by preaching a single sermon on the whole book, his experience of that book sermon is exactly opposite to the congregation's experience of it. They meet it first; he came by it last.

The chapters of this book are designed to stand between the second and third papers. The first section of each chapter, entitled "Working Your Way into the Book," is a kind of conducted workshop by means of which a minister goes beyond his cursory reading of the book itself, and beyond a census of the experts, to "dig in" and "come to grasp" with the book itself, as a student in his own right. This stage of the study must not be skimped; each man must do it for himself, using the chapter only as a set of suggestions and helps, never as a substitute for firsthand digging. The section on "Preparing Your Book Sermon" is intended only to stimulate the fifth category of the "Third Paper"—the sparking of ideas for sermons on the whole book. Since this is a difficult task, the illustrations of possible developments which are presented in "Preparing Your Book Sermon" are specific; but they are intended only to be illustrative and suggestive. In no case are they ready to be used without further development. It is the purpose of this section not to give ready-made outlines but to show a way and impel travelers to take that way as their own adventure.

The method of working just outlined has this advantage for the preacher himself: On the way to an adequate grasp of a whole book for the purposes of one sermon, he comes into possession of a vast treasury of biblical sermons of all sorts. It is inconceivable that his pulpit ministry will not be the richer for it.

How this is shared with one's congregation is a matter which may be variously determined. One man may wish to preach a series of book sermons; but if he is to do this adequately, he must put months of study into his preparation. He cannot assume that he can start from the beginning and come up with a book sermon between two Sundays. If he tries to do so, he will almost certainly become frustrated and end up with a sermon that is confused or shallow, or both. The method that seems most natural is to plan for a period of preaching from one biblical book, starting with a book sermon to set the perspective. Again let it be stressed that the preaching itself must be preceded by weeks or months of quiet preparation in the study.

37

HOW TEACHERS MAY USE THIS BOOK

ALTHOUGH *Preaching on the Books of the New Testament* was written primarily for preachers, I discovered after publication that many teachers of Bible—in the church school, in various church fellowships, and even in colleges—were using it in programs of group study. I should like to encourage the same use of the present volume.

The teacher who plans to present an Old Testament book as a whole to a class or group will need to make a distinction between preparation and presentation. His minimum preparation will be a conscientious reading of the section entitled "Working Your Way into the Book" plus a reading of all the italicized Scripture references, to be followed by the reading of the whole biblical book at least once from beginning to end. Fuller preparation may well follow the steps designated "First Paper" and "Second Paper" in the preceding chapter. Quite obviously, the teacher will find little value in taking the steps outlined under "Third Paper" and "Fourth Paper."

Presentation of a biblical book in a class session may assume little or no advance information about the book on the part of the class members. In that case the class will begin at once with a systematic study of the material entitled "Working Your Way into the Book." Each passage of Scripture should be read aloud as it is called for, preferably by various members in turn. The interpretive material of the chapter may be presented in the teacher's lecture, or by individual reports assigned in advance, or it may even be read from the book—the last being the least desirable method. The aim of this session is to send class members home eager to read the biblical book which they have thus studied.

Some classes will want to prepare for such a study in advance of each session. Their best preparation is simply the reading of the biblical book itself. Many members will find this easier and more rewarding if they use a modern-speech translation, like the Revised Standard Version or *The Complete Bible: An American Translation*.

When the members of a class have read the biblical book in advance of the class session they will probably move more quickly in their group study, thus allowing time for class discussion following the presentation. This discussion should do more than review biblical events and sayings; it should penetrate to the meaning of those events and sayings on the level of personal and social challenge. When God speaks through the pages of Scripture he comes to meet us—he in his infinite majesty and love, we in our finite need. This meeting calls for a deepening insight into self, and for decision and commitment. Only upon this level of personal claim and personal response is the truth of the Bible to be experienced in its own terms.

Teachers and classes will be drawn to such a study by a growing desire on the part of thoughtful Christians really to know the Bible by reading it as we now have it, book by book.

INDEX